14

WI

RAWN

WITHDRAWN

VIETNAM VETERAN FILMS

by
Mark Walker

The Scarecrow Press, Inc.
Metuchen, N.J., & London
1991

British Library Cataloguing-in-Publication data available

Library of Congress Cataloging-in-Publication Data

Walker, Mark, 1960-
    Vietnam veteran films / by Mark Walker.
        p.   cm.
    Includes bibliographical references and index.
    ISBN 0-8108-2475-2 (alk. paper)
    1. Veterans in motion pictures.   2. Vietnamese Conflict, 1961-
1975--Motion pictures and the conflict.   3. Vietnamese Conflict,
1961-1975--Veterans.   I. Title.
PN1995.9.V44W35 1991
791.43'658--dc20   91-28813

Dedication

This book is dedicated to my wife. I love you, Mary.

Contents

Acknowledgments

I would like to thank my friends and colleagues:

Stuart Kaminsky

Lawrence Lichty

Janice Mouton

Dan Patterson

Gene Phillips

Jim Schwoch

Mimi White

and

My family.

Introduction

In essence this is an image study. This book traces the change of the American narrative film image of the Vietnam veteran (Vietvet) over time, from its first appearance in the mid-1960s to the present. In effect, thus, the main thrust of this book is a historical one, although I will make reference to film theoretical concepts when and where they seem helpful. More specifically, the particular image under consideration is that of the returning or returned Vietvet. That is, the focus of this book is upon those soldiers in narrative film who have completed their active duty in the Armed Forces.

In order to attempt a comprehensive picture of this question as it concerns fiction film, I have studied the veteran image across American film genres. In this way this book can trace the Vietvet image in at least three ways: over time in all instances, within film genres, and among film genres. The genres examined will be the following: the biker film, the vigilante film, the caper film, the police film, the war film, the horror film, the comedy, the melodrama, and the art film. This list suggests that this book will be diverging from some of the traditionally studied genres such as the Western and the gangster film and indeed it will be, although some of the standbys will also be discussed.

The genres listed above contain enough films with Vietvet characters to make my hypotheses concerning them more specific than they would be involving other genres, which by the way, will not be ignored but rather mentioned in appropriate contexts. As Tzvetan Todorov maintains in the introduction to his study of the fantastic: "We actually deal with a relatively limited number of cases, from them we deduce a general hypothesis, and we verify this hypothesis by other cases, correcting (or rejecting) it as need be."[1] In this sense, my hypotheses can be modified or rejected based upon further research. Also, the hypotheses within genres

ix

can be added toward making conclusions about the Vietvet image in narrative film as a whole.

For the purposes of this discussion, narrative film refers to those feature films apart from the other major modes, documentary and experimental film. Formulaic film refers to those films studied by genre theorists such as Stuart Kaminsky, Thomas Schatz, and Michael Wood, what John Cawelti refers to as "popular genres."[2] Non-formulaic film refers to what is often called "art film," which for purposes of this analysis will be treated as a genre.

The foundations provided by the genre theorists can provide a quite sound beginning for a methodological framework. By comparing the convention/invention interplay of genre films containing Vietvets with films of the same genre that do not, much light can be shed on important societal concerns and the Vietvet image will start to emerge. By comparing this interplay with certain archetypes, what Joseph Campbell calls "the common ideas of myths,"[3] it will become apparent that filmmakers have placed contemporary masks on what are ancient character types and have fashioned modern twists on centuries-old stories. In this regard the filmic Vietvet image represents only variations upon, not breaks from, archetypal conventions.

The genre and mythic framework, though, is only a part of my organizing methodology. I envision this book as an examination of several interlocking and overlapping systems, "system" being used in the strict sense of Ervin Laszlo and the system theorists.[4] The Vietvet films themselves, the film genres that incorporate them, and narrative film in general can be seen as systems of increasing complexity that interconnect and overlap. I will argue that the way films basically do this is by economic exchange and will show that the Vietvet filmic system has been quite economically viable over the period under examination.

Notes

[1]Tzvetan Todorov, *The Fantastic: A Structural Approach to a Literary Genre*, trans. Richard Howard (Ithaca, NY: Cornell University Press, 1975), p. 4.

[2]Stuart M. Kaminsky, *American Film Genres*, 2nd. ed. (Chicago: Nelson-Hall, 1985); Thomas Schatz, *Hollywood Genres: Formulas, Filmmaking, and the Studio System* (Philadelphia: Temple University Press, 1981); Michael Wood, *America in the Movies: Or, "Santa Maria, It Had Slipped My Mind!"* (New York: Basic Books, 1975; reprint ed., New York: Dell, 1978); John G. Cawelti, *Adventure, Mystery, and Romance* (Chicago: University of Chicago Press, 1976), p. 6.

[3]Joseph Campbell with Bill Moyers, *The Power of Myth* (New York: Doubleday, 1988), p. 51.

[4]As in Ervin Laszlo, *The Systems View of the World* (New York: George Braziller, 1972).

Tom Laughlin as Billy Jack in *Born Losers*.

The Films Themselves

The Vietvet films themselves are the primary sources for this book, and this section explains the research methodology in deriving the films that portray the Vietvet image system, as well as the reasons other groups of films were not included.

While the filmography does not necessarily contain every American feature fiction film that has a Vietvet as a character, it does contain enough of a sample to reach some at least tentative conclusions within and without the genres discussed. These conclusions can be made more solid if and when more data turn up. As Todorov maintains, "[w]hatever the number of phenomena (of literary works, in this case) studied, we are never justified in extrapolating universal laws from them; it is not the quantity of observations, but the logical coherence of a theory that finally matters."[1] I have, however, included in the filmography all those films found that do include a Vietvet character regardless of that character's perceived importance.

That is, I did not reject a film because a commentator describes a character as "minor," although I will make a distinction between minor and major characters. Further, I did not reject a film due to the perceived importance of a Vietvet character's experience in Vietnam to that character's life in film, although I will discuss whether that experience is foregrounded in the narrative or not. In both cases it can be significant where Vietvets are represented as minor or major characters or when their experiences are foregrounded or not, and whether these occurrences are more common in some genres rather than others.

This book will argue that this body of films performs a mythic function, a negotiation of important symbols about Vietnam between film and audience, better than any other group of films of the period. One could also argue that the

1

group of films both set in Vietnam and set during the Vietnam War would also perform this mythic function and perhaps do so in a clearer way. These films were not the subject of study for a number of problems that they present, all of which the Vietvet group of films avoids.

First, all the Vietnam War films, obviously enough, can be more or less easily incorporated into the war film genre, negating the advantages gained by cross-generic analysis. One would not avoid this problem by comparing them to other war films. Even if one were to torture numerous genres out of this small body of film, the question of gaps during the period arises. There are certain periods in recent history when there simply are not any Vietnam War films to analyze.

As commentators have frequently noted, only one American fiction film, *The Green Berets* (1968), about the Vietnam War was made while the fighting was going on. A few others, including *A Yank in Vietnam* (1963), *Last Message from Saigon* (1965), and *To the Shores of Hell* (1966), deal with the pre-history of the conflict. For the 1960s, though, these films are the run of those that could reasonably be discussed in this generic context.

The issue of the war was studiously avoided during the first part of the next decade. *The Losers* (1970) has a group of bikers, not officially associated with the military, sneak into Cambodia to rescue a group of CIA agents. *Hi, Mom!* (1971) contains a very brief segment set in Vietnam. *Clay Pigeon* (1971) and *There is No 13* (1974) both ostensibly set away from Vietnam can be seen as representations of extended hallucinations of soldiers fighting there.[2]

That is about the extent of it until the late 1970s and *The Boys in Company C* (1977), *The Deer Hunter* (1978), *Go Tell the Spartans* (1978), *Apocalypse Now* (1979), and to lesser extents *More American Graffiti* (1979) and *Who'll Stop the Rain?* (1979), which devote only part of their running time to the Vietnam War, curiously dovetailing with the films at the beginning of the decade.

Only very recently--and about ten years after the withdrawal of troops--has there been a burgeoning number of Vietnam War films, starting in 1982 with *Don't Cry, It's*

Only Thunder. The mid-1980s saw *Missing in Action II: The Beginning* (1984), *Purple Hearts* (1984), *The Hanoi Hilton* (1986), *Platoon* (1986), and *P.O.W.: The Escape* (1986). Later films include *Hamburger Hill* (1987), *Full Metal Jacket* (1987), *Good Morning, Vietnam* (1987), *Bat 21* (1988), *Off Limits* (1988), *84 Charlie Mopic* (1989), *Jacob's Ladder* (1990), and *Flight of the Intruder* (1991). All of these films are included in their own separate filmography. Some of these films reflect current trends in the Vietvet films. The Vietvet films, however, overcome the problem of generic uniformity, and many exist in periods where Vietnam War films do not, particularly in the mid-1960s to late 1970s.

While the Vietnam War has not been a popular subject for feature film until very recently, it is certainly inaccurate to say that war in general has been an unpopular subject during the period under study. Comments like "The Vietnam War played as it happened on home screens"; [t]hus, no one needed story films about Vietnam itself,"[3] do not attempt to answer the question of whether the other war films of the period, which range in war-as-subject from the Revolutionary War to the Korean, perform a mythological function concerning the relationship between the audience and the Vietnam War that I will argue the Vietvet films do. A brief, closer look at these films tends to bear out an indication that they indeed might, especially in the case of World War II films.

Films concerning America's wars from the Revolution to World War I are fairly common during the period under examination. Films about the Revolutionary War include *1776* (1972), a musical, and *Revolution* (1985), a war film. Films about the Civil War in the period include *A Time for Killing* (1968), *The Beguiled* (1971), *The Scavengers* (1971), and *Glory* (1989). Films containing representations of veterans of that war include *Rio Lobo* (1970), *Bad Company* (1972), *The Outlaw Josey Wales* (1976), *The Long Riders* (1980), and *Rebel Love* (1986).

Films dealing with the Indian wars, such as *Little Big Man* (1970), *Soldier Blue* (1970), and *Ulzana's Raid* (1972), have often been approached by commentators as allegories for Vietnam. One, writing about the trend in another allegorical western, *The Wild Bunch* (1969), points out that this film, "released during the Vietnam War, has more to say about our involvement in Vietnam than the film actually set there [*The Deer Hunter* (1978)]."[4]

Films centering around WWI during the period under study--*The Guns of August* (1964), *Oh! What a Lovely War* (1969), *Shout at the Devil* (1976), *1918* (1985) and vets of that war--*Johnny Got His Gun* (1971), *High Road to China* (1983), and *The Razor's Edge* (1984) do not seem nearly as common as those revolving around WWII.

Many of these latter films are set in the Pacific Theater, including *The Thin Red Line* (1964), *Beach Red* (1967), *Hell in the Pacific* (1968), *Tora! Tora! Tora!* (1970), *A Taste of Hell* (1973), *Midway* (1976), and *MacArthur* (1977). Some other WWII films can perhaps be seen as allegories of Vietnam. These films include *Castle Keep* (1969), *Catch-22* (1970), and *Slaughterhouse-Five* (1972).

Many of the rest are comedies, including *What Did You Do in the War, Daddy?* (1966), *The Secret War of Harry Frigg* (1968), *Welcome to the Club* (1971), *1941* (1979), *To Be or Not To Be* (1983), and *Shanghai Surprise* (1986). Of the remaining films some are highly nostalgized melodramas dealing with either the homefront: *Summer of '42* (1971), *The Class of '44* (1973), *The Way We Were* (1973), *Swing Shift* (1984), *Racing with the Moon* (1984); or romances set during the war: *Yanks* (1979), *Hanover Street* (1979), *Eye of the Needle* (1981), *Plenty* (1985), and *A Time of Destiny* (1988).

Films that represent WWII veterans have also been fairly common during the period under study. These are fairly cross-generic as well, including representatives in the gangster film, the melodrama, the vigilante film, the horror film, and even an instance in a musical, *New York, New York* (1977). *The Godfather* (1972) and *The Godfather, Part II* (1974) are gangster films in this category. Melodramas include *Baby Blue Marine* (1976), *Greased Lightning* (1977), *Maria's Lovers* (1985), and *Desert Bloom* (1986). Vigilante films that represent a WWII vet in this period include *The Farmer* (1977), *A Time to Die* (1983), *Stand Alone* (1985), and *Armed Response* (1987). Finally, a horror film that includes a deadly WWII vet is *Pet Sematary* (1989). While these films are fairly cross-generic, the Vietvet films are more so, and more directly related to the issues at hand.

Similar problems arise when the Korean war films of the period are examined. Films like *M*A*S*H* (1970), *Inchon* (1982), and *Field of Honor* (1985) are similar generically and apparently quite limited in number. Films representing Korean veterans such as *Thunderbolt and Lightfoot* (1974), *Remo Williams: The Adventure Begins* (1985), *52 Pick-Up* (1986), and *Road House* (1989) are generically varied but similarly limited in quantity, too limited for any kind of specific hypothesis to be generated about Korean vets represented in the period that this book covers.

Getting back to films perhaps more directly related to Vietnam, but not representing the war, similar problems arise. During the period a handful of films represented contemporary members of the national guard--*Earthquake* (1974), *Shoot* (1976), and *Southern Comfort* (1981)--and of the merchant marine--*Cinderella Liberty* (1973) and *The Last Detail* (1973)--and in none of these examples is a character's service in Vietnam made explicit. There have also been representations of the fighting in Cambodia with *The Losers*, as mentioned above, and *The Killing Fields* (1984). There is even at least one film representation of the French forces in Indochina, *The Lost Command* (1965).

Films of the period representing draft dodgers are nearly all melodramas. These include *Hail, Hero!* (1969), *Cowards* (1970), *Prism* (1971), *Summertree* (1971), *Outside In* (1972), and *Journey Through Rosebud* (1972). These latter two represent Vietvets as well and will be discussed later.

The many homefront films, from *The Activist* (1969) and *The Strawberry Statement* (1970) to *Four Friends* (1981), *Fandango* (1984), and *1969* (1988) are still limited in number when compared to the Vietvet films, not as cross-generic, and limited to representing a certain point in time as well. Those films that represent the homefront during the Vietnam War and that represent a Vietvet will be discussed where appropriate in the main body of this book.

During the period then, a great many films have as a focal point the issue of war. Of these films, only during and after the late 1970s are very many set in Vietnam during the War. Those can be shown to mythologize the war in a fairly direct way. Those that are not set there during the war, but that still evoke war, can be seen to exist in a slightly different mythological relationship, linking film audiences to conceptions of Vietnam. Of the groups of films that perform this mythological function, none appears to be as cross-generic and consistent in release pattern over this time as the Vietvet films.

My historiographical method will not include a mere listing of these films chronologically, nor simply an attempt to describe the films and their aesthetic merits. Rather, my generic/mythic/systemic analysis will be informed by a specific method. It is to that method I now turn.

Genre

Within the formulaic films, the "popular genres" in Cawelti's sense, I will use a division suggested by Thomas Schatz--genres of order and genres of integration--so named to describe the resolutions each group invariably portrays. The genres of order are marked by lone, usually male protagonists, embattled settings, and violent conflicts. On the other hand the genres of integration are marked by dual protagonists, usually with a strong female as one of them, genteel settings, and gentle conflicts.[5]

Then, the biker, vigilante, caper, gangster, police, horror, and war genres can be seen as genres of order. The comedy and the melodrama can be seen as genres of integration. The art film can be seen as non-formulaic film. I see fluidity between and among these genres, and placement of a Vietvet film, when it seems necessary, will be argued with qualifications. Within these genres I will refer to a short period of activity over a defined number of years as a "cycle."

In *Vietnam in Prose and Film* James Wilson makes an aesthetic argument that I disagree with by blending film and literature criticism with a vague notion of historiography.[6] The author here holds that Vietnam-related fiction and movies are mostly flawed because they are not true to his notion of history, which is based on ideas of realism which he does not fully explain. His argument runs as follows: "good" fiction and film should uphold the demands of "good" history. Specifically, Vietnam-related literature, according to Wilson, should describe and discuss the background that led to America's involvement and trouble in Vietnam. This background, according to Wilson, includes such things as Vietnamese cultural history, the French involvement in Indochina, and the American foreign policy decisions following World War II that led to escalation in Vietnam. It therefore comes as no surprise that Wilson holds that the nonfiction about the war from 1965 to 1980 was more successful than the fiction.[7]

First of all, Wilson does not seem even to consider that the concerns of "good" historiography need not necessarily be the concerns of "good" filmmaking. *Grand Illusion* (1937) and *Paths of Glory* (1957) do not mention the mobilization of Russia's train system. Does *Full Metal Jacket* have to deal with Dienbienphu to be considered a "good" film? His assumptions and mine on this point are quite different. I believe that "true" history need not necessarily have to have anything to do with mythic function.

In any case my approach differs from Wilson's. I am not concerned with what the films studied below should or should not do. Rather, as a starting point for analysis of the Vietvet image system, I will describe and discuss *what* they do. Thus, my descriptive approach differs fundamentally from Wilson's prescriptive one. Also, I would like to add something to this basically aesthetic work of film history, by introducing concepts from both social and economic film history.

Myth

The interplay mentioned above between convention and invention is the starting point for generic analysis. This way of looking at types of films helps one to describe recent historical trends within genres. If concepts from myth studies are added to this notion of generic interplay, broader cultural patterns can also emerge.

In a sense, according to Joseph Campbell, both of these

processes can be seen as belonging to the orders of mythology. In the first sense, the convention/invention interplay is a type of mythology "that is strictly sociological, linking you to a particular society." In the second, broader sense, a mythology can be seen "that relates you to your nature and to the natural world."[8]

According to Campbell, myths "are archetypal dreams and deal with great human problems."[9] These fundamental myths include such things as the creation of the world, virgin births, negotiating the stages of one's life, death and resurrection, and ascension into heaven. Societies mold these great themes into shapes that make sense to them.[10] The Vietvet films do not make systematic use of all of these fundamental myths. The ones they do use are those in the middle of the list above, regarding the stages of life and death.

Campbell also describes certain subsidiary types of myth, including certain archetypal narrative patterns, characters, and objects. Some of these myths range centuries back in time; others have appeared in more modern times, as updates of older archetypes. Automobiles, airplanes, and weapons are examples of "myths to incorporate the machine into the new world."[11] These objects will have iconic significance in various Vietvet genres. Certain narrative patterns have existed for a much longer time than have these objects.

For example, "the lance that delivers the wound" myth involving a narrative point that "only when that lance can touch the wound again that the wound can be healed," dates back at least to medieval times. This myth can be seen in many Vietvet films, especially in the genres of order. A current societal twist is that the Vietvet, traumatized by his war experience, must again face that experience in order to be purged of his "wound." In the genres of integration, an important mythic narrative concept is compassion, used in the sense of two lovers "suffering with" each other.[12]

Vietvets can also nearly always be seen as archetypal characters.[13] The archetypes of special importance to this book are the hero, the monster, the bureaucrat, and the shaman. Campbell gives definition to all of these terms. For example, the hero can be one of two types: "some that choose to undertake the journey and some that don't." I will call the former an "intentional hero" and the latter an "adventurer," following Campbell's distinction.[14]

The hero experiences a "supernormal" range of human activity and either remains apart from the world he left, or else tries to return to that world with his new information. In the Vietvet image system, heroes of these general types populate many of the genres of order and of integration. Opposing figures to these heroes can be either monsters or bureaucrats. A bureaucrat in mythic terms, one "living not in terms of himself but in terms of an imposed system,"[15] only very rarely is a major Vietvet character within this system.

Examples of the Vietvet as monster, "some horrendous presence or apparition that explodes all of your standards for harmony, order, and ethical conduct,"[16] are even more rare within the image system. Within the horror film, however, many Vietvets can be seen as a type of horrendous presence in human form. That shape then greatly disrupts the social order. These I will call "human monsters." Somewhat related to the archetypal monster is the shaman; both are often associated with madness, although the latter figure is not as socially disruptive.

According to Campbell, the shaman in "late childhood or early youth has an overwhelming psychological experience that turns him totally inward. It's a kind of schizophrenic crack-up." Rather than the destroyer of social order, the shaman "becomes the interpreter of the heritage of mythical life."[17] Vietvets as shaman archetypes, deeply touched by their experiences in Vietnam, figure into both the comedy and art film genres.

In regard to how specifically this myth system mediates between film and audience, I will argue the Vietvet films act as purveyors of fragments of myths that "[w]e translate and interpret and transfer from films back to life, but we do it instantly and intuitively, working at a level of awareness somewhere just below full consciousness."[18] Campbell's ideas do not seem incompatible in this regard.

While he claims that film can be a purveyor of "stories about gods," one of his central definitions of myth, he also claims that most "movies are made simply to make money."[19] Accordingly, following Campbell, it is not enough that a Vietvet character appears in a film to hold that the character performs a mythic function. Rather, that character's function must be analyzed and compared to the function of other characters.

Some writers of nonfiction regarding the Vietvet state that their purpose is to clear up the distinction between "myth" and "fact." Quite to the contrary, I do not believe it is possible or even healthy to try to get myths totally out of people's minds. Rather, this is where the importance of the book lies: to dissect those myths, to see how they function in film. This book will usually be approaching somewhat different myths than commentators like Ghislaine Boulanger and Charles Kadushin evoke.[20]

For example, when they say that there are myths about the relationship of group cohesion to post-traumatic stress disorder (PTSD), it is clear that they and I are talking about different systems of myth, although they might not be incompatible in the largest of myth supersystems. The main application of this last work to this book lies in the area of social support groups available to Vietvets. I will repeatedly check how Vietvet characters function regarding these groups, which can include friends of both sexes, people at work, and immediate and extended families.

In this sense, many of these films, instead of being places we can go to escape, become a distant, distanced battlefield where we can go to think about Vietnam. These movies often seem to provide pieces of myth that are shadowy, vague, and tripping over each other instead of firmly reconciled. In this sense I agree with Michael Wood.[21] Again, Campbell's thoughts do not seem incompatible in this regard. His points about the economics of the film industry also need examination, especially in light of the fairly recent trends towards homogenization of the theatrical market and the recent growth of new ancillary markets.

System

A genre is more than the individual films that comprise it; it can only be said to be a genre when the relationships among those films are expressed. The same things can be said about the Vietvet image within a particular genre and across genres. These systems and subsystems, used in the sense following Ervin Laszlo, can be seen as related to bigger systems, the supersystem of film itself, and the even bigger system of the things outside film that film represents.

As films can be grouped into genres, the power of one filmmaker to change the course of that genre is limited, although an influential film can inspire imitators that help the genre progress. For example, if a filmmaker decided to "revolutionize" the western by making a film that makes absolutely no overt reference to the conventions of that genre, no one, apart from the filmmaker perhaps, would recognize the resulting film as belonging to that genre.

Genre theorists have shown that a systems approach can be applied to the study of film genre and genre films as intersecting systems. Another concern of this book is to show that a similar process can be applied to an image study by examining two different systems, the Vietvet image as it relates to certain film genres, and the Vietvet images collectively, across genres. These first systems are subsystems of the various film genres. The second system is a supersystem made up of those subsystems.

Other systems can be cross-checked, including myth, as discussed above, and audience reaction based on economics, a subject about which I need to define a few terms.

For the purposes of this study, major studios will be the following: Columbia, Metro Goldwyn Mayer, Paramount, Twentieth Century Fox, United Artists (or, depending on the year, MGM/UA), Universal, and Warner Bros. All the others will be called independent studios, with qualifications for American International Pictures, Buena Vista, Cannon, Orion, and Tri-Star when appropriate. Also, those films on *Variety*'s "All-Time Rental Champs" lists for the period under examination will be considered popularly successful films, with the following provisos.

First, the notion of "popularly successful" is from the point of view of movie rentals returned from exhibitors based upon ticket sales. This notion of success is not necessarily shared by the distributing company. There, deductions based upon the distribution fee, upon distribution cost, and upon negative cost must be taken out of the figure for combined domestic and foreign rentals. Only if something remains after profit participation will a distributing company consider the film a financial success.

In other words one must know the contract arrangements for the distribution fee and for profit participation as well as the distribution costs and the negative cost and compare them with both foreign and domestic rentals to get a notion of whether a film is financially successful in this sense. Since studios are almost always reluctant to part with this information, as the recent Art Buchwald case shows, this question is often impossible to answer.

Second, this rental figure should be adjusted over time, by dividing it by the average ticket cost for the year in which the film is released. This will result in a reasonable indication of the number of admissions to the film in the year of its biggest theatrical return. Still, this method will only give an indication of theatrical success, and not a very clear picture of success in ancillary markets.

Accordingly, one can check a film's availability on video against the film's initial release date. As video tapes have only in the 1980s and later been released as nearly a matter of course after a film's theatrical run, or released as "video only" without a theatrical run, a film culled from libraries of 1960s and 1970s films implies a strong assumption on the part of the video releaser that that film will find a market in the present. Conversely, a "video only" film implies a strong assumption on the part of a distributor that that film would not find a suitable market at the theaters. With these qualifications in mind, the rental chart and video availability can be taken as thumbnail indications of a film's popularity with the initial paying audience and in ancillary markets in the 1980s and 1990s.

I will refer to this notion of "popular success" throughout the book. In this area film audiences get a chance to make their feelings known to filmmakers, at least in a general way, about whether they will support or do not support certain types of films. The filmmakers, by making or not making more films of a particular type, can be seen as at least partially responding to this popular support. This economic feedback system provides another checkpoint for the Vietvet films, along with the generic and mythic ways described above.

Notes

[1]Todorov, *The Fantastic*, p. 4.

[2]Generically, there is nothing particularly unusual about this trend. As Kaminsky notes in *American Film Genres*, p. 229, most war films are made when the represented war is over.

[3]Jeanine Basinger, *The World War II Combat Film: Anatomy of a Genre* (New York: Ballantine, 1985), p. 212.

[4]William Galperin, "History into Allegory: *The Wild Bunch* as Vietnam Movie," *Western Humanities Review*, Summer 1981, p. 171.

[5]Schatz, *Hollywood Genres*, p. 35.

[6]James Wilson, *Vietnam in Prose and Film* (Jefferson, NC: McFarland & Company, 1982).

[7]Wilson, *Vietnam in Prose and Film*, p. 5.

[8]Campbell, *The Power of Myth*, pp. 22-23.

[9]Ibid., p. 15.

[10]Ibid., pp. 10-11 and p. 32.

[11]Ibid., p. 18.

[12]Ibid., pp. 195 and 198.

[13]Something, again, that this cross-generic analysis points out, and that other types of analysis might miss.

[14]Campbell, *The Power of Myth*, pp. 123-129.

[15]Ibid., p. 144.

[16]Ibid., p. 222.

[17]Ibid., pp. 85 and 88.

[18]Wood, *America in the Movies*, p. 16.

[19]Campbell holds that movies show actors who have multiple presences, a condition of the gods, and that they are shown in special temples. *The Power of Myth*, p. 15. The point about film economics is on page 82.

[20]Ghislaine Boulanger and Charles Kadushin, eds., *The Vietnam Veteran Redefined* (Hillsdale, NJ: Erlbaum, 1986).

[21]Wood, *America in the Movies*, pp. 20-21.

(L-R, foreground) Danny Glover and Mel Gibson in *Lethal Weapon*.

The Vietvet and the Biker Film

While Vietvet characters have very frequently appeared in films representing crime, as Stuart Kaminsky has pointed out, "crime" is much too broad a categorization to sensibly be called a genre, for too many different types of film have to do with crime.[1] Although this section's focus will be upon the biker, the vigilante, the caper, and the police film, I would also like to point out some films that contain Vietvet characters, dealing with crime in some way, apart from those genres.

These include the gangster film and the hard-boiled detective film. Regarding these films, there have not been enough instances of Vietvet characters within them to make strong generalizations about them. Regarding the other genres of crime, these groups provide initial views of the Vietvet as intentional hero, as adventurer, and as human monster. Further, the police film is perhaps the most popularly successful group with the Vietvet filmic image system. The genres of crime will provide the beginnings of this image; the other genres of order, the war and horror films, will supplement it.

The biker films represent the Vietvet in some important ways. For one thing, they are the main film vehicle that carried the Vietvet image from the mid-1960s to the early 1970s. By examining the Vietvet characters along mythic lines, a similarity emerges regarding heroism. By comparing this characterization to that in films within the genre but without the Vietvet subsystem, one can see that this characterization is not carried throughout the genre.

This analysis by character also shows that the biker film represents a Vietvet who comes home to find himself more or less unaffected by his war experiences. This representation will not be picked up by other genres initially. Biker

Vietvets often use skills or weapons acquired in Vietnam, but never seem deeply troubled by their experiences there.

An examination of the settings and of the icons of the genre further shows major differences both within the genre and without it. For example, the genre only very rarely represents a Vietvet as a drug-user or addict within a genre rife with such representations. On a somewhat larger scale, the genres of order often represent characters who are expelled from contested space. While the biker film follows this trend, the characters are often pre-figured as expelled; often the settings are on the fringes of civilization.

The biker film, as a genre, remained viable for about a decade starting in 1964. 1966 to 1971 was a period of special productivity, as more than forty biker films were made over those six years. American International Pictures (AIP) produced the bulk of these films. According to Thomas McGee, after *The Wild Angels* (1966) was released, AIP followed with a flurry of biker films, starting with *Devil's Angels* (1967).[2]

Biker films offered independents another collection of stories with the "torn from today's headlines" quality that they produce with regularity. For example, *Born Losers* (1967) was reportedly based upon two newspaper items from the mid-1960s, and its plot does seem similar to them. One involved a Marine who wounded two men who were attacking three women in Philadelphia. The Marine was sentenced to six months in jail and a $1400 fine. The two men were fined $50 a piece and released. The other was the Kitty Genovese story. She was stabbed several times while many onlookers did nothing to help.[3]

Using these kinds of sources for stories can have strange repercussions for the independent studios. For example, The Hell's Angels sued Roger Corman for defamation of character, arguing that what was consistently being portrayed in these films as an outlaw gang was in actuality a harmless social organization. The strength of their $2,000,000 suit was perhaps realized by the sporting club-- they settled out of court for $2000.[4]

Much has been made about the speed and efficiency, the overall economy and single-mindedness, with which AIP worked. This idea of single-mindedness can be taken a step further and helps the films to be seen as a distinct genre. From the titles alone, such as *Hell's Angels on Wheels* (1967), *Hell's Angels '69* (1969), *Angels From Hell* (1968), *Hell's Bloody Devils* (1970), *Devil's Angels*, *The Wild Angels*, *The Wild Rebels* (1967), *Wild Wheels* (1969), and *Wild Ones on Wheels* (1967), it can be safely assumed that studios were trying to sell what they thought was a basically undifferentiated product. Further, this mind-set is not at all incompatible with a number of films in a few short years becoming a recognizable genre.

Not until after the success of *Easy Rider* (1969) did a major studio release a film that could fall into this category, and the few that were attempted, for example *Little Fauss and Big Halsy* (1970), did not fare well enough for very many more attempts to be made. It should be noted in these instances, as well as in *Electra Glide in Blue* (1973), a police film with biker film and detective film elements, that the majors seemed quite leery of making a biker film containing a biker gang. Independents made several attempts to revive the genre. For example, George Romero's *Knightriders* (1981), *Hell's Angels Forever* (1983), *The Danger Zone* (1987) and its sequels, and *Easy Wheels* (1989), a parody which contains three Vietvets, are all biker films, but the productivity of the late sixties is a thing of the past.

Before turning to the Vietvet biker films' contributions to the genre, I will discuss the genre more broadly. It can be seen as a part of many youth/rebellion films current during the late 1960s and early 1970s. Among these are various drug-trip films, campus unrest films, and homefront films, which dealt with opposition to the Vietnam War.

Vietvet characters rarely appear in these films, except in a few of the homefront films. One drug-trip film containing a Vietvet is *The Initiation* (1968), an obscure picture from Original Films. In it Kelly (Rick Strausser), a Vietvet drug addict, likes beer parties and engages in orgies with his siblings. He gets arrested by federal agents for trying to buy heroin.[5] The following discussion of the biker films along the lines of icons, settings, character and conflict, and theme, will show that this type of representation of a Vietvet is very rare.

The central icons of these films are the motorcycles themselves and the gang colors, worn on leather jackets. People's lives are often subordinated to these objects. Invariably, weapons are also linked to one of these central icons in the form of bike chains, although knives and inexpensive guns are also sometimes used. Drugs, especially marijuana and LSD, are also very important objects in these films, along with drug paraphernalia.

The biker films generally take place in the area bounded by California, Nevada, and the Mexican Border. Within these states the small towns, beaches, and deserts provide the setting for a majority of the biker pictures. Very occasionally Los Angeles or Las Vegas will provide a backdrop for these films, but then only the fringes of these cities. Exteriors are made use of much more frequently than are interiors, probably for both narrative and economic reasons. A large part of these films' stories involves rival gangs chasing back and forth at each other. Exteriors can be shot more cheaply than interiors, and these, in particular, were close to the independent studios' headquarters. Very few of these pictures were shot on big budgets.

The main interiors include places for the gangs to crash, fight, or encounter the law. These can include shacks and caretaker's sheds for the gang's headquarters, bars for places of rough socializing and fights, and police stations for being charged, making bail, and serving time. Thus, both the exteriors--unincorporated, fringe, wild--and the interiors --places to battle and rest exhausted--can be seen as contested rather than civilized space in the biker films.

Character and conflict can be treated together because the central conflicts nearly always arise from two groups in opposition with each other. Sometimes these groups include the biker gangs made up of veterans, blacks, Mexicans, American Indians, and often, mechanics and other filling station workers, or some combination thereof. In some cases one biker gang will confront non-biker characters from the list above, as is always the case involving three other groups: hippies, surfers, and police.

Bikers interacting with hippies in film is not at all common until after *Easy Rider*, which can be seen as a merger of those two until then disparate groups. After that, we have *Angel Unchained* (1970) and *Angels Hard As They Come* (1971). In both these films bikers and hippies are involved in conflicts.

When surfers and bikers are set in conflict, the opposition is generally played for comedy. Films like *Bikini Beach* (1964), *Beach Blanket Bingo* (1965), and *How to Stuff a Wild Bikini* (1965) are the chief examples of this tendency. *Pajama Party* (1964), a "beach party"-type movie shot mainly using interiors, is a variation of this trend. This type of film does not figure prominently later in the cycle. *Wild Wheels*, in an action variation, pits a biker gang against peace-loving dune-buggy enthusiasts. In the 1980s in a few isolated instances, bikers reappeared in a comic context, notably in the Clint Eastwood *Which Way* pictures.

Police, however, figure in most biker films all throughout the genre's run. The most common crimes by biker characters are murder and rape, and the police try to track them down, often ineffectually, in many films including *The Wild Angels*, *Shanty Tramp* (1967), *The Wild Rebels*, *Angels From Hell*, *Wild Wheels*, and *Angels Die Hard* (1970). Later in the biker cycle there seems to be a marked tendency towards either absence of police or representation of very weak police forces.

In these instances and many others the central conflict is gang against gang. For example, in *The Glory Stompers* (1967), the Black Souls fight the title group. In many cases the gangs are comprised of the character types listed above. In other instances single members of those groups battle gangs.

Single blacks fighting against gangs figure into *Shanty Tramp* and *Big Enough n' Old Enough* (1968). In *The Black Angels* (1970), the white Serpents battle the black Choppers, with a policeman acting like Yojimbo in the background. *The Black Six* (1974) also features a black gang battling a white gang, with the police remaining out of it.

In *The Wild Angels* the Hell's Angels fight a Mexican biker club. Mexican slave traders figure into *The Glory Stompers*. In *Rebel Rousers* (1970) a Mexican family fights off the title group with pitchforks when the police are late in arriving. Also, a single Mexican-American takes on the Black Angels in *Big Enough n' Old Enough*.

Single American Indians have been represented as gang members in *Satan's Sadists* (1969). In *The Savage Seven* (1968) a group of American Indians is terrorized by a gang in a town in the California desert. Also, Billy Jack (Tom Laughlin), half Indian, fights against a biker gang in *Born Losers*.

Mechanics and gas station workers figure into *Hell's Angels on Wheels* in two ways. First, the owner of a station is attacked by the gang; later, a worker from the station joins them. *Big Enough n' Old Enough* shows a variation. Here, while the owner is beat up, the worker battles the bikers. In *Five the Hard Way* (1969) a garage owner forms a gang to battle a rival gang.

Veterans appear as characters both singly--*Motor Psycho* (1965), *Born Losers*, *The Angry Breed* (1968), *Satan's Sadists*, and *The Hard Ride* (1971)--and in groups--*Angels From Hell*, *Chrome and Hot Leather* (1971), *The Black Six*, and *Easy Wheels*.

As the outline of characters and conflicts starts to indicate, these films belong firmly to Schatz's genres of order. The conflicts here are nearly always externalized and violent. The characters are outsiders, outlaws. Also, the resolutions offer no hope of the characters' integration, if indeed they even survive. These films are generally static in terms of location, especially before *Easy Rider*, and end when they start, with a character or group set apart, alone, away from anyone else.

Russ Meyer's *Motor Psycho* appears early in the cycle and displays enough of the biker film conventions to include it in the genre.[6] The gang in this case has only three members, smaller than would become the pattern in later years. It consists of Brahmin (Stephen Oliver), a Vietvet out on a medical discharge and his two cohorts, Slick and Dante. This group terrorizes the townspeople of a typical setting, a desert town in California. The central conflict arises when they rape the wife of a veterinarian named Corey (Alex Rocco). The local sheriff offers Corey no help, so Corey tracks down the bikers himself, finally killing Brahmin with dynamite. Along the way, Brahmin kills Slick in an argument. Bikers this far on the wrong side of the law will not often be represented as Vietvets, as other biker films will show.

Born Losers begins with a voice-over description of Billy Jack: "He had just returned from the war. One of those Green Beret Rangers. A trained killer, people were to say later," a description out of sorts with the action of the film, for the townspeople generally support Billy Jack's battle with the outlaw bikers, although they offer no effective help. It seems that the opening titles on current video prints of the film may have been re-shot, and added on to the film for its re-release after the success of *Billy Jack* (1971).[7] The stock footage that runs under the credits lends support to this inference. By then, too, other filmmakers were starting to make different assumptions about how audiences wanted Vietvets represented.

Billy Jack's first run-in with the bikers comes as he tries, after being unable to rouse the police, to prevent them from assaulting a townsperson. The gang and Billy both get arrested; they for assault and he for "vigilantism," which nets him a stern warning from the judge and a larger fine than the bikers get. This sentence is one instance in a long line of representations of flawed institutions in the Vietvet films, especially the law and the family.

Beside the wrongheaded judicial branch, the executive fares no better. Jack Starrett plays Fred, a policeman, amidst lines such as, "You're the weakest sheriff we've ever seen!" In an quirk of casting, Starrett also portrays the officer who particularly torments John Rambo (Sylvester Stallone) during the shaving scene in *First Blood* (1982). Here, however, he tries to help the Vietvet character and fails

miserably. After refusing to help Billy Jack in his final encounter with the bikers, Fred stays outside and then shoots
Billy by mistake when he emerges from the gang's headquarters.

The feud between Billy Jack and the gang had escalated
to this point because Billy befriended and protected Vicky,
one of the many town girls the bikers had sexually attacked
and terrified into keeping silent. One of the conflicts of the
film is whether these girls should "do their duties as citizens"
and testify against the gang. The girls get practically no help
in these matters from their families. Vicky's father disap-
pears from the film in the beginning, never to be seen again.
Other parents offer conflicting advice. One parent complains
to Billy, "If only one of us had the guts to cut 'em down."
Billy Jack replies, "Yeah. I tried that once."

On the one hand, testifying against these criminals is
held up as a positive good by all the townspeople and Billy
Jack. Yet, Billy knows from first-hand experience that the
legal system operates badly in his world. Further, to save
Vicky's life and ostensibly allow her to testify, Billy Jack
does precisely the same thing he did to get in trouble in the
first place. That is, act as a vigilante. None of these problems is reconciled; they merely coexist in the film. Testifying is good, but it isn't. Vigilantism isn't good, but it is.

At closure Vicky's testimony is rendered moot by the
fact that the principals who committed the crime are now
dead. Billy Jack is literally carried away from the community, his deeds netting him nothing but a cop's bullet. Like a
gunfighter in a western, Billy's skills are barely tolerated
until his job is done, and then the people are glad to see him
leave.

Throughout, Billy Jack's fighting skills are tied to his
experience in Vietnam. At one point a biker asks, "You
think you can get away with those Green Beret heroics in
here?" Billy replies, "Yeah. Yeah, as a matter of fact." This
exchange points out a certain nonchalance about the Vietvet's
war experience that will be represented quite commonly in
these films over the next few years. This exchange and the

voice-over at the beginning, in fact, are about the extent of the discussion of Billy Jack's military service.

In an atypical representation of work in a biker picture, Johnny Taylor (Murray McLeod), tries to sell a script to Hollywood in *The Angry Breed*. He's not really a scriptwriter; he got the work from a war buddy who died in Vietnam. After Johnny saves a producer's daughter from some bikers, he thinks he has made a sale. Ultimately, though, the producer declines. Later, the bikers meet Johnny again and decide *they'll* produce the screenplay, resulting in a fairly rare merging of drug-trip and biker movies.

Angels From Hell is the only example of a Vietvet forming a biker gang and thus being in direct opposition to the police. Here, Mike (Tom Stern) "establishe[s] himself as uncontested gang leader" in his area of small-town California, then "decides to unite all the cycle gangs in the state."[8] He dies opposing the Establishment that sent him to war.

Satan's Sadists, far from showing the political consciousness apparent in *Angels From Hell*, has its central character, Johnny Mardin (Gary Kent), utter lines such as, "Christ, in Vietnam, at least they paid me when I killed someone," after dispatching one of the Sadists. This takes the nonchalance exhibited in *Born Losers* to a new level.

Mardin single-handedly battles a gang in a desert, after antagonizing them by protecting a girl from their attacks. The mentions of his service are more frequent than Billy Jack's, though the nonchalance becomes exhibited to a greater degree. He sums up his war experience by saying, "It's pretty rough over there.... I can thank the Marines. They taught me that the most important thing is to stay alive. Then you can find out what you're looking for."

His attitude toward stateside violence is equally casual. After killing one of the Sadists by throwing a snake on him, he returns to the girl whom he is protecting. She asks what happened, and he replies, "Oh, there's not really that much to tell."

Private Duty Nurses (1972) represents a variation. In it Domino (Dennis Redfield) is a Vietvet who suffers a serious head wound in Vietnam, but will not give up motorbike racing, the thing he thinks he needs to reintegrate. The representation here is different from the main one in biker pictures, for Domino says he smoked grass in country, and he is much more politicized than the typical biker within their genre. He talks of returned vets running the country and mentions that he hates the people who "hid" during the war as much as those who sent him over.

The Hard Ride, a more typical presentation, is interesting to this study in at least two ways, for it presents a story line that will be picked up in later Vietvet films--a soldier returning home to bury his war friend--and serves as a link to the remaining Vietvet films that feature blacks in central roles. Robert Fuller portrays Phil, who returns to bring his black friend Lenny's body back to his hometown for burial. Lenny has left his prized possession, his motorcycle, to Phil, who must battle Lenny's old gang when it becomes the object of their attention.

All Phil wants to do is get people to go to Lenny's funeral, and he even offers the coveted bike to the gang in exchange for their attendance. Phil goes about his humble ambition quite calmly and good-naturedly. When a biker tells him that "Nam must have made you crazy," it is because Phil dares resist them, not because of any symptoms of psychopathology. This veteran character is calm through and through, about life ("For me, everyone's entitled to do their own thing."), about drug use at home and in Vietnam ("It was there if you wanted it."), and about readjustment ("As I reach out for peace at home, I find another kind of war," as the film's main song goes.), and so forth.

As the song suggests there is no peace to be found for this returning veteran. His attempts to pay his friend's memory a proper tribute result in his getting caught in the middle of a rumble that kills him. Ironically, some of Lenny's old gang shows up at the subsequent double funeral, underscoring the trouble this heroic Vietvet has to undergo to complete his humble task.

Chrome and Hot Leather takes another step in the representation of black Vietvets as bikers. Actually, Mitch (Tony

Young), T.J. (William Smith), Al (Peter Brown), and Jim (Marvin Gaye) are Green Beret instructors on leave, posing as bikers to track down the gang that killed Mitch's fiancée. Their combat experience is not as much discussed as shown in their actions declaring war on the other group of bikers.

For, as Gilbert Adair points out, they use a combination of "tear gas, rockets, smoke grenades, explosion simulators...radios, walkie-talkies, field rations and a command post tent" to do so.[9] This is quite an early example of film Vietvets so arming themselves, something to get much more common in the 1980s. This film is also a fairly early example of an independent genre film featuring black lead characters, commonly termed "blaxploitation," the subject to which I will now briefly turn.

As McGee points out, "[i]n the early 1970s much of...[AIP's] revenue was garnered by tapping the black exploitation market."[10] In a sense, then, *Chrome and Hot Leather* can be seen in this company's history as the point where one major product line descended, the biker film, and another, the black genre film, ascended.

The other independents followed suit as well, as the black genre film was enormously popular from about 1971 to about 1975. For example, *Shaft* (1971), *Superfly* (1972), *Black Caesar* (1973), *Blacula* (1973), and *Coffy* (1973) all generated sequels that came out the year after the initial film was released. I mention this now to point out the fact that I will not treat black Vietvet film as a separate genre as Thomas Cripps does, rather I will discuss the representations of black Vietvets within the genres that portray them. There are quite a few films that fall into this category, all within the genres of order, including *Slaughter* (1972), *Gordon's War* (1973), *Slaughter's Big Rip-Off* (1973), *Tom* (1973), *Solomon King* (1974), *Youngblood* (1978), *Rage* (1980), and another biker picture, *The Black Six*.

The film introduces the Black Six in an uncharacteristically homey light for the genre. These six bikers, all portrayed by professional football stars of the time, are busy finishing up farm chores for an old widow. She is so pleased with their work that she invites them in for a country supper and admonishes them to save room for her home-made apple pie. The woman again tells them how much help they have been and that she wishes she could pay them more and keep them on as permanent hands. To round out their introduction they accept permission to sleep in her barn, fix the barn door for free before dawn, and roar off without even waking her up.

One of them, before they leave, makes an apparently contradictory remark that "the Army gave us a home and we never gave it up." This seems odd because they are obvi-ously nomads. It soon becomes clear that he means "bikes, open road, $150 a month from Uncle Sam, and no hassles." As they continue their nomadic existence they do, however, run into some conflict. Bubba (Gene Washington) finds out by way of his general delivery mail that a white biker gang has chain-whipped his brother Eddie (Robert Howard) to death because he was dating the gang leader's sister.

Bubba, and then the rest of the Six, decide to ride west to Menlo, California, to look into Eddie's death. Once there they encounter representatives of the two central institutions portrayed in *Born Losers*, the family and the law, though here the emphasis is slightly different. For one thing Bubba's sister Sissy's initial characterization is one of a black militant. She tells her brother he is nothing but "a bad memory, a dead memory" and calls him an Uncle Tom for fighting in a white man's war. His mother, more typically of the biker genre, tells him to let the police handle the case.

The police, similarly and symptomatically, are of no help whatsoever and the Six decide to investigate on their own. Questioning in the black community, at a bar and a poolhall, turns up no leads. On the contrary those questioned at these places are openly hostile to Bubba. One of these characters includes a 4-F reject named Copperhead. There is some de-fensive interplay, on his part, about his avoiding the service. Before the Six get anywhere in their investigation, they have to turn to the white community.

Once they find Jenny (Cynthia Daly), Eddie's girlfriend and the sister of the white gang's leader, she immediately tells them who and where the gang is. Before the rumble,

Bubba returns to his family. There is a character change apparent in Sissy, who now agrees with her mother that the Black Six should not fight the rival white gang. Her earlier militant stance appears to have vanished. In the ensuing gang fight the Six easily defeat the rival gang, killing many of them.

This film has an uneasy relationship with race. This trend is most apparent surrounding the idea of black militancy and the character Sissy. Her ardent party line, that blacks should rely on blacks only, fails as the black community turns its back on Bubba when he needs help. Further, after this failure, when Sissy next appears she is no longer militant.

The film also has a fairly uneasy relationship in this regard with the idea of racism. All the groups the Six fight are guilty of prejudice against blacks. This notion is summed up in an end title card that reads "Honky...Look out...Hassle a brother and the Black Six will return!!!"

In a sense the many gang-related films that came after the biker genre lost its viability can be seen as a continuation of a trend that portrayed groups of youths outside the law in confrontation with the law, with other groups, or with individuals. Most of these films were made by independents ranging from *Assault on Precinct 13* (1976) to *China Girl* (1987). The financial success of *The Warriors* (1979) and the relative failure of *Streets of Fire* (1984) represents the run of the the majors' apparent interest in this trend. The independent films *Band of the Hand* (1986) and *Enemy Territory* (1987) are rare examples of these films that represent Vietvets, and Orion's *Colors* (1988) could be another, although that picture is better seen as a police film.

As for the biker film Vietvet subsystem, most of these films are today fairly obscure. All of these films were made by independent producers. Of them only *Born Losers* is on *Variety*'s rental-champs list, and only it, *Satan's Sadists*, *Private Duty Nurses*, *The Black Six*, *Savage Dawn* (1985), and *Easy Wheels* are currently available on video tape. Accordingly, the rest of the 1960s-1970s subsystem cannot be said to have sustained itself through history in a strong way, taking economic exchange as the primary exchange of energy in this case.

Still, throughout the historical period in which this image was more viable than currently, and even then this system produced no major hits, certain generalizations can be made. These Vietvet representations occurred at the fringes of the film industry. To much of the film audience these images remained unknown, and remain unknown today to audiences of ancillary markets. Certain parallels can be drawn between this industrial background and the way these independent films portray Vietvets.

In many ways they represent Vietvets as relating to other groups found in these films as similar to the other characters found in the genre. That is, Vietvets relate to police, to other gangs, and so on, the way other characters in the genre do. There does not seem to be a clear trend toward representing Vietvets as individuals opposed to biker gangs, or toward representing groups of Vietvet gangs, although Vietvets in opposition with each other does not appear at all common. In other ways, though, these vet characters can be seen as distinct from others in the genre.

The icons involved with vet characters within this subsystem reflect this separation from other characters found within the genre. This trend can be seen in the Vietvet characters' relationships with bikes themselves, weapons, and drugs. As for the motorcycles, these can be seen in opposition to one of the icons of modern mythology, the automobile.[11]

The Vietvets in this subsystem seem leery of the motorcycle. Often, as in films from *Satan's Sadists* to *The Hard Ride*, the Vietvet will oppose a bike gang without frequent recourse to one, if the vet character uses one at all. Even when they use these objects to pursue their goals, as in *Chrome and Hot Leather*, the motorcycles sometimes rebel against them. This distinguishing feature moves them away from other bikers in the genre and perhaps slightly toward the larger society, which generally also seems leery of the bikes and bikers.

Another distinguishing feature involving icons involves the use of weapons. Vietvets within this subsystem seem never to use the bikes and extensions of them as weapons, as other bikers within the genre frequently do. As opposed to bikes and chains, Vietvets use the skills and weapons of war to do battle. On a different note, drugs are an icon of the genre, often used and sold by bikers. Again, Vietvets within this system are almost never users or sellers of drugs. In both these ways Vietvets can be seen as distinct from other characters in the genre.

In mythic terms, the Vietvets represented can nearly all be seen as adventurers, as heros who get drawn into trials and are ready to face them. The same cannot be said for biker characters generally within the genre. The Vietvets are often represented as initially trying to reintegrate into society, although on its outskirts. When even this minimal reintegration is resisted, these vet characters always turn to violence, but not often directly against that society.

Their violence is often displaced away from the society and towards other outcasts, and the Vietvets usually triumph over these characters but remain apart from the society. These adventurers perform almost exclusively physical deeds, with the general implication that these skills were learned in combat. The image that results is one of a returned hero who remains apart, but not of his own choosing and not due directly to anything that happened in Vietnam.

Notes

[1]Kaminsky, *American Film Genres*, p. 7.

[2]Mark Thomas McGee, *Fast and Furious: The Story of American International Pictures* (Jefferson, NC: McFarland, 1984), p. 171.

[3]Ibid., p. 172.

[4]Ibid., p. 171.

[5]As described in Richard P. Kratsus, ed., *The American*

Film Institute Catalogue of Motion Pictures: Feature Films 1961-1970 (New York and London: R.R. Bowker Co., 1976).

[6]As described in Kratsus, *The AFI Catalogue, 1961-1970.*

[7]Billy Jack's appearances are cross-generic. In the 1971 film he again appears as a vigilante, away from the biker context. In his other two film appearances, the films are melodramas. *The Trial of Billy Jack* (1974) is also a homefront film. *Billy Jack Goes to Washington* (1977), as the title implies, is quite Capraesque.

[8]Kratsus, *AFI Catalogue 1961-1970*, p. 33.

[9]Gilbert Adair, *Hollywood's Vietnam: From "The Green Berets" to "Apocalypse Now"* (London: Proteus, 1981), p. 87.

[10]McGee, *Fast and Furious*, p. 187.

[11]Campbell, in *The Power of Myth*, p. 18, includes this icon as one that serves to incorporate the machine into the new world.

The Vietvet and the Vigilante Film

The Vietvet characters within the subsystem drawn from the vigilante film genre represent some similarities to those found in the biker film genre. For one thing, in another genre rife with illegal drug users and sellers, Vietvets are nearly never represented as such. Further, very common within this genre are vigilantes who actively battle these drug sellers. Another similarity is the Vietvet vigilante's relationship with weapons, which within this subsystem have even a stronger personal association than do the weapons found in the Vietvet biker subsystem.

The Vietvets in the vigilante subsystem show a remarkable consistency in mythic representation, as intentional heroes. These heroes, pitted against bureaucrats, evil-doers, or both, go about their trials quite efficiently. While they are technically outlaws, they can still be considered heroes, as anti-heroes, a term that became common during the Vietnam era. In this sense these characters can be seen to be variations on archetypal characters, updated to make sense to their contemporary audiences. The vets within this subsystem are almost always these characters. Not until very late in the cycle do Vietvets also appear as the ones the Vietvet vigilante opposes.

Within this genre a myth that does not appear in the biker films begins to become evident, the myth of "the lance that delivers the wound."[1] Simply, this myth portrays a wounded hero able to be cured only by the same instrument that created the wound in the first place. For a film to reasonably fall into this category, the Vietvet character has both to be wounded and to be cured by a similar thing, in this case his experiences in Vietnam. Again, these conditions will not be met until very late in the cycle.

One of the salient features of the vigilante genre, as mentioned above, is the nearly total absence of the police, either literally, or figuratively, in the representation of a weak, useless, or totally corrupt police force. This distinguishes the genre from the western, where there is often an absence of the law. That is, I will consider as vigilante tales only those films that take place in a historical period past that of the Western, in which a breakdown or absence of police service is represented, and that void is filled by the vigilante.

The protagonist, almost always male, operates outside an ineffective legal system, generally the way he wishes the police would behave.[2] The settings for these films are often urban streets overcome with crime, and the vigilante walks down those mean streets being mean. The vigilante is generally spurred on to action by a violent attack upon someone quite close to him, usually members of his family.[3] The weapons the vigilante uses generally have some personal meaning to him, be they a gun he swore he would never pick up again or even his own hands and feet.

The Vietvet image in vigilante films can be traced in a number of ways, for example, along the lines of stars. Chuck Norris is one who has played this type of role repeatedly in a number of films for independent studios. In *Good Guys Wear Black* (1978), *A Force of One* (1979), and *Forced Vengeance* (1982) he plays vets who battle, respectively, corrupt politicians, drug warlords, and the Mafia.

Thus, his characters have single-handedly combatted three of the main concerns of these films. Charles Bronson has also been in similar roles often, notably in the *Death Wish* pictures, but only once as a Vietvet. Grouping by film stars, then, does not give as complete a Vietvet image as does an analysis by genre, myth, and system.

The black genre films in this category often deal with the Mafia, the problem of drugs on the ghetto streets, or both. For example, *Slaughter* (1972) and *Slaughter's Big Rip-Off* (1973) have the title character (Jim Brown), another ex-Green Beret, battling the mob. In a variation Brown plays the title role in *Black Gunn* (1972), a nightclub owner who joins with a group of black militant Vietvets to battle the mob, who have killed his brother, an ex-member of BAG, the Black Action Group. *Mean Johnny Barrows* (1976) follows a basically similar plot.

Gordon's War (1973) tackles both these problems, as Gordon (Paul Winfield) reforms with his old unit, ex-Green Berets in a group variation, because "it would take an army to get the dope out of Harlem," and "we're experts. We're gonna use all the tools of the trade. We're gonna drive those bastards out." They then wage an effective war on the drug-supplying New York Mafia.

Youngblood (1978) has Rommel (Lawrence-Hilton Jacobs), a Vietvet, again fighting his own personal war with the help of an Los Angeles street gang. Rommel and his gang are on a mission to try to eradicate drugs from their ghetto. In an earlier film the central problem also has a gang theme, with a black militant group battling corrupt cops.

In *The Bus is Coming* (1971) Billy Mitchell (Mike Simms) comes home to find that his brother has been murdered. Rather than join the militants in the murder investigation, Billy conducts his own investigation but dies before he can prove the corrupt police were responsible. Order has to be restored by the white chief of police.

Another early example involving corrupt police is *Tiger by the Tail* (1970). Steve Michaelis (Christopher George) returns home hoping to become a partner in a racetrack his brother owns, but finds that his brother has been killed in an apparent robbery there. Unsatisfied with the police investigation, he conducts his own and finds out that the sheriff was behind the killing. This time Steve restores order by shooting the sheriff.

A couple of films that fall under this rubric feature a working class emphasis, *Mr. Majestyk* (1974) and *White Line Fever* (1975). Charles Bronson plays Mr. Majestyk, a melon grower who irritates a mob hitman and spends the rest of the movie alternating between fighting the killer and the police, and getting his crop in. Again, the implication in this film is that Majestyk is so proficient in his fighting skills because he proved himself so in Vietnam.

This information is conveyed in a standard way, read aloud from a policeman from the character's rap sheet. This is another Vietvet character, along with one in *The Big Bounce* (1969), connected to agriculture. The similarity here can possibly be attributed to the fact that Elmore Leonard wrote the novels from which both of the films were adapted.

Carol Joe Hummer (Jan-Michael Vincent) in *White Line Fever* is an ex-Air Force pilot who takes the law into his own hands because of a conspiracy between his local police and a corporation to allow truck smuggling to carry on. The information about his service is presented in another standard way ("Don't try your flyboy heroics around here."), in the context of a fight. Still, the representation of a Vietvet as a working class hero (the other truckers go on strike to stop the illegal hauling due to Hummer's actions) is fairly rare.

Cutter's Way (1981) contains a character that also bypasses the police to challenge a corporation, in the figure of a corporate head who arrogantly tries to avoid punishment after killing a young woman. Alex Cutter (John Heard) is an intriguing blend of both old and new characteristics, both within and without this genre. He is aimless and anti-social, not uncommon within the genres of order. He, however, is also physically disabled, alcoholic, and extremely articulate. These traits in combination are extremely rare anywhere in the Vietvet image system.

An earlier film also portrays a Vietvet with a physical disability, but not one directly related to his experiences in Vietnam. Charles Rane (William Devane) in *Rolling Thunder* (1977) loses his hand, but only after he returns from being a POW. The film provides another Vietvet character, Johnny Vohden (Tommy Lee Jones), who is not physically disabled. These two track down, despite an ineffectual policeman who is tailing them, the gang that injured Rane and killed his family. Some later films pick up these threads.

Duggai (Sonny Landham) in the little-seen *Fleshburn* (1984) served three tours in Vietnam, where at that point, he started torturing the enemy. He escapes from an institution for the criminally insane, where he was having an *Apocalypse Now* (1979) inspired flashback very similar to the taunting sniper scene. He goes to seek vengeance upon four psychiatrists who put him there for leaving people to die in a desert over a dispute about Indian magic. He hitches a ride with Brody (Robert Alan Browne), a vet who didn't see much action. After some chat about the deer Brody has shot, quite reminiscent of talks in *The Deer Hunter* (1978),

Duggai takes the truck and shoots Brody with his own deer rifle. Duggai collects the psychiatrists and then leaves them to die in the same desert he left the others. The film waffles over the point about whether Duggai is evil or mad. While the great weight of the film suggests that the institutions he has come in contact with are the mad ones, that they should have left Indian problems to the Indians, the events at closure do not support this reading.

Vietvets in film have often sought to come to the aid of entire cities and towns. For example, in *Vigilante Force* (1976) a Vietvet, Aaron Arnold (Kris Kristofferson), is hired by a small town to restore order from oilfield ruffians who are running wild, and he does so by marshaling a corrupt police force to break the law at nearly every opportunity. Borrowing a twist from Westerns like *Invitation to a Gunfighter* (1964) and *High Plains Drifter* (1973), once he completes his job the town has trouble expelling the mercenary. Aaron's brother, a non-Vietvet, Ben (Jan-Michael Vincent), has to mobilize the citizens to depose him.

John Eastland (Robert Ginty) in the *The Exterminator* (1980) and *Exterminator II* (1984) battles assorted criminals and a specific gang, respectively. These films pick up the thread of Vietvet characters using weapons common in jungle fighting. Here, the Exterminator's weapon of choice is a flame thrower, which he gained proficiency using in Vietnam. His vigilante tactics have a similar effect on the crime rate of New York City to the exploits of Paul Kersey (Charles Bronson) in these films' close model, *Death Wish* (1974).

Similarly, *The Annihilators* (1985) offers the Vietvet-as-vigilante, but with a group variation. Sarge (Christopher Stonc), Ray (Gerrit Graham), Flash (Lawrence-Hilton Jacobs), and Woody (Andy Wood) regroup outside Atlanta, when a mob-supplied, drug-selling gang kills their war buddy, Joey (Dennis Redfield). They teach the community self-defense techniques that they learned in the war, and direct mentions of their war experience abound. For example, during one group strategy session, the conversation goes as follows: "We have got to make a plan and follow it through." "Like Nam?" "Just like Nam."

Then, *Armed Response* (1985) features a whole family of veteran characters, three of whom are Vietvets: Jim Roth (David Carradine) and his brothers, Clay (David Goss) and Tommy (Brent Huff). Their father Burt (Lee Van Cleef), a WWII veteran, joins in to battle the gang that killed various members of their family. This battle is clearly linked to the Vietvets' battles in country. At one point, Jim says, "Well, Dad, back to the jungle."

Although Jim suffers from a PTSD-like disease (his brothers do not), and is plagued by visions similar to those in the French film *Sundays and Cybele* (1962) and *Firefox* (1982),[4] he longs for the days of Vietnam. He mentions that it made more sense than things do for him presently. To refight it, he and his dad attack the gang with Vietnam War-issue weapons.

Later variations mark the emergence of a new image of the Vietvet in film, especially regarding the veteran character's relationship to the war. In most cases these films provide a bare glimpse of an increasingly well-adjusted veteran, in terms of the character's relations to family and work. The partial characterization is shown in a number of ways.

Steele Justice (1987), however, is a bit of a throwback. Its plot is very similar to that of *Search and Destroy* (1981). In these films, the object of revenge directly links back to the character's experiences in Vietnam, and specifically to the representation of a Vietnamese advisor to American troops during the war. These films portray the advisors as corrupt, subordinating the interests of the American troops to their own.

The troops then turn on the advisor, due to his breach of faith. In the battle that ensues the Vietnamese is left for dead. Then, in these films that advisor comes to the United States, where it falls to the protagonist to avenge the death of the friend that the Vietnamese character kills stateside. This portrayal of the Vietnamese, negative as it is, seems to prevail with very few exceptions.

The main difference between the earlier film and the later one is that the Vietvet character is made less harsh in many ways. John Steele (Martin Kove), perhaps in an allusion to the *Billy Jack* films, is a member of the "Wild Horse Management Bureau." He has a habit of losing jobs, including one as a cop and the wildlife-related one, but this latter firing comes because he will not allow horses to be mistreated. Similarly, he drinks but seems to keep it under control. Also, his wife left him but there is a chance they will get back together, and so on.

This softening of typical Vietvet character traits is somewhat mirrored by the representation of Vietnamese veterans. The venal, evil Kwan (Soon-Teck Oh) is matched by the virtuous Lee (Robert Kim), Steele's good friend and ex-partner. So, while the negative stereotype is still present, it is matched by a positive one.

Also, Steele's actions often seem to be played for comedy. For example, after some of Kwan's men try to kill Steele, he instead kills them. Steele deadpans, "They're having doughnuts with Buddha," when someone asks about the thugs. Later, during a fight at a restaurant Steele injures his arm and cauterizes the wound with a hot skillet from a handy buffet table.

Steele also has success in reclaiming some of the things he lost after Vietnam, after refighting his old nemesis from the war using the implements of that war. The resolution of the film pushes back together the husband and wife. Along with the reintegration of his family, Steele gets the promise of his old job back as a policeman. This new type of characterization continues through the 1980s.

For example, in *Eye of the Tiger* (1987) Buck Matthews (Gary Busey) makes a *High Noon*-like speech to his neighbors. Buck, out of prison for a crime he did not commit, wants them to help him track down the outlaw bikers that killed his wife and injured his child. The gang has bought off the sheriff, so the police provide him no help. To elicit the townspeople's support Buck tells them that when they asked him to fight, he did so willingly, in Vietnam. These two things, an overt reference to Vietnam-as-the-people's-will and to the debt a veteran's community owes him are quite rare up to this time.

Also, the film presents Buck Matthews as, in most respects, quite well-adjusted. Although he is just out of prison, the film modifies that point as noted above. Further,

he easily obtains and holds a job and gets along with nearly
everyone he comes into contact with, including his co-workers, his family, and an old ex-police sergeant friend. Everyone, that is, but some outlaw bikers, whom he quite successfully and violently dispatches.

Somewhat similarly, the title character (Burt Reynolds)
in *Malone* (1987) is an introspective CIA man trying to break
away from the Agency. His mysterious past is partially un-
covered in a conversation with Paul Barlow (Scott Wilson)
when Malone tells him that he started his service in 1961.
When Barlow mentions that that seems a little early, Malone
replies, "Not for what I was doing."

It later comes out that Malone fought in Vietnam as well
as in Laos and Cambodia. Barlow also served in Vietnam
and came back with a physical handicap, a limp. Malone,
while helping Barlow and his daughter fight off some land-
developer/survivalists, is reading *Dispatches*, perhaps trying
to make some sense of his war experience.

Nowhere to Hide (1987) contains two clear Vietvet characters, Rob Cutter (Daniel Hugh Kelly) and Ben (Michael
Ironside), a recluse who lives in a cabin in the woods. Rob
Cutter, on the other hand, is a family man and his wife, Barbara (Amy Madigan), is a rare character in American film, a
woman veteran. The film does not mention clearly whether
she is a Vietnam era veteran, but she is a retired Marine,
wins the war games she plays with active Marines, and can
fly a helicopter through tricky maneuvers.

Her husband in the film is killed off early by Army con-
tractor conspirators, which fits him into the trend of the representation of partially well-adjusted Vietvet characters late in
this cycle. That is, Rob Cutter's readjustment to society, as
good as it may seem, is represented as not lasting very long.

On the other hand, in *Dangerously Close* (1986), the
Vietvet Corrigan (Madison Mason) tells his neo-Fascist
group, the Sentinels, how easy it was for him to kill Vietcong, and is suspected for the murder of a high school drug
dealer when one of their vigilante sessions in the woods
goes too far. The student leader of the group, anyway,
wants the rest of the group to see it that way. Corrigan
comes to a warehouse when some innocents are about to fall

into the clutches of the Sentinels, the leader tussles with him, and Corrigan is shot. It turns out that the leader of the group was behind the murder after all, and the film provides an example of a character's war service providing a possible but misleading motivation for murder.

Omega Syndrome (1987) presents a split pair of Vietvets. One, Jack (Ken Wahl), is a decorated soldier, able to put the war behind him and start a career as a journalist. He does have some problems, but they are not war-related. His family broke up when his wife died of leukemia. On the other hand, Phil (George DiCenzo) has not been able to put the war away and still deals in illegal weapons. The two are reunited when the Omega terrorist group kidnaps Jack's daughter. During one scene they joke about setting fire to the Vietcong, tricking one of the neo-Nazi gang into giving them the information they want. They threaten him with their trusty Zippo lighters.

Ministry of Vengeance (1989), another film with a split presentation, is also one of three films that represent a Vietvet who has turned to the priesthood after the war. Here, David Miller (John Schneider) suffers from PTSD-like symptoms, stemming from the time when he had to kill a child Vietcong who was about to throw a grenade at him. His troubles do not end there, as soon his family is murdered by terrorists at an airport. When the State Department is no help, he enlists in a survival camp run by his old commander, Freeman (James Tolkan), and ships out to Lebanon to seek vengeance upon the terrorists, getting himself involved in a complicated CIA plot. Even with all these troubles, Miller remains remarkably unaffected, as is the norm late in this cycle.

Father McCain (Robert Ginty), in *Vietnam Texas* (1990), also has ostensibly tormenting Vietnam flashbacks that have very little outward effect on him, triggered by seeing a Vietnamese woman at Mass and a Vietnamese girl in a schoolyard. It seems that he became a POW after fathering a child with a Vietnamese woman, whom he subsequently "didn't think much about" for the next fifteen years or so. He then abruptly goes to Houston's Little Saigon to try to find her, resulting in her death and the deaths of many others when it turns out that her new husband is active in the Vietnamese Mafia and does not appreciate the presence of McCain. The title apparently refers to *Paris, Texas* (1984), although *Little Saigon, Texas* would avoid the problem of parallelism in the title as it stands. *Last Rites* (1988), a melodrama, is the third film that contains a Vietvet priest as a character.

These vigilante films, as well as some Italian and Filipino exports such as *Fighting Mad* (1977), *Rage* (1978), *The Devastator* (1985), *Kill Zone* (1985), and *Ultimax Force* (1987), and some more obscure ones from the United States such as *The No Mercy Man* (1975) AKA: *Trained to Kill*, *Delirium* (1979), *The Executioner Part II* (1984), *Fear* (1988), and *Ghettoblaster* (1989), represent Vietvets taking the law into their own hands in the face of a useless or absent police force. In terms of economics, the Vietvet vigilante subsystem has peaked, with *White Line Fever*, *Good Guys Wear Black*, *A Force of One*, and *The Exterminator* being the last popular successes. The most recent films in this subsystem have been released almost directly to video. The vigilante films, however, have faired better in ancillary markets than have the biker films; most of the vigilante films are currently available on video tape. They have also lasted for a longer historical period than have the biker films.

In that later period a Vietvet character would become a vigilante, due at least partially to events that occurred in Vietnam during the war. From the early 1970s to the mid-1980s, however, becoming a vigilante was incidental to the character's service in Vietnam, except in the sense that the skills learned in and weapons brought from Vietnam greatly aided the vigilante in his tasks.

Welcome Home, Soldier Boys (1972) is unusual for its time within this subsystem in that the characters become vigilantes and destroy the entire town of Hope, New Mexico, for reasons closely linked to their service in Vietnam. It involves four ex-Green Berets who decide to attack Hope when nobody earlier--including a car salesman, a prostitute, an auto mechanic, a group of Korean War veterans, a small-town sheriff, and a hotel manager--treats them fairly or shows them any gratitude for their wartime service. When in Hope they rebel against a merchant, a policeman, the whole town, and finally against the Army itself. When what was keeping them going was found out to be a big lie, represented by the farm in Napa Valley they hoped to own being a fiction invented to keep them going in battle, they went berserk and went to get their vengeance.

Another icon of the genre, drugs, sheds light on the Vietvet vigilante as a mythic figure. The Vietvets within this subsystem are the heroes who use their skills to battle those, among others, who would supply drugs. When, in the later films, an evil Vietvet would appear, he is always matched with a heroic Vietvet. The main thrust of this consistent representation is to homogenize the Vietvet character as an intentional hero. Throughout the cycle, heroic Vietvets have also appeared in groups.

This splitting of the hero does not seem common in vigilante films outside the Vietvet subsystem. For instance, *Death Wish, Ms. 45* (1981), and *Stand Alone* (1985) all contain lone vigilante characters. Many of the Vietvet vigilante films, though, contain groups of vets battling the evildoers, perhaps in an effort to associate those Vietvets with those commonly found in group hero war films.

The impetus for these characters' revenge has only recently, and rarely, been something that happened in Vietnam. In films like *Search and Destroy* and especially *Steele Justice*, the Vietvet characters battle Vietnamese veteran characters stateside. *Steele Justice* also represents a somewhat better adjusted vet character than does the earlier film, and *Ministry of Vengeance* and *Vietnam Texas* show characters better adjusted still.

The "lance that delivers the wound" myth can be seen partially in these films, as the Vietvet characters can partially reintegrate, but only after they, in a metaphorical sense, refight the war that caused them their problems of reintegration in the first place. The notion of refighting due to a wound, and its associated myth, becomes clearer in other genres during this time.

Notes
[1]As mentioned above and in Campbell, *The Power of*

Myth, p. 195.

[2]Any film within the Vietvet system that contains a vigilante/cop will be treated in the section on the police film.

[3]To react violently when harshly provoked is not a symptom of psychosis. That Vietvet characters included under the genre of vigilante films all respond to such a stimulus is one of the major reasons for excluding them from the category of horror of personality films, to be discussed later.

[4]In all these films the veteran characters are plagued by visions of the death of a young Vietnamese girl. The later representations are similar to the one in the news media of the napalmed Vietnamese girl running down a road.

Charles Bronson (with shotgun) as the title character in *Mr. Majestyk*.

The Vietvet and the Caper Film

While "the lance that delivers the wound" myth is only weakly represented in the Vietvet subsystem of the caper film, the iconic use of certain props points to another line of mythic analysis. In the caper films, vet characters start to be associated with flying machines.[1] Although the beginnings of this association are clear within this subsystem, it can be seen even more clearly in other genres, which will be discussed in later chapters.

These films also show an unusual relationship between Vietvet characters and weapons, in most instances disassociating those characters from them, which is not particularly unusual for the genre as a whole. The major departure from this trend will be noted in the case of *Black Sunday* (1976). Again, the subsystem shows nearly complete uniformity in representing Vietvets as intentional heroes.

Caper films are those which portray a group's intricate planning to pull off a major crime. The central characters in the caper film are often a diverse lot, each with his or her own specialty: the driver, the demolitions expert, the safecracker, the "face," the "brain," and so on, depending on the crime. The group's own internal squabbling can sometimes put the outcome of their crime in jeopardy. Films in this category include the French film *Rififi* (1954), *Five Against the House* (1955),[2] *The Killing* (1956), *Topkapi* (1964), *The Hot Rock* (1972), and *Thief* (1981).

Use of weapons, except upon inanimate objects, is generally considered bad form, as the emphasis is usually on the intricate planning of the caper as opposed to the use of brute force. Even upon safes, bank vaults, and cars, these weapons are often used with great precision, by experts. The "trigger-happy" members of these groups are often eliminated by the more stable members, who see them as a threat to group unity and thus to the successful completion of the

43

caper.

The 1970s saw a handful of these films containing Vietvet characters, generally using the skills they learned in Vietnam in order to pull off the caper. For example, Barney (Hal Reed) in *The Doberman Gang* (1972) gets duped by a gang of bank robbers into training a group of Dobermans in order to pull off a bank heist. His service is mentioned only briefly, at the initial meeting between him and the leader of the gang. Barney tells him that he owes his life to a dog, one that knowingly stepped on a land mine to protect his master. He is described as clean-cut, All-American, and he turns the tables on the gang by closure. He appears quite well-adjusted, and is not in it for the money. Barney is motivated by two things when he double-crosses the double-crossers: revenge against the people who offered him the American Dream and then snatched it away from him, and protection for the kind of animal that saved his life in Vietnam.

Charley Varrick (1973) contains a minor character who served in Vietnam, Harman (Andy Robinson). Harman was a demolitions expert in the war and carries over his skills learned there to help Charley Varrick (Walter Matthau) rob banks. An overt mention of the war comes when Charley is apprehensive about Harman's setup of a diversionary explosion. Harman replies, "No sweat. I've blown up a lot of gooks with this crap, and I'm still here." Although Harman shows no signs of serious mental trouble, he does seem plagued by memories of the war. When the bank robbers are making their getaway, Harman worries out loud, "Some chopper's gonna throw a net over us."

Black Sunday helps perpetuate the representation of the mad Vietvet. Bruce Dern plays Lander, a disturbed ex-fighter pilot, who finds a job flying a blimp. Lander, deeply resentful about his life in the States after Vietnam, looks for a way to strike back at his native country. When terrorists approach him, he finds a scheme suitable for his twisted psyche: They plan and attempt to blow up the football stadium hosting the Super Bowl and the President.

In *Special Delivery* (1976) Jack Murdock (Bo Svenson) leads a group of Vietvets in a string of bank robberies. In a fairly rare representation for the time within the genres of order, Murdock has a sustained relationship with a woman, Mary Jane (Cybill Shepherd). In this respect and some others, this film can be seen as a caper-comedy. More typically, his group does not hold regular jobs and seems to relate well only to those who also served in Vietnam, survived, and returned. A different type of film came out the same year.

Ransom (1976) AKA: *Maniac!* features an embittered Vietvet whose plans to compete in the Olympics were cut short by the war. He disguises himself as an Indian, and takes revenge against a wealthy town, killing policemen with arrows from a crossbow and threatening to do more if not paid a million dollars. Two of the people who track him are also Vietvets, but practically nothing is made of their service. The implication that the war made the extortionist go crazy is very strong, but the main way the information about him is conveyed is very strange. It comes from the picture's theme song. A high-level intrigue picture also belongs in this group.

Twilight's Last Gleaming (1976) centers around an angry ex-Air Force Officer (Burt Lancaster), who with the help of cohorts, seizes a missile silo and threatens to launch the rockets unless the United States makes public its "hidden agenda" about the Vietnam War. Similarly, *The Domino Principle* (1977) came in the midst of a wave of post-Watergate high-government conspiracy thrillers which includes films like *The Parallax View* (1974), *Three Days of the Condor* (1975), and of course the docudrama *All the President's Men* (1976).

In *The Domino Principle* Tucker (Gene Hackman) gets recruited out of jail by a governmental conspiracy group to perform a political assassination, using the marksmanship skills he learned in Vietnam. Typical of the representation of the time, Tucker intones that killing is like making love: "After the first time it comes easy." Somewhat atypically, he refuses to cooperate with the conspirators.

That this conspiracy variation had mainly been played out by the mid-1980s can be seen in the obscurity of the sequel to the novel from which the film was adapted. *The*

Domino Vendetta,[3] in which Tucker battles yet another conspiracy, was not a best seller and no film adaptation of it has
been made. Similarly, the lack of financial success of
Flashpoint (1984),[4] which represents a Vietvet, Bog Logan
(Kris Kristofferson), being hunted down by government
agents when he uncovers their conspiracy, and the dearth of
other high-government conspiracy films by this time suggests that this theme was no longer viable, although variations of it can be seen running through films as late as
Rambo: First Blood Part II (1985), and in two other not-
quite-successful films a bit later.

In *Betrayed* (1988) Tom Berenger plays Gary Simmons,
a Vietvet "war hero" who is now in a murderous white
supremacy group. He almost won the medal of honor, and
did win a purple heart. Simmons says that his marriage
might have been broken up due to the war. His war background is not presented as motivation for his violent nature
though; quite the opposite, it is mentioned that this background might make him hard to be found guilty, because
war heroes are "fashionable now." Also, the FBI agents in-
terested in his case suggest that this type of background
makes it unlikely for him to be the murderous racist that he
actually is.

Betrayed contains a strong implication that Gary and
Bobby Flynn (Jeffrey DeMunn), a high-level political advisor, are playing out the war. They say that it is not over and
that this time they will win, which, within the context of this
film, is a very liberal echo of Rambo's main concern about
Vietnam. Bobby, by the way, was Gary's platoon leader in
Vietnam. Gary was the point man; Bobby was into
"formations." The leader here does not, however, completely trust his proclaimed best point man, as he arranges
for backup for the assassination they are plotting.

The Package (1989) also involves a high-level political
conspiracy, this time to scuttle plans for nuclear disarmament
through assassination. A trio of vets, Gallagher (Gene
Hackman), Boyette (Tommy Lee Jones), and Milan (Dennis
Franz) are involved. Gallagher's job is to deliver Boyette, a
hit man under deep cover, from Germany to the United
States. When Gallagher loses his "package," he goes to his

old war buddy Milan, a Chicago policeman who helps Johnny at great risk on the basis that they served together: "I got eighteen years invested here. And you come walking up outta my past like saying the one year we spent in country is all that counts.... And I agree with ya. And that's, like, some kinda weird shit." The film portrays a deep bond between Gallagher and Boyette as well, as Gallagher somehow "knows" Boyette served in Vietnam, and as Boyette helps Gallagher as much as he can within his circumstances. For example, Boyette discourages a plan to kill Gallagher. *The Package* is quite similar in plot to a police film, *Above the Law* (1988), also directed by Andrew Davis.

In an earlier caper film both a partially heroic Vietvet, Ray (Nick Nolte), and a venal Vietnam journalist, John (Michael Moriarty), are portrayed. *Who'll Stop the Rain?* (1978) involves smuggling drugs from Vietnam to California. The main characters, and practically everyone else in the film, are criminals, but Ray has a strong moral sense, an identifiable code to which he adheres. He also knows a lot about drugs, apparently from experience in Vietnam, but does not take any onscreen.

In *The Pursuit of D.B. Cooper* (1981) Treat Williams plays Meade, an ex-Green Beret who, as in the modern legend, hijacks a plane, demands and gets $200,000 and a parachute, jumps out, and gets away. While theoretically on the wrong side of the law, the film presents Meade as thoroughly sympathetic, friendly, helping people along his way, and so on. Conversely, Meade's former Green Beret sergeant, Gruen (Robert Duvall), takes the role of antagonist. Still, this film represents a Vietvet in at least a somewhat heroic light.

In Dangerous Company (1986) has a Vietvet hit man meeting his old flame and getting involved in an art forgery ring. Blake (Cliff DeYoung) lives in L.A.'s Little Saigon and has Vietnamese-American friends, including Peggy (Catherine Ai), who owns the Pleiku Bar, and Truong (Dana Lee), who was also in country. He has a friend in Chris (Chris Mulkey), also a Vietvet, a shady character who commissions hits and sells armaments. Blake says that he resolved Vietnam years ago and refers to it as a "crusade."

He saved Chris's life in Vietnam and cannot kill him at the film's end. Blake had initially turned down a hit on Evelyn (Tracy Scoggins), who along with Raymond (Steven Keats), has angered rich people with all their counterfeit art, and Chris takes on the assignment. Blake prevails, but will not kill either Chris or Evelyn because he still cares for both of them. He does, however, get a nice Mercedes and a lot of cash, showing that a moral decision does not cost him any money.

Code Name: Zebra (1987) shows a few variations, especially concerning violence against people. Basically a caper film with both vigilante and gangster film elements, it fits within the category of this chapter because the vet group's main goal is the mob's money. It is also partially a vigilante film because the group takes the law into its own hands to clean "some scum off the streets." In the battle with the gangsters, most of the Vietvet group is killed off astonishingly quickly, and then just as quickly replaced by a multinational group of out-of-work mercenaries. Only one of the Vietvets survives until the end. *Kill Squad* (1982) has a somewhat similar plot. Two earlier caper films represent Vietvets as pilots.

In *Firefox* (1982) Clint Eastwood plays Mitchell Gant, an ex-ace fighter pilot who suffers from PTSD-like flashbacks at dramatic moments. He suffers from one similar to that in the French film *Sundays and Cybele* (1962), where a French veteran is plagued by the death of a young Vietnamese girl, just before the precise moment when he must go to the hangar and steal the MIG airplane from the Russians in order for the caper to work. The main generic variation here is that Gant is acting, albeit reluctantly, on behalf of the United States government, and not against it.

In *Iron Eagle* (1986), Chappy (Louis Gossett, Jr.), an Air Force vet, goes to the aid of a man he does not know personally, out of a fraternal bond for his fellow soldier. He also does it because he likes the man's son, after the son tells him how his father was taken hostage by an Arab country for engaging some of their jets in a dogfight outside their territorial airspace. With the help of other children of pilots at an air force base, these two go through intricate planning to pull off the caper, the rescue of the father.[5] Chappy cannot complete the mission and passes on the banner of "right man" to the son, who is not a Vietvet. *Iron Eagle 2* (1988) represents Chappy again, but this time he leads a mixed group of Soviets and Americans on another bombing run.

This invocation of the "right man" myth, central to the war film,[6] points out that the caper film and the war film share certain similarities. This myth, that the right man in the right place in war can change the world, can be seen as an updating of the figure of the intentional hero, as identified by Joseph Campbell, for use within the war genre. None of the Vietvet figures within this subsystem can said to be the "right man" in this sense, although nearly all can be seen to be intentional, although at times quite reluctant, heroes. Exceptions in this regard can be seen only in the minor Vietvet characters in *Charley Varrick* and *Special Delivery*. Also, the pairing and grouping of Vietvets does not occur as frequently within this subsystem as it does within others.

Another major difference between these genres comes in the icons, as in the war film the weapons of war are generally directed against people. In the caper films, as mentioned above, weapons are only in certain instances directed against people. For example, Dell (Burt Lancaster) in *Twilight's Last Gleaming* shoots a murderous Vietvet member of his gang. When a Vietvet acts as a would-be assassin, that attempt almost always fails. Otherwise, these vets use their skills only toward inanimate objects. A major variation in this regard comes in the character Lander in *Black Sunday*.

Lander wants to use his skills as a pilot, learned in Vietnam, to kill thousands of people, including the President of the United States. In direct contrast to the use of skills elsewhere in the genre, his plan can be seen as all the more twisted and shocking. Lander's character also represents an early association of a Vietvet character with flying machines, something that is picked up strongly within this genre in *Firefox* and *Iron Eagle*, and less so with *The Domino Principle*.

Joseph Campbell holds that the airplane can be seen as a modern mythic image, standing in for the eagle, which represents a flight away from the constraints of the world.[7] By association, fliers in Vietnam can be seen as those farthest away from the battles and by implication from the responsibilities of the war. The notion that even these removed figures can be so affected is their chief mythic function. In Lander's case, his removed encounter with the war and traumatic homecoming were presumably enough to make him turn psychopathically against the United States.

In *Firefox* Mitchell Gant (Clint Eastwood) turns not so much against as away from his country. Content to live the life of a hermit, Gant has to be coerced to return to service for the U.S. His reluctance is associated with his flawed psyche, as mentioned above. In this regard, his mental trauma seems to stem from the witnessing of an atrocity, which he does not partake in. This association of hero Vietvet with atrocities is mirrored in generically diverse films such as *Blue Thunder* and *Armed Response*. By the time of *Firefox* and these later films, in contrast to the earlier image in *Black Sunday*, Vietvets were starting to be represented as traditional, pre-Vietnam heroes and no longer as anti-heroes. This trend becomes much clearer when one looks at the police film and the war film.

As for caper films, this traditional heroic image is only partial. Their popular success is only partial as a group as well, although *Firefox* can be considered extremely popular as it ranks among the top of *Variety*'s "All-Time Rental Champs" list. Nearly all of these films are also currently available on video tape, and most of them were theatrically distributed by the major studios. In these senses, then, it seems safe to assume that this subsystem is more popularly "known" than are those found within either the biker or the vigilante genres.

Notes

[1]Campbell points out importance of the airplane as a myth to introduce the machine into the modern age. *The Power of Myth*, p. 18.

[2]This film involves five Korean veterans in a caper film.

[3]Adam Kennedy, *The Domino Vendetta* (New York: Beaufort Books, 1984).

[4]*Flashpoint* is not on the *Variety* "All-Time Rental Champs" list, nor did it have a long theatrical run before being released on video.

[5]The myth of searching for the father, which Campbell dates back to at least the *Odyssey* (*The Power of Myth*, p. 166), is not a strong part of the Vietvet subsystem for the caper film, although it seems more important in the melodrama.

[6]Norman Kagan, *The War Film* (New York: Pyramid Publications, 1974), p. 23.

[7]Campbell, *The Power of Myth*, p. 37.

Clint Eastwood in *Firefox*.

The Gangster Film and the Detective Film

Vietvet characters are sparse in both these genres. In the case of the detective film, there seem to be none that contain a Vietvet as a detective character, although in a few instances Vietvet characters appear in detective hybrid films. As for the gangster film, there also seem to be only a few examples of Vietvet characters in that genre.

Regarding central characters in the traditional gangster genre: the gang is usually portrayed as a business; the central gangster undergoes a decline and fall, and the general public is usually nowhere to be seen. The settings are almost always urban. Important icons include big-bore weapons, such as Tommy guns and .45s.[1]

Examples of Vietvet characters within the traditional gangster genre seem quite sparse. While such films as *The Stone Killer* (1973) and *Year of the Dragon* (1985) portray both Vietvet and gangster film elements, I prefer to treat them with the other police tales. Similarly, *Some Kind of Hero* (1982) represents both those things, but I will treat it as an individual comedy. The only clear examples are early ones, *The Brotherhood* (1968) and *Mean Streets* (1973).

In the earlier gangster picture Alex Cord plays Vince Ginetta, a returning Vietvet who wants to join the outfit run by his brother Frank (Kirk Douglas). His war experience seems to have left him completely unaffected, which, as the biker films show, is typical of Vietvet films of this time. The only real discussion of the war takes place at Frank's home, sparked by a newspaper headline that reads, "Ho Chi Minh Escalates War."

The conversation that follows contains the lines "I told you Ho Chi Minh wouldn't sit still," and "You're lucky you got out when you did. They've got snakes that can kill with one bite. That jungle malaria. Who'd want to live there? They can have it." These are by Frank, who did not even serve there. As such, they can be seen as developing Frank's know-it-all character perhaps more than cogent statements about the war itself. In any case not much is made of Vince's service.

Much the same can be said for Martin Scorsese's absolutely stunning *Mean Streets*, in that not much is made of Jerry's (Harry Northup) service. Jerry, in his only scene, comes home and his old neighborhood friends, mostly small-time gangsters, throw him a private party. The Vietvet here gets lots of presents and a nice dinner. The guys give him an American flag, and Michael (Harvey Keitel) says he can make a shirt out of it. One of the gang points out Jerry's silver star, then Michael quotes a John Garfield WWII picture. A little later Jerry slams his hands down on the dinner table and attacks a woman. The guys surround him and remind him he's back in America now.

While Michael's references to the flag and to WWII might not have been particularly sensitive, one cannot say for certain if these remarks, or ones like them, made Jerry go momentarily berserk. This scene, powerful as it is, is not the focus of the film by any means. Jerry is presented as an outsider, and the picture's central concern is the rise and fall of Michael, in both a spiritual and a business sense. Vietvet portrayals in gangster films apart from these seem very rare.

The bandit gangster film can be seen as a variation upon traditional gangster film, while including within itself many of the elements of the main genre. Some variations appear in terms of the characters and settings. The characters here usually involve a couple, a man and a woman in a love relationship who go on a crime spree. The settings are often rural. The resolution often sees both killed during the commission of their last crime.[2]

As for bandit gangster films with Vietvet characters, the showing seems about equally sparse as that in the traditional gangster film. The only good candidates include *The Big Bounce* (1969) and *Vanishing Point* (1971). Both these films can be seen as coming in the middle of the Youth/Rebellion cycle starting in the 1960s. In the earlier film Jack Ryan (Ryan O'Neal), a cucumber picker, goes on a crime spree with Nancy Barker (Leigh Taylor-Young).

Julian Smith marks this film as the first from a major studio to deal with returned veterans' problems,[3] but he is leaving out *Bus Riley's Back in Town* (1965). The overt mentions of the war in *The Big Bounce* are pretty much limited to Nancy's salacious inquiries as to whether Jack has ever killed anyone.

Vanishing Point can be put in the context of the Youth/Rebellion pictures, with certain links to the biker and trip pictures. Kowalski (Barry Newman) is an ex-Marine, decorated for bravery under fire, who served in Mekong at the beginning of the war. The character is also a number of other "ex's"--an ex-motorcycle racer, ex-race-car driver, and an ex-San Diego cop, where he was also a hero in that role. As is typical of the time, the information about his war service is passed along second-hand, as one policeman reads his rap sheet out loud to another. This film does mark the quite rare onscreen drug-use of a Vietvet character, as Kowalski takes amphetamines to help him on his trip from Denver to San Francisco.

Detective films, like gangster films, apparently lack many Vietvet characters and can be divided into two categories. In the private detective film, as opposed to the classic detective film, the protagonist generally exists on the fringes of a violent urban environment. The detective takes on a case which takes him or her deeper and deeper into an increasingly complicated mystery. Once the case is solved, the implication usually is that the detective returns to the fringes, and the environment goes on more or less unaffected.[4]

The relationship between Vietvet characters and the detective genres is perhaps even more tenuous than that in the gangster film. As far as I can tell no classical detective film with a Vietvet character has been made, although the chief ones made during the period revolve around characters created by Arthur Conan Doyle and Agatha Christie, which puts them out of the relevant story time frame.

Eyewitness (1981) and *Blow Out* (1981) come close to falling within the category of private-detective, but there are problems with categorization as such for each film.[5] Daryll Deever (William Hurt) appears as a remarkably atypical

Vietvet character for the time. He holds a steady job, has no obvious alcohol-dependency problem, exhibits no observable symptoms of a PTSD-like disease, and gets along well with the major social groups: friends of both sexes, family, and co-workers. Not until 1985 and after will Vietvet character types similar to Daryll start to appear with the slightest resemblance of regularity. In the film there is a mystery to be solved, but the pattern of the narrative does not fit well into that of a detective film, nor does anyone within it function clearly as a private-detective type.

As for *Blow Out*, its narrative can perhaps be reconciled with the private-detective genre, but there is not a strong indication that the character who is represented quite like other Vietvets of the time definitely is represented as such. In speech and manner, Burke (John Lithgow) fits into the mold of one who has served in the military. Further, his characterization is not at all inconsistent with the one discussed in the horror of personality section of the chapter on horror film, but there is no hard evidence for his inclusion into the ranks of filmic Vietvets.

A fairly clear private detective film, *Tough Guys Don't Dance* (1987), can be seen as a reversion to a Vietvet that in other genres seems to be dying out. Wings Hauser plays Regency, a secondary character, who is clearly psychotic. He is an ex-Green Beret whose best friend in Vietnam was his machete and who carries some of these tendencies back to the States with him.

These characteristics are among those that Norman Mailer changed during the adaptation of his novel into his screenplay. In the novel of the same name, Regency's character is not so overdrawn. Perhaps Mailer felt that what would work in a film would be a cliché in a novel, although the representations in other movies tend to indicate that other filmmakers already thought this type of characterization was a cliché, as an examination of the Vietvet representation in the police-procedural tale might bear out.

Later, in *Suspect* (1987), Liam Neeson plays a deaf-mute Vietvet who had moral questions about why he killed when there, and was psychiatrically discharged. He spent six years in the psychiatric ward of a VA hospital, and subsequently contracted meningitis, which led to his affliction. He also lost his family and became homeless. When he is falsely accused of murder, his defense attorney and one of the members of his jury perform typical functions of a private detective and uncover a conspiracy within the judicial system. Neeson plays his part with dignity in a small but important role. He is presented as a good soldier who gave up when he returned. His service is not offered as an excuse for his later behavior in any way.

Backfire (1989) is a mystery with affiliations to *Diabolique* (1955). In it Donny (Jeff Fahey), a very rare Vietvet portrayed as extremely wealthy, suffers from a PTSD-like disease stemming from witnessing atrocities in Vietnam. His wife, Mara (Karen Allen), wants to do him in for his money and starts a campaign of psychological torture based on his fears from the war, centering around disembodied eyeballs. Affiliations from the war play a very strong role in the outcome.

Finally, *Gleaming the Cube* (1989) also has tenuous relations with the detective film. Here, Christian Slater plays a skateboard wizard who tries to solve the murder of his adopted Vietnamese brother. As the story unfolds, a couple of Vietvet characters are introduced, one a Vietnamese veteran of the war, and one a policeman who tricks members of a Vietnamese gang because he can speak their language and they do not know it.

The dearth of Vietvet characters as gangsters or as private detectives seems to indicate that filmmakers were hesitant to position them as such traditionally clear representatives of crime, on the one hand, and moral order, on the other. The ambiguous nature of the relationship of the Vietvet to the law has already been shown in the cases of the biker, vigilante, and caper film.

With the police tale, the Vietvet can be seen to be represented as a much more clear representative of the law, but only very recently. The scarcity of Vietvet characters in the gangster and detective genres could perhaps be due to the general scarcity of these genres as filmic vehicles in a time period when Vietvet representations clearly on one side of the law are common in other film genres. Early in the relevant cycle of the police tale, a more ambiguous relation to the law is the norm for Vietvet characters as well.

Notes

[1]These conventions are from Kaminsky, *American Film Genres*, pp. 26-39.

[2]These conventions are from Kaminsky, *American Film Genres*, n., p. 41.

[3]Julian Smith, *Looking Away: Hollywood and Vietnam* (New York: Scribner's, 1975), p. 160.

[4]These narrative elements were suggested in a "Studies in Genre" class, Stuart M. Kaminsky, professor, Northwestern University, Spring 1985.

[5]The central problem is that neither of these films has a detective as a central figure, although the actions of the main characters can be seen as acts of detection.

The Vietvet and the Police Film

Initially in the cycle, the Vietvet character in the police tale functions uneasily in relationship to the genre. That is, the early Vietvets within the genre appear either as main characters in generic hybrids or else as fringe criminal characters in films that can be seen as "purer" examples of the police film. Into the 1980s, especially recently, the Vietvet character has begun to function as a policeman within films that are clear examples of the police tale, although in these instances the Vietvet cop is invariably mirrored by more shadowy Vietvet figures.

This type of character opposition, partially shown in the vigilante films, becomes more common in the police genre. Again, I call attention to the opposing nature of these Vietvet characters late in the cycle, in contrast to the hero-grouping common in the late 1960s and early 1970s. In this sense, the police tale shows something new, Vietvet characters consistently pitted against other Vietvet characters. This multiplicity of representation departs from the uniformity common in the other genres of crime analyzed previously.

This subsystem shows an affinity with the private detective genre, at least in those films containing a Vietvet as a policeman. This trend is true throughout the cycle from *Electra Glide in Blue* (1973) to *Lethal Weapon 2* (1989). This affinity can be seen in these Vietvet police officer characters straining to make moral choices and in the narrative structure of the films, which often start as mysteries to be solved. Both of these elements are generally associated with the private detective story.

Filmic representations of the police officer, in either plainclothes or uniform, often will show the character to function similarly to a vigilante. In his or her pursuit of a criminal, the legal system generally proves too restrictive, and the police officer will investigate outside of it. The police officer sometimes has a mentor who tells him he is proceeding at the risk of his job.[1]

The criminal will often be known early in the film, unlike the private detective film in which there is always a mystery to solve. The policeman often becomes obsessed with the criminal, starts to identify with him or her, and usually sees his dark side reflected in the criminal, although the policeman tends to remain solidly a middle-class citizen. A common means to foster this emotional connection between these two character types is to have the criminal kill, injure, or at least threaten part of the policeman's family. The resolution often has the policeman encountering the criminal one-on-one and the policeman's elimination of the criminal can be seen as the major way he rejects the identification process he has undergone.[2]

Three police-related films came out in 1973 containing Vietvet characters: *The Stone Killer*, *Magnum Force*, and *Electra Glide in Blue*. In the former two, Vietvets are represented as criminal, fringe figures. In the latter picture, several Vietvets are represented, including a central figure with a steady job, as a policeman.

The young vigilante-cops in *Magnum Force*, Sweet (Tim Matheson), Grimes (Robert Urich), Davis (David Soul), and Astrachan (Kip Niven), met in the Army and at least Sweet was in the Special Forces as an Airborne Ranger. This information is conveyed to Dirty Harry Callahan (Clint Eastwood) as he remarks upon their great shooting skill and combat stances. Later, he has to hunt them down.

Similarly, Detective Torrey (Charles Bronson) in *The Stone Killer* is in hot pursuit of a whole army of Vietvet characters: "Forty men. They're all well-trained in combat, transportation, and communications. All of them anonymous. Not one of them has a criminal record." Lawrence (Stuart Margolin) thus tries to sell their services to the Mafia, highlighting their war experience as a selling point. Torrey's higher-ups refuse to believe that a gang of veterans could be behind the crimes, favoring such then-fashionable culprits as black militants.

There is some indication of Vietvets as potentially insane, as one of the group, Gus Lipper (David Moody), goes berserk and smashes up a bar. Once incarcerated, he compares the Vietnam War to a lobotomy. Finally, his psychiatrist concludes, "He's one of the wounded with no noticeable wounds. Vietnam doesn't make heroes, it makes a generation of Lippers." Overall, though, Lawrence's army appears to be very efficient and traditionally soldierly.

In both these films the vet characters can be seen to function as bureaucrats. In Joseph Campbell's definition, a bureaucrat lives "not in terms of himself [as does the hero] but in terms of an imposed system."[3] The vets in these films serve as functionaries within such oppressive systems and are opposed by non-Vietvet intentional heroes. Vietvets as bureaucrats seem rare anywhere else in the system apart from the melodrama. Also, in the genres of integration, Vietvet characters often oppose non-Vietvet bureaucrats.

Electra Glide in Blue, a hybrid police/detective film with biker film elements, offers a variety of Vietvet characters, two minor and one major. Of the minor characters, one is a truck driver (Michael Butler) and one is a drug dealer (Peter Cetera). The major character is a motorcycle policeman, Wintergreen (Robert Blake). Early in the film, Wintergreen, who has already resisted a fraternal bond by giving a fellow policeman a speeding ticket, resists another by ticketing the trucker. In the small talk of this transaction, the trucker finds out that both he and the cop are Vietvets. The trucker bemoans the fact that he has been back only six weeks and that he is already having trouble holding onto jobs. Wintergreen tells him, "I'm gonna to give you in six weeks what it took me six months to get: nothing."

Wintergreen wants to become a detective, and he gets the chance by toadying to one over him, Harve Poole (Mitchell Ryan). When Wintergreen solves a murder without Detective Poole's involvement and further antagonizes him in their mutual relationship with a woman, he gets demoted back to the motorcycle cop. Wintergreen, after this turn of events, apparently makes the moral observation that being promoted to plainclothes will not make him any better as a human being.

Back on patrol he seems to apply this realization. He

tries to give a break to a hippie whom he encounters in traffic, and to whom he and his partner were unfair earlier. The hippie, unknown to Wintergreen, is now smuggling drugs in his van. The motorcycle cop lets him off with a warning this time, but neglects to give him back his license. When Wintergreen chases after him to give it back and reaches out to someone outside any of his fraternities, the hippie panics and shoots him.

While it is tempting to read this narrative as a statement that moral choice is something impossible for returning Vietvets, it has to be limited to this one instance until a number of years later. This is because Vietvet characters appeared only in minor roles throughout the rest of the 1970s. For example, this is the case in *The Choirboys* (1977), which features two Vietvet war buddies who had a frightening encounter with the Vietcong in a cave in a prologue to the film. When Lyles (Don Stroud) and Bloomguard (James Woods) become cops, the war comes back to haunt them. During one of their "choir practices," Lyles gets drunk and is locked in the back of a paddy wagon by an officer who does not know that he cannot stand confined spaces since the war. Lyles shoots a passerby who tries to let him out, mistaking him for a Vietcong soldier, and the whole gang gets into serious trouble. Also, Ed Harris plays Hotchkiss in *Borderline* (1980), a murderous Vietvet who runs illegal aliens across the Mexican border without any regard for their lives.

Then came a spate of films that represented Vietvets as flawed heroes. *Ruckus* (1981) has Kyle Hanson (Dirk Benedict) acting very much like Rambo, but this film was released before *First Blood* (1982). Hanson starts off as a seriously disturbed character: he wears face paint, eats raw meat at a roadside diner, and will not talk to anyone even when directly questioned. After he assaults a group sent after him, the sheriff (Richard Farnsworth) discovers that he was in a VA mental hospital, and that he twice escaped the Vietcong. He then escapes to the woods and starts bettering the forces of the law sent against him. At this point the film veers away from *First Blood*. Once Hanson clears off his war paint, he and Jenny (Linda Blair), a young woman he meets while on the run, fall quickly in love. *Ruckus* is very unusual within this subsystem in that the main character could fashion such a romance.

First Blood also has John Rambo chased through the woods of the Northwest after being arrested for vagrancy, but no such embrace is suggested here. Thus, he is technically an outlaw but fits into the tradition of a common type of post-Vietnam hero, commonly called the "anti-hero." While the anti-heroes in especially the biker and vigilante films exhibit some of these tendencies, none perhaps is a better example than the first film appearance of Rambo. This point is perhaps set in better relief with reference to other representations of this same character.

For example, in the other *Rambo* films the character shows more traits of a traditional or pre-Vietnam hero, as set out by Hellman: "a desire to 'do good,' a conception of the world as a battleground between the forces of Light and Darkness,...knowledge of a savage landscape and enemy,...and an absolute faith in America's righteousness and 'mission.'"[4] In the 1972 novel from which this film was adapted, Rambo is more clearly a crazed killer. That character kills more than a dozen people, including, apart from police, some innocent bystanders.

The first characterization of Rambo on film seems somewhat in between these extremes. In *First Blood* not one single person is represented as dying onscreen directly from Rambo's hand. This film represents a pair of veterans, with the image of the insane Rambo, especially at closure, matched by the calm, commanding Trautman (Richard Crenna).

Blue Thunder (1983) again represents more than one image of the Vietvet. On the one hand there is Murphy (Roy Scheider), who doubts his sanity. Murphy learned to fly a helicopter in Vietnam and in some ways his characterization is similar to that of Mitchell Gant in *Firefox* (1982). He exhibits PTSD-like symptoms and seems plagued by visions of Vietnam, especially those involving the "body bombing" of a non-cooperative North Vietnamese during questioning by the evil Cochrane (Malcom McDowell), another ex-helicopter pilot. Like Gant, Murphy was a witness to this atrocity; he did not cause it to happen.

Murphy, now a helicopter cop, obtains evidence that the corporation behind the Blue Thunder helicopter is trying to provoke a riot in the Barrio so that they can go in, show the effectiveness of their killing machine, and thus increase sales. Cochrane, now working for the corporation, reappears to try to eliminate Murphy and the evidence from the scene. In an aerial battle over Los Angeles, Murphy gets to exorcise both his demons of Vietnam and Cochrane with an air-to-air missile. The chief figure that plagued him now gone, the implication is that Murphy will now be "cured" of his ailment.

In *Year of the Dragon* (1985) Mickey Rourke plays Stanley White, a Vietvet who is now a cop, who wants to get rid of his lingering memories another way. He seems to feel that the reason the United States lost in Vietnam was because the nation did not attempt to understand the Vietnamese culture. In his battles with the Chinese Mafia in New York, he attempts to avoid a similar mistake by immersing himself in Chinese culture, which somewhat dubiously includes having an affair with a Chinese newscaster. As he gets more and more carried away, his obsession costs him his job, his wife, and very nearly his life. Ironically, then, this film represents a Vietvet whose intellectual decision costs him what many other films represent the Vietnam War has cost other Vietvets, a good chance to reintegrate into society.

Extreme Prejudice (1987) presents another type of mixture, the Zombie squad, a group of ex-soldiers officially dead, made up of both Vietvet characters--Hackett (Michael Ironside) and McRose (Clancy Brown) --and representations of post-Vietvets--Atwater (Bill Forsythe), Biddle (Larry B. Scott), Fry (Dan Tullis Jr.), and Coker (Matt Mulhern). This group's job is to perform clandestine operations for the Army, usually outside the States. Hackett, unbeknownst to the rest of the squad, plans to rob Cash Bailey (Powers Boothe) of his drug money, which involves a Texas policeman, Jack (Nick Nolte), in the matter.

McRose, the younger Vietvet and the moral voice of the group, objects to the operation, which takes place partially on American soil. Hackett, the older Vietvet, comes off as a

Nixonian figure, pledging duty and country while committing a crime. The others remain neutral at first, then join in with McRose, but none of them survive the mission. Thus, the film depicts Vietvets making a moral choice but not surviving.

The interplay between an older Vietvet character and a younger one comes up again in *Lethal Weapon* (1987). The younger Martin Riggs (Mel Gibson) is initially characterized as potentially crazy. He is suicidal, wifeless, generally unstable. The older Roger Murtaugh (Danny Glover) gets a much calmer treatment. He is a family man, and generally much more steady. One metaphor for this difference can be seen in one of the icons of the police genre, their choice of weapons. Riggs prefers the more sleek, more powerful 9mm automatic, which is more likely to jam and misfire than is the gun Murtaugh uses, the old standby .38 revolver.

Both of these characters are mirrored by criminal Vietvets. In a minor role Tom Atkins plays an Army friend of Murtaugh's, a businessman turned bureaucrat/criminal who tries to tell the cop duo about the heroin smuggling ring lead by Joshua (Gary Busey), but is killed before he can. Joshua, a wild-eyed and vicious criminal, after threatening Murtaugh's family, is eliminated by Riggs. In this sense, Murtaugh's family is made whole, and the implication is that Riggs, who had started coming over to their house socially, is now a part of it.

Lethal Weapon 2 (1989) carries over the implication that Riggs is a part of Murtaugh's family; he practically lives with them now. On the other hand Vietnam is practically a non-issue in the later film. The motif about the guns is brought up again in a joking context, and the idea that Riggs is insane is also brought up as a joke. He wins a bet by getting out of a straitjacket. These matters come up in a film played for more laughs than the first in the series.

Above the Law (1988), as does *The Package* (1989), introduces a set of three Vietvet characters and brings up the question of moral choice again. These are Nico Toscani (Steven Seagal), a Vietvet Chicago policeman; the evil Zagon (Henry Silva), an ex-CIA operative now into the drug business; and a strangely bland Vietvet, Fox (Chelcie Ross), now a government agent, a bureaucrat, who mediates between the other two Vietvets. Nico is, in the film's present, a dedicated family man with a new baby. He's also a churchgoer and a protector of Central American refugees.

The title of the film is taken from a speech by Nixon: "No one is above the law, no one is below the law...." Nico holds that Zagon's drug runners, who want to kill a Senator who vows to break up their crime ring, must be stopped because, more than anything else, no one should act above the law. Nico, though, is suspended from the police department himself as he tracks them down and stops them. Nico is a rare Vietvet within these films who makes a moral choice, carries it out, and survives.

Marked for Death (1990) presents a variation, as Steven Seagal again plays a law enforcer, this time for the DEA, who goes after Jamaican drug-runners, among other lawbreakers. He is paired with an old war buddy from Vietnam (Keith David), and they seem to have absolutely no lingering effects from their experiences there. The moral element from *Above the Law* is dropped out here, and the film plays like a more standard police tale.

In some of these later films, one can get a brief glimpse of Vietvet-as-human monster. Campbell defines a monster as a "horrendous presence or apparition that explodes all of your standards for harmony, order, and ethical conduct."[5] There is a certain similarity to the way that Hackett, Joshua, and Zagon are represented; makeup and lighting conspire to emphasize these actors' sharp looks. Hackett and Zagon try to explode their governmental trust, and Joshua tries to destroy a family. This representation of the Vietvet can be seen much more clearly in the genres of horror.

There also seems to be a trend in the police genre in which current films represent Vietvet characters in minor roles again. In *Colors* (1988), for example, a man (Tom Todd) at a neighborhood meeting dealing with gang warfare stands up and introduces himself as a Vietvet before stating his objection to the way the police are limiting crime. He seems perfectly normal, no residue of any of crazy vet stereotype presented earlier in the genre, justifiably upset at conditions on the streets. There are also minor characters in

Die Hard (1988) who were Vietvets, now working for the FBI.

The Presidio (1988) again offers a mixture. Caldwell (Sean Connery) is a major Vietvet character, seemingly unaffected by the whole affair. Maclure (Jack Warden) is a minor one, but one represented as having won the Congressional Medal of Honor. His life after Vietnam is not as spectacular, and he seems rather sad as the curator of the small war museum in the Presidio itself. He gives tours to children who have no idea what Vietnam is. This character cannot endure the transition from hero to bureaucrat. He turns to crime after the war, although he redeems himself the way he made himself a hero in the war, under fire.

Finally, in *Cage* (1989), a film with police elements, two Vietvets are trying to reintegrate and run their business, the Incoming Bar. Two mobsters see their fighting prowess at the bar, though, and try to get them to fight in the illegal "cage" fights in Chinatown on which they bet great sums of money. In order to do so, they kidnap Billy (Lou Ferrigno), who has brain damage from a head wound in Vietnam. His partner Scott (Reb Brown), who owes Billy for saving his life in Vietnam, tries to rescue him, but both get involved in the cage fights. When Billy fights, he has a PTSD-like flashback resulting from the old head wound being aggravated. Recovering in the dressing room Billy says, "I died a long time ago." When all the gangsters shoot each other, an undercover policeman gives Billy and Scott the money from the gambling, and they open a fancy oyster bar.

The consistent multiplicity of representation of the Vietvets within single films in this subsystem suggests that filmmakers, in this case nearly all major studios, were hedging their bets as they made guesses about what the audience would want in this regard. The genre blending that is evident in the Vietvet police subsystem can also be seen to support this suggestion. In any case, audiences have responded to this set of films perhaps better than any other in the Vietvet system.

A majority of these Vietvet police films appear on the "All-Time Rental Champs" list, the only time in the system that this comes close to happening. *Lethal Weapon 2, Die*

Hard, *Lethal Weapon*, *First Blood*, and *Blue Thunder* are all near the top of the Vietvet list. Also, each and every one of these films is now available on video, something extremely unusual for any of the Vietvet subsystems. For these reasons, the police Vietvet subsystem is the most popularly successful to date.

What this subsystem represents is a spectrum of Vietvets from monster to bureaucrat to hero. Late in the cycle all three of these character types co-exist in the same film. A message that filmmakers seem to be giving and one audiences seem to be receiving is that a monolithic interpretation of the war experience upon returning vets is not presently viable, and that the Vietvet should wear many different masks at once to be properly understood. In many of the latest of these films, such as *Lethal Weapon* and *Above the Law*, the Vietvet intentional hero prevails. Much the same can be said for the representation found within the war film genre.

Notes

[1] These conventions are from Kaminsky, *American Film Genres*, p. 230.

[2] These conventions are from Kaminsky, *American Film Genres*, pp. 230-31.

[3] Campbell, *The Power of Myth*, p. 144.

[4] John Hellman, *American Myth and the Legacy of Vietnam* (New York: Columbia University Press, 1986), p. 14.

[5] Campbell, *The Power of Myth*, p. 222.

The Vietvet and the War Film

Refighting the Vietnam War is an important theme in the Vietvet war film subsystem. In mythic terms, then, Campbell's "the lance that delivers the wound" myth is central to this subsystem, at least when the heroes in these films are intentional heroes and not adventurers. In this latter case, when Vietvets are represented as mercenaries drawn into their quests, refighting does not seem to be as important as when Vietvets return to Vietnam or fight other wars. Unlike the police film's representation of multiple Vietvet character types, war film representation of the Vietvet as anything but an archetypal hero seems very rare.

Another important myth related to heroism in the war film is the "right man" myth, mentioned earlier in the context of the caper film. This myth comes to the forefront in this Vietvet subsystem, especially in the mid-1980s with the re-emergence of Rambo and other heroes who harken back to earlier eras in American history, especially WWII. At this point, the anti-hero tendencies of much of the 1970s become rare regarding the representation of the Vietvet. A mythic theme of more limited importance to this subsystem is that of the search for the father, also mentioned earlier in the context of the caper film.

Analysis of certain icons, such as the helicopter and the various weapons used by Vietvets, tends to illuminate the changes that the Vietvet hero undergoes through this cycle. A brief outline of the war genre will serve as a point of departure.

The war genre can clearly be seen as an example of a genre of order. The conflicts are externalized and violent. The central character is normally a group, diverse in both ethnic makeup and personality type. A conflict within this group is often whether they can all put their differences aside

68

in order to overcome their common enemy, who is often corrupt. Before Vietnam American troops were nearly always represented as supporting "a recognizable ally against a clearly discernable enemy." Within this group there is often a single discernible hero, who is often outnumbered, and a group mascot of one sort or another.[1]

Important icons are the weapons and machines of war, although after Vietnam these machines are often represented as "monstrosities." "Likewise, the moral justifications of a 'good' war are missing." Post-Vietnam war films, for instance, sometimes portray American soldiers as taking part in atrocities. These elements often lead to a combat finale as resolution.[2]

The settings, the backdrops for war, are contested, uncivilized spaces. Traditionally, they have been "stark...open landscapes" that feature "bombed-out houses, and an almost expressionistic reduction of detail." Again, after Vietnam these settings begin to change. Often, lush jungles provide the backdrop for post-Vietnam war films whether they represent the Vietnam War or some other war. The idea that nature is the enemy comes to the forefront often in these films.[3]

Other thematics include the sense of group unity, the journey towards the last stand, and the notion that the "right man at the right time can solve everything." This last notion will be examined as the central way the war film representing the Vietvet character mythologizes war, whether that character becomes a mercenary, returns to Vietnam after the war to fight again, or fights some other type of war as a post-Vietnam soldier.[4]

Vietvets as mercenaries

A number of films represent Vietvets as mercenaries, those used to fighting who turn their skills over in order to gain financial profit, revenge, and usually both. The title character (Sal Watts) of *Solomon King* (1974), for instance, demonstrates actions which fit in this film with the vigilante films discussed previously. King, yet another ex-Green Beret, leads a mercenary group comprised of his old squadron against an Arab sheik. In this instance the main motive for reversion to war activities is one of personal re-venge; the sheik has murdered an old girlfriend of King's.

Clifford Baumgartner (Ben Gazzara), on the other hand, does not want to fight again in *High Velocity* (1977). But when a wealthy industrialist is kidnapped, Baumgartner gets blackmailed into using his martial skills to recapture him. Baumgartner rejoins his war buddy, Watson (Paul Winfield), and they talk frequently about their war experiences. One of their central topics of discussion is how out-of-shape the two already feel, just ten years out of combat.

Once back in the chase, these two have the following typical exchange: (Baumgartner to Watson) "You love it, don't you?" "I suppose you don't." "Yeah, but I don't like loving it." After a cleverly staged attack in the jungles of South America, none of the principals, Baumgartner, Watson, nor the industrialist survive. They do complete their mission; however, they get betrayed.

A British film, *The Dogs of War* (1980), provides a similar set of characters and conflict, though in a different setting, Africa. Shannon (Christopher Walken) leads a group of Vietvet characters to war in a village there. They, again, have stayed in a military profession, though not in the legitimate military. This time they are fighting for profit, not for vengeance or as the result of being blackmailed.

Near the end of this part of the Vietvet war cycle and after, many films represented American commandos with no mention of service in Vietnam. These films include *The Wild Geese* (1978), *The Soldier* (1982), *Invasion U.S.A.* (1985), *The Wild Geese II* (1985), *Commando* (1986), and *Predator* (1987). Many others contain Vietvets but remain obscure.

The publicity material for another Vietvet-as-mercenary film, *Mission Kill* (1985), describes Coop (Robert Ginty) as a "good natured" gunrunner and demolitions expert. This description, his very name (others to which he answers include Kennedy and Robin Hood), and the actions of other characters toward him throughout the film indicate that a change is in the wind. Specifically, the Vietvet is becoming represented as a traditional pre-Vietnam war hero,[5] chiefly by associating him with a host of past heroes.

The associations with "Coop" continue as the narrative of *Mission Kill* follows very closely that of a Gary Cooper film, *For Whom the Bell Tolls* (1943). Here, Coop reluctantly stays in a country in Central America, the fictional Santa Maria, to help the freedom fighters battle a rightist regime. He ultimately uses his demolition skills to help the freedom fighters win the final big battle by blowing up a vital bridge, but only after he witnesses and responds to the shooting of a child by the right-wing forces. He asks, "Whose side of the revolution was she on, huh?"

After seeing Coop fight, one of the freedom fighters, whose favorite movie is *Sands of Iwo Jima* (1949), compares Coop to John Wayne, from then on referring to him as Duke. As if this were not enough, all the while a newspaperman is busy printing the legend of Coop and telling him things like "You are a natural hero." Finally, Coop makes his credo on war apparent: "It is worth dying for somebody you love, but it is not worth dying for somebody you hate."

In spite of these mechanisms associating Coop with pre-Vietnam heroes, this characterization is not consistent. The major indication of this inconsistency comes at the end of the film. At closure, Coop gains access to the new President's helicopter and tosses the President from a great height to his death. It would be hard to miss the association here with the "body bombers" of both the Vietvet and Vietnam War films and their distance from pre-Vietnam heroes.

Vietvets returning to Vietnam

Next come a number of films featuring returned vets who go back to Vietnam. Nearly all of them were popularly successful at the box office. Some commentators read these films as messages that "America was right in Vietnam."[6] None of these Vietvet characters, however, is acting in any official capacity for the government. Other popular commentators such as Gene Siskel and Roger Ebert have labeled this trend the "this time we win" films, but closer examination can make this nomenclature more specific.[7]

When these characters and their central conflicts are examined, furthermore, a clearer message emerges: "We may have lost, but it was not the combat soldier's fault." Thus, Rambo's lament that "somebody wouldn't let us win" is addressed in these films, with that somebody being precisely representatives of the U.S. government, politicians and bureaucrats.

The film to which Freedman refers is *Uncommon Valor* (1983). Here, Colonel Rhodes (Gene Hackman) is convinced that his son is among a number of officially designated MIAs that are really being held by the Vietnamese as POWs. His efforts to go through official channels are thoroughly thwarted. Frustrated, he gets a wealthy industrialist to fund a rescue mission.

He then regroups members of his old platoon, an ethnically and socioeconomically diverse group, who then retrain for their mission back to Vietnam. The pre-Vietnam Army and the post-Vietnam Army are linked, with Scott (Patrick Swayze), the representative of the untested new Army accepted by the others once he shows his mettle, and once they find out his father died in Vietnam. The group is then partially successful; they get out most of the POWs alive but not Rhodes's son.

Missing In Action (1984) follows a quite similar narrative. Braddock (Chuck Norris) knows from first-hand experience, as a MIA/POW for seven years, that the Vietnamese are holding prisoners, which they will not admit. At a hearing about this in Ho Chi Minh City, Braddock, there as an advisor, openly insults the Vietnamese, calling them liars about the issue. Senator Porter (David Tress) and Fitzgerald (Lenore Kasdorf) are there in a more official capacity, and they, typically in this cycle, accept the Vietnamese's story without much questioning. Fitzgerald's character changes a bit throughout the film, but at one point she tells Braddock that he is "the most undiplomatic man" she has ever met.

Braddock, rejecting the diplomatic, official channels that he presumedly believes led to America's loss in Vietnam, disregards the negotiating table and goes off pretty much on his own to recapture the MIA/POWs. The actions, then, of the central character here fit in with the other films in this cycle, although more emphasis is given to Braddock as a lone figure than any one figure in *Uncommon Valor*.

Braddock is clearly given more of a hero's portrayal than is the Hackman character. The most overt instance of this aspect of his character comes in a linkage of Braddock to a cartoon hero, Spiderman. Braddock is seen watching both the nightly news and Spiderman on television in his hotel room before the conference mentioned above. After the conference, Braddock climbs outside his hotel on a wire high above the street, à la Spiderman, to escape detection from Vietnamese police.

A variation from the genre as a whole comes as Braddock battles the Vietnamese troops more or less single-handedly. He does pick up some minimal support from the MIA/POWs he frees and from Tuck (M. Emmet Walsh), another Vietvet character, whose main function is to arm Braddock. In a rare portrayal of ex-ARVN soldiers in a Vietvet film, these POWs do not come off very well. Braddock, freeing these men as he looks for the Americans, is thanked warmly. They promise undying support to him and nobly promise, "We will fight for our freedom." Then they all promptly disappear, and in an absurd way continue the representation of ARVN members from the Vietnam War films as not trustworthy.

Heated Vengeance (1984) contains elements of the return-to-the-war theme. Here, Hoffman (Richard Hatch) returns to Thailand, where he was stationed during the war, to meet the Thai woman who bore his child after he was shipped out. While there he runs into his old nemesis, Bingo (Ron Max), whom he tried to get court-martialed for sexually assaulting a young Thai girl. Bingo has reformed a group of mainly Vietvet misfits to run drugs through the Golden Triangle. After a chance meeting, the two old adversaries once again do battle, this time in the jungles of Thailand. This action picture contains a rare portrait of a woman, Hoffman's love interest, who is a Vietvet.

Rambo: First Blood Part II (1985) presents a minor variation. Rambo, the most popular Vietvet character in American film history to the present, does follow official channels but with grave suspicions, especially after he finds out that the head bureaucrat Murdock (Charles Napier) lied about his own service in Vietnam. A central line in this respect is "Do we get to win this time?" Here, the implication is that vague governmental forces prevented a victory in Southeast Asia and that the group of bureaucrats led by Murdock, now positioned as a non-Vietvet, are set to continue the trend.

They do, indeed, betray Rambo, refusing to pick him up after he leads a group of MIA/POWs to safety, bucking great odds. This action comes after a great number of trials. Rambo is supposed only to take pictures, but the mission is a setup. Rambo rescues the POWs at great personal peril, but as a variation of the intentional hero, he is represented as indestructible. That is, over the course of these films, the character can jump off cliffs, repair his wounds with a fish-hook and fishing line, fight off whole armies with a bow and arrow, and so on.

The film also represents something quite rare, a Vietnamese woman who is a veteran of the war. Co (Julia Nickson) plays an agent working for the Americans and served a similar function during the war. She is tough, resourceful, and provides Rambo with someone he has not before or since been represented as having, a friend of the opposite sex. Their attraction does not come to much, though, as Co dies.

In a variation *White Ghost* (1988) features Steve Shepard (William Katt) as a Vietvet who never left Vietnam. He was a Special Forces soldier in Vietnam in 1972 who witnessed a Mylai-type atrocity led by the evil Walker (Wayne Crawford), but when he tries to report it no one wants the bad publicity. So, for obscure reasons, Shepard decides to stay in Vietnam for the next fifteen years. When questioned about it later he just says that Vietnam is his home now. Walker was asked to leave the service quietly and became a mercenary in Central America. When the Pentagon gets word that a White Ghost is roaming around Vietnam, they send in Walker to bring him home. He goes to Vietnam and lots of fighting ensues, centering around a Vietnamese border war and the attempts to kill Shepard and his Vietnamese wife, Thi Hau (Rosalind Chao), who is about to have their child. Shepard and Thi Hau make it to the helicopter, and an

Army Major (Reb Brown) says, "Welcome home," underlining the mixed messages of the film.

Braddock: Missing in Action III (1988) provides a similar character to Co or Thi Hau, but reverts to the pattern of an angry vet returning to Vietnam in disregard of official channels. Braddock sneaks back into Vietnam to take out his Vietnamese wife, whom he thought had died during the evacuation of Saigon. Again, once the Vietnamese character encounters the Vietvet character, she dies. Braddock does, however, manage to get out a group of American/Vietnamese children, orphans of the war.

Vietvets in other wars

In *Latino* (1985) Guerrero (Robert Beltran) and Trevino (Tony Plana) are fairly rare character types: Vietvets who decided to re-enlist after the war. They are sent to Honduras as advisors and accompany Contras over the border into Nicaragua to do battle with the Sandinistas. Their characterizations are not traditionally heroic, as they stand by as murderous Contras kill Nicaraguan civilians, and they do nothing but give knowing nods. Earlier, Guerrero has an ill-fated romance with a Nicaraguan woman.

In another film with Vietvets remaining in the service, *Opposing Force* (1987), a military survival skills course turns to a shooting war. Becker (Anthony Zerbe), the leader of the camp where this takes place, is so evil that he rapes the only woman soldier (Lisa Eichhorn) there, so she could get used to it if it happened in the field. Becker, an infantryman in Vietnam, also has a major conflict with Logan (Tom Skeritt), a pilot there. Becker gives him a by-then standard tongue lashing about bombing civilians and being back at the base for lunch, saying that even if the blood reached the clouds it would never touch him or those like him. The film thus presents a fairly typical split presentation of Vietvets.

Rambo III (1988) again has John Rambo going off to fight a war, this time within the uneasy auspices of the U.S. government. The CIA, represented in the figure of Griggs (Kurtwood Smith), offers Rambo help in his mission to Afghanistan, but no official recognition. Rambo, for his part, does not trust the CIA man, linking him ("I'm used to it/Sounds familiar") to his experiences with other bureaucrats and operatives.

Rambo himself, however, shows some character changes. The reason he goes this time, as the tag line reads, "is for his friend." As Braddock went to Vietnam for his wife, so now Rambo goes to fight for a different member of the basic social support group, a friend, in this case Trautman. If Trautman can be seen as a father figure, then Rambo can also be seen as searching for his father.

There seems to be evidence to support Trautman as a father figure across the three films. For example, in *First Blood* (1982) Trautman says he "made" Rambo, and Rambo almost always calls Trautman "Sir." In this sense Rambo, over three films, can be seen to change from an anti-hero bringing back an unwelcome message, to a more traditional hero fighting for his society and then for his own father.

In the ensuing battle finale, Rambo alludes to *Shoulder Arms*, the film Kagan refers to in isolating the "dark current" in American war films that "the right man in the right place" can overcome any obstacle.[8] Impossibly outnumbered, Trautman asks Rambo how they should proceed. Rambo responds, "Surrounding them's out." This joke, a close variation of the one used at the end of the Chaplin film, shows another change, a sense of humor, in Rambo's character. While that may be a change, the notion that the right man in the right place can win any battle, certainly central to the *Rambo* films, is simply underlined.

Gunney Burns (Fred Dryer) also embodies the right man myth in *Death Before Dishonor* (1987). Burns risks court-martial to rescue his Colonel (Brian Keith) from Arab terrorists in the Middle East. In doing so he finds himself right in the middle of a shooting war. His service in Vietnam is alluded to only lightly, as the Colonel tells the American Ambassador (Paul Winfield) that Burns cannot help his nature towards getting involved in such things, that it is just a matter of the combat instincts that he honed while in country.

In a related film Gunney Highway (Clint Eastwood), the protagonist of *Heartbreak Ridge* (1986), also fits the mold of the "right man in the right place." By his own estimation he "eats concertina wire and pisses napalm." He is a warrior who seems to need a war to function. Conversely, without a war Gunney is a menace. As a judge tells him as he hands down a sentence for brawling, "Just because there's no war going on, doesn't mean you've got a right to start one every time you're drunk."

Gunney seems out of place even within the military in his role as a supply clerk. He hates the job and wants to train men, to be closer to wartime activities. Still, he is loyal to his "family," the Marines, as evidenced by his honesty when approached with a smuggler's offer of Cuban cigars for "looking the other way" when valuables are to be checked in. Later, during the Grenada invasion Gunney will take a Cuban cigar from the corpse of a Cuban regular, whom he has shot rather than take prisoner, which it appears he could have done. What was contraband is now the spoils of war, where apparently all is indeed fair, at least to Gunney. His thinking seems to be that there is nothing civilized about war, and acting civilized can get not only him, but his men, killed.

Gunney is consistent in his Marine credo that his job is to "improvise, overcome, and adapt." This consistency keeps him constantly at odds with his by-the-book, pointedly post-Vietnam commanding officer, Major Powers (Everett McGill). Powers tells him, echoing the words of the judge, that he "should be sealed in a case that reads: Break glass only in the event of war." Powers also mentions that in Gunney's new post as trainer of a reconnaissance platoon, any violations of the rules will be his last as a Marine.

In this sense Gunney's unorthodox training methods can be seen as a moral choice. He risks his job in order to do the job the way he thinks it will save the lives of his recruits, all the time being consistent with his credo. These recruits, an ethnically diverse lot, offer him no help at first, either. They think Gunney's ordered lifestyle foreign, to say the least. Again, he does this in the light of the Marines being his only stable family.

His wife Aggie (Marsha Mason) has left him, although he tries to win her back. To do so he has been reading women's magazines. In a comic confrontation with her, talking about their marriage he asks her "Did we mutually nurture each other?" and other things straight out of those magazines. Aggie seems to sense that he wants to renew their relationship to replace the one that is ending for him in the Marines; Gunney is close to mandatory retirement age. She accuses him of giving up "the old frontal assault" and of trying to "outflank" her with the quotes from magazines he uses to try to get them back together.

In the meantime, Gunney has the Marines. Not all the representatives of this branch of the service fall into the post-Vietnam camp. Choozo (Arlen Dean Synder) was with Gunney in Korea in the ridge that gives the film its name, and where Gunney won his Congressional Medal of Honor. Choozo relates to Gunney that Major Powers considers their group "0-1-1. No wins. One tie, Korea. One loss, Vietnam." Gunney counters that he will ignore Power's by-the-book wishes to play a professedly small part: "I'm not gonna lose the next one because my men aren't ready."

The gunnery sergeant proves as good as his word. His use of the Russian AK-47 and live ammunition is unorthodox but effective, again almost costing him his job. Also, by a cunning mixture of cheating, improvising, and adapting, his formerly misfit platoon is able to overcome the Major's pet landing unit. The real test for his platoon, however, is the invasion of Grenada.

There, Gunney's unit is under Powers' strict orders to do nothing but reconnaissance work. Gunney's unit, however, carries out the invasion nearly single-handedly. They engage an initial assault, capture a bridge, free the American medical school students there, and call in a bombing mission, improvising, adapting, and overcoming the whole way. Major Powers, furious that his orders were again ignored, is about to read the riot act to Gunney when a general, also a Vietvet, intervenes and scares him off.

In a curious way the ranks that have some stability--private, sergeant, general, as opposed to those marked by possible upward mobility: lieutenant through colonel--have been traditionally represented as having "common sense" and an ability to communicate with each other. This representation

holds here and elsewhere. Further, it can be seen as analo-
gous in rank as families are to generations, as grandparents
and grandchildren are said to be able to communicate in a
similar way.

Whatever the case about rank, the right man myth is at
work here. Gunney clearly thinks this is a war on a par with
Korea and Vietnam. He says, "Well, Chooz, I guess we're
not 0-1-1 now, huh." Before he had said he just wanted to
do his little part, train his men. But his training leads to the
single-handed capture of the whole island, which by implication is a full-scale war. In a sense then, Gunney fits right
in with the right man myth.

Also, this characterization can be seen as another in a line
of making Gunney fit a mold of the pre-Vietnam hero.
Gunney and his men get kisses from the freed medical
school students and a parade upon their homecoming,
something which Gunney points out is a first for him. Actors with the star personae of Clint Eastwood and Sylvester
Stallone seem always to play heroes of one type or another,
but over these years, the specific type of hero they have portrayed has changed, and the films have moved from non-war
genre to war genre, from *First Blood* to *Rambo III* and from
Firefox to *Heartbreak Ridge*.

Knowles (Roy Scheider) in *The Fourth War* (1990) can
be seen as Gunney Highway without a Grenada. Knowles
won the Distinguished Service Cross while in country.
General Hackworth (Harry Dean Stanton), his friend, clearly
tries to make him into a traditional hero: "You're the off-
spring of the war in Vietnam. Now mind you you're not the
only one. That war also begat loonies, and cowards, and
dink heroin traffickers. Iowa farmboys with their first dose
of clap. But most important it begat heroes. And you are
one of them." As Knowles has no role in peace, he makes
his own war with a hero from another doomed enterprise,
the Afghan/Soviet war. As this private war escalates,
Hackworth is no longer able to save Knowles as he has done
numerous times in the past, as the general narrates the film
from Knowles's court-martial.

Top Gun (1986), finally, is another in a cross-generic
line of recent films that represents a well-adjusted Vietvet in

a minor role. Viper (Tom Skeritt) is a family man and an instructor at Top Gun, the naval flying school. He flew in Vietnam with Maverick's (Tom Cruise) father, who bravely fought with a damaged plane, giving up his life to save Viper's. This dogfight, further, took place on the "wrong" side of the Vietnamese/Cambodian border, and according to the State Department, never took place. This incident reaches out to affect Maverick, adding to his reputation for not following the rules. Maverick's father also thus fits in with the representations of dead, absent vets that are fairly common in the genres of integration.

The clearly glamorous weapons, the sleek fighter jets, represented in *Top Gun* are about as far removed from Smith's notion of war weapons as "monstrosities" as can be imagined. Indeed, even during the 1970s the notion of weapons as such in war films have occurred only outside the Vietvet war film subsystem. Throughout this cycle weapons are generally represented as in a range from functional to nearly fetishized, as in the back-lit introduction of the equipment in *Rambo: First Blood Part II*.

This representation is not carried through in the film, however, as Rambo is quickly stripped of all the weapons except the basics, his knife and bow. There is still some interplay here. These weapons, based on ancient models, have high-tech twists, such as the highly efficient and relatively modern compound bow that he uses. Rambo employs these and other basic weapons against an icon with which he has an ambiguous relationship, the helicopter.

The helicopter is a central icon representing the Vietnam War, both within and without systems of filmic representation.[9] This flying machine can be seen in mythic terms as a variation of the airplane with some important differences. The helicopter in operation occupies a middle ground when compared to the airplane; it is closer to the action. Helicopter operators, then, can also be seen as closer to the action, and by implication, more affected by their experiences in the war. In these terms Rambo only reluctantly uses helicopters, as last-ditch escape vehicles. He can fly them, but only as a result of his multifaceted training, not because it was his specialty. When he does they always seem on the brink of failure. Anyway, Rambo much prefers to destroy helicopters than to fly them, as the narrative of *Rambo III* bears out.

These airships can also be seen as more ambiguous than the straight-ahead, unidirectional fighter planes found in *Top Gun* and WWII aviator films. Helicopters are omnidirectional and can hover over spaces. In this regard helicopters can be seen as an important representation of the ambiguity of the war itself. That Rambo would seek to destroy these icons of ambiguity, and do so to a greater degree later in the cycle, is in keeping with his positioning as a pre-Vietnam hero.

This positioning of Vietvets as traditional, pre-Vietnam, filmic war heroes is apparent whether the Vietvet is an adventurer, as in *Mission Kill*, or an intentional hero as in *Missing in Action*. These Vietvets often have minor battles with non-Vietvet bureaucrats, but their major battles are with fairly traditional enemies, sometimes North Vietnamese who resemble representations of the Japanese in WWII films as in *Rambo: First Blood Part II* and *Braddock: Missing in Action III*.

There is also an apparent split in the representation of these heroic Vietvets. Sometimes, in a generic variation, these vets will fight battles basically single-handedly, as in *Rambo: First Blood Part II* and *Missing in Action*. Other times Vietvets will appear in groups, most clearly in *The Dogs of War* and *Uncommon Valor*, which is more in keeping with the conventions of the war film genre.

This subsystem has enjoyed great popularity in the mid-1980s to the present, as many of the films can be found on the "Rental Champs" list. These include two of the top grossers to date, *Top Gun* and *Rambo: First Blood Part II*. Nearly all of these films are also available on video, including *High Velocity*, which was culled from a mid-1970s film library. The later films' popularity shows that the Vietvet's return to representation as a traditional war hero has struck a nerve in the popular consciousness.

Notes
[1]The comments about group make-up come from

Basinger, *The World War II Combat Film*, p. 16, and Kaminsky, *American Film Genres*, p. 229. The comments about the enemy come from Kaminsky, p. 229, and about the corrupt enemy from Kagan, *The War Film*, p. 101. The comment about the pre-Vietnam enemy is from Smith, *Looking Away*, p. 22. The last comments about the group are from Basinger, p. 16.

[2]The comments about war machines are from Smith, *Looking Away*, p. 23. The comments about resolution are from Basinger, *The WWII Combat Film*, p. 66.

[3]The quote about settings comes from Kaminsky, *American Film Genres*, p. 229. The comments about nature come from Basinger, *The WWII Combat Film*, p. 16.

[4]The comment about group unity comes from Kaminsky, *American Film Genres*, p. 229. The comment about the journey comes from Basinger, *The WWII Combat Film*, p. 66. The quote about the "right man" is from Kagan, *The War Film*, p. 20.

[5]Please see the discussion of the "traditional" hero above, in the context of the police film.

[6]Samuel G. Freedman, "The War and the Arts," The *New York Times Magazine*, 31 March 1985, p. 50.

[7]On *At the Movies* (Syndicated television program), June 1985.

[8]Kagan, *The War Film*, p. 23.

[9]For example, Michael Herr in *Dispatches* (New York: Alfred A. Knopf, 1977) speaks of "a collective meta-chopper," p. 9.
Frank McConnell in "A Name for Loss: Memorials of Vietnam," *Commonweal*, 9 August 1985, pp. 441-42, also treats the helicopter this way. McConnell also notices a

distinction between helicopters and fighter planes similar to the one mentioned above, p. 442.

Fred Dryer (in uniform) in *Death Before Dishonor*.

The Vietvet and the Horror Film

There has been a recent trend in art, especially fiction, in the representation of Vietvets and POWs toward equating those groups with ghosts and zombies, although not actually representing them as such. In these cases, these characters can be seen as metaphors for monsters in Campbell's sense, as "apparitions" who attack social standards. For example, in Larry Heinemann's *Paco's Story*, Paco, a Vietvet, is haunted by the ghosts of his dead comrades, and David Morrell's novelization of *Rambo: First Blood Part II* (1985) contains this characterization of a POW : "The hand had almost no flesh. It might have belonged to a corpse come back from the grave to seek revenge."[1] Horror films representing Vietvets have generally followed this trend, in representing vets mainly as monsters in human shape.

In a film market, however, saturated over the period with horror and science fiction films representing demons of horror and monsters of science, only a handful of these pictures have contained Vietvet characters as this type of monster character. Further, no major company has yet made a film containing a Vietvet monster in this sense. Before turning to a discussion of those few films that do, however, I will discuss the generic groundwork for this section.

Charles Derry has formulated in *Dark Dreams* and refined in a later article a generic triptych that encompasses what have been often been treated as separate genres, the horror film and the science fiction film. His three part formula is "horror of personality," "horror of Armageddon," and "horror of the demonic."[2] The horror of personality films show a consistent representation of a human monster vet. The horror of Armageddon and of the demonic films are much more rare within the subsystem of Vietvet horror films.

Horror of personality films

According to Derry, in the horror of personality film the conflicts are generally externalized and violent, with a special emphasis towards bodily mutilation, although the violence often is an outgrowth of a character's mental problems. Thus, the horror comes not from without, supernaturally or preternaturally, but from within. Central characters with split personalities and alter-egos are often represented, although quite often everyone is represented as "potentially insane."[3]

Other characters include crippling parental figures, sometimes in abnormal sexual roles, and investigators who are often killed. Icons include claw-like weapons such as knives, hatchets, and axes. Resolutions often take the form of a reversal, in which "the disguised monster is shockingly revealed." In horror of personality films, as Derry points out, everyone is potentially insane. In Vietvet horrors of personality, the Vietvet character almost always is portrayed *as* insane.

Psycho a Go-Go! (1965) is a horror of personality film and one of the earliest Vietvet pictures. A certain Dr. Vanard (John Carradine) implants a device into Vietvet Joe Corey's (Roy Morton) brain, causing the veteran to become deranged. Thus, the cause of Corey's insane behavior comes literally from without, but does not come directly from his experiences in Vietnam. As more Vietvet films within this genre were made, the image of the mad veteran continues, but the Vietnam War will more and more assume an apparent causal role in this process. Corey terrorizes a family and murders a go-go dancer, whence the movie gets one of its titles.

The fact that the movie is also known by a variety of titles suggests that it was quite a difficult sell. Indeed, throughout its life, its distributor tried to sell it by emphasizing violence (*Blood of Ghastly Horror*), sex (*The Love Maniac*), and science fiction (*The Fiend with the Atomic Brain*, *The Man with the Synthetic Brain*). While none of these titles helped turn it into a hit film, the film is available on video cassette currently. Also, in 1987 a similar plot was used for *No Dead Heroes*, in which a Vietvet gets a microchip planted at the base of his skull by some Russians. He then goes on a murder spree that includes his estranged family and that of his best friend from Vietnam. This film also owes a debt to *The Manchurian Candidate*, as the Russians have more global plans in mind for the Vietvet--they want him to kill the Pope.

The central way that the image of the mad vet was carried over this period was in a spate of horror of personality films, by far the most common way for a Vietvet to be represented within the genres of horror. After *Psycho A Go-Go* many Vietvet horror of personality films appeared in the 1970s, of which *The Ravager* (1970) is perhaps the most obscure.

The Ravager contains a representation of a Vietvet whose psychopathology is directly linked to his experiences in Vietnam. Joe Salkow (Pierre Gostin or Gaston; there is controversy over the proper name), a demolitions expert in the war, sees the Vietcong rape and murder a Vietnamese woman. Upon Joe's return home, he becomes deranged whenever he witnesses sex, and dynamites the young lovers involved. In a remarkable description of the film, the AFI film guide remarks, "Soon, running low on money and dynamite, Joe is forced to become simply a voyeur."[4] After this film, variations on the mad vet became common.

For example, in *Glory Boy* (1972) AKA: *My Old Man's Place*, Trubee Pell (Michael Moriarty) invites two of his war buddies, Martin Flood (Mitchell Ryan) and Jimmy Pilgrim (William Devane), to his father's farm. *Variety* describes the film as an updating of "essentially an old motorcycle gang exploitation package." The review goes on to say that Flood "reverts to insanity and tries to wipe...out" Pell, Pilgrim, and a social worker they meet.[5] Pell, in an early representation of a vet plagued by noncombat deaths in Vietnam, is tormented by the memory of a Vietnamese woman he killed during his service.

Similarly, *The Visitors* (1972) presents a small-town milieu in which veteran characters turn upon other veteran characters. The theme of atrocities is again picked up here as two vets, Mike Nickerson (Steve Railsback) and Tony Rodriguez (Chico Martinez), terrorize a third, Bill Schmidt (James Woods), after he testifies against them in the rape and killing of a young Vietnamese woman. Their first stop after the penitentiary is Schmidt's home, where they attack him and rape his wife. Two films feature vets with killer animals.

Stanley (1972) came in the aftermath of *Willard* and in the midst of a whole host of animals-gone-mad films including those involving snakes, grizzly bears, and even rabbits and frogs. Tim Ochopee (Chris Robinson) is a returned vet who does not relate to other people very well. When someone offends him or hurts snakes in some way, Ochopee gains his revenge by unleashing his pet poisonous snakes, including Stanley, his favorite.

Second, *To Kill a Clown* (1972) has Alan Alda playing Major Ritchie, a sort of Hawkeye gone berserk. In it he holds a callow young couple hostage in and around his beach house with the aid of his two Dobermans, Charlie and Rice. He lost his kneecaps in Vietnam, and much more. Suggestions abound that he is impotent, that he blames the war for this, and that he resents those who did not participate in the struggle. Apparently, he got the impression from his upbringing that only those who fight can gain manhood, and the idea that the fight in Vietnam deprived him of his drives him insane.

In a twist, *Have a Nice Weekend* (1975) represents a recently returned vet who is not the killer, although the film positions him as a suspect. Paul (M.B. Miller) calls his family to a meeting on a New England island. He acts unstably, as if his war experience still troubles him, at one point burning his old uniform. Thus, he seems the prime suspect when one of the group is knifed to death. But Paul is not the slasher; he is the second to be claimed as a victim.

Jim (Hugh Feagin) is a slasher in *Poor White Trash II* (1976) AKA: *Scum of the Earth.* He is a Vietvet thought killed but actually held as a POW. In typical slasher style, he kills off his wife's new husband upon his escape from a mental ward, and then systematically kills off the members of the title family, at whose shack his wife has taken refuge. *Nightflowers* (1979) also represents a return to the old form. In this independent horror of personality film two veterans (Jose Perez, Gabriel Walsh), one Hispanic and one Irish-

American, both show symptoms of their psychosis by raping and killing a girl and killing an intruder, respectively. *Variety* describes the film as "focused on the seedy, sordid and psychotic aspects of urban society."[6]

This stereotype was so pervasive that some commentators labeled killers of this type as Vietvets when there is no direct evidence in the texts surveyed that this was in fact the case. For example, this is the case with at least the current video tape versions of *Targets* (1968), *Rollercoaster* (1977), and *Far From Home* (1989), although the discrepancies could be due to textual variation. Indeed, by 1980 *Variety* was calling "a Vietvet with scars on the brain...a cliched affliction."[7]

This remark was made in *Variety*'s review of *Don't Answer the Phone*, another Vietvet horror of personality film. The film's script seems to share these assumptions, as it contains the line "Sick son of a bitch--maybe we're looking for a Vietnam vet," immediately after a policeman sees the killer's first victim. Kirk Smith (Nicholas Worth) has other problems as well, with his self-image and with his religion, and he strangles about a half dozen women before he is stopped.

This trend of representation has carried on into the 1980s. Larry Cohen's *Perfect Strangers* (1984) contains the portrayal of a disturbed, switchblade-wielding Mafia killer recently back from Vietnam. The more recent examples are increasingly baroque ones, and can be seen as moving into parody. One, *Combat Shock* (1986), comes from the Troma Team and executive producers Lloyd Kaufman and Michael Herz, who are more or less responsible for *The Toxic Avenger* (1985), *Class of Nuke 'Em High* (1986), and *Surf Nazis Must Die* (1987) among many others.

In *Combat Shock* Frankie (Ricky Giovinazzo) awakens from a Vietnam War atrocity-dream, in which a whole village of Vietnamese is slaughtered, to a world of bleak poverty. He is out of work, has a wife who cannot stand him, and a baby straight out of *It's Alive* (1974) or *Eraserhead* (1978). During his time in Vietnam Frankie was a POW and spent many months recuperating in the hospital.

Desperate because his family is starving and his father

will not help, Frankie turns to crime and ultimately murders his loan shark and the loan shark's henchmen. This violence triggers more violence and Frankie returns home and kills his family, including graphically murdering the baby and cooking it in the oven. Frankie then shoots himself in the head, and the question of whether the atrocities he dreams about were real and whether Frankie himself committed them remains unresolved.

Perhaps even stranger is the representation found in *The Texas Chainsaw Massacre Part 2* (1987). After his brother Leatherface (Bill Johnson) clips him in the head with his chainsaw, Chop Top (Bill Moseley) screams, "Nam flashback! Nam flashback! You're gonna send me back to the VA hospital with a dent in my plate!" Then, as Chop Top hits a victim with a hammer, he yells out, "Time for incoming mail!" and "Ho Chi Minh!"

While this could be a portrayal of the delusions of a very demented mind, within the context of the film it appears that Chop Top actually did serve in Vietnam. As he explains to his father and brother during a family squabble, "No lucky gook with a machete, no head wound. No head wound, no fancy rolling grill a go-go. This chrome dome bankrolled this food business." These lines are almost hidden in the film; they are spoken offscreen and buried low in the mix of the sound track. The original picture in this series and its second sequel do not contain this representation, although the third film of the series is in some ways suggestive of other representations of Vietnam.

While much less baroque, *Moon in Scorpio* (1987) has a Byzantine plot structure, which involves three vets: Burt (William Smith), who killed a civilian Vietnamese woman; Allen (John Phillip Law), who stood by and did nothing; and Mark (Louis Van Bergen), who is linked to them only by friendship. Allen is plagued by his inaction, and has acquired a related fear of water that he wants to conquer. In order to do so, he takes his new bride Linda (Britt Ekland) on a trip on Mark's yacht with Burt, Mark, and their girlfriends. Killings and red herrings start multiplying, with many of the false clues indicating that one of the Vietvets is the murderer. For example, Linda says that the men had "bombs going off inside their brains," that it was a war they couldn't forget, and that what was a honeymoon turned into a war, "another war for the survivors."

Although, as Derry points out, the horror of personality film has been viable through the 1970s and into 1980s,[8] an enormous number of them in this time frame do not represent a Vietvet. These include *Halloween* (1978) and its four (so far) sequels, *Friday the 13th* (1980) and its seven (so far) sequels, and many others including *Prom Night* (1980) and its sequel, *Terror Train* (1980), *Silent Rage* (1982), *Silent Night, Deadly Night* (1984), *Return to Horror High* (1987), and the parodies of these films including *Student Bodies* (1981), *National Lampoon's Class Reunion* (1982), *Thursday the Twelfth* (1983), and *April Fool's Day* (1986).

While the Vietvet horror of personality films represent just a portion of these films, the image resulting from them is clear. Either the Vietvet is a deranged killer, or else is a prime suspect. The picture in the horror of Armageddon films is only slightly different.

Horror of Armageddon films

Derry sees the twin roots of the horror of Armageddon film in the independent science fiction films of the 1950s as well as in the theater of the absurd. In these films the conflicts are externalized and violent as the world or a good part of it is destroyed by "multiplying, nonindividualized non-human creatures," often due to a breakdown in our ecosystem or else due to nuclear escalation. The thematics of the horror of Armageddon film include "proliferation, besiegement, and death."[9]

A rare horror of Armageddon film that represents a returned vet is *The Crazies* (1973). This film did not enjoy much commercial or critical success during its theatrical release. Like *Psycho A Go-Go* this film is known by more than one title. It is also know as *Code Name: Trixie*, suggesting as well that it had marketing trouble. Nearly fifteen years after its initial release *The Crazies* became available on video tape under that title.

The Crazies can clearly be seen as a horror of Armageddon film. This film also contains a recurring image in the

Vietvet genres of order, the representation of the disin-
tegration of a family. In the precredit sequence a father kills
his wife and sets fire to his house, injuring his children. He
is the victim of an awful disease.

Vincent Canby, writing in *The New York Times*, shows
the inattention the mainstream press has generally shown the
horror film by confusing an important plot point about this
disease in his review of *The Crazies*. He complains about an
"error of logic" that does not exist in the film, by stating that
the soldiers wear gas masks although the poison is in the
water supply.[10]

It is true that the poison is in the water supply, but the
contagion, Code name: Trixie, once ingested, is highly con-
tagious. Trixie, a bacteriological weapon insinuated into
Evans City's water supply as a result of an Army transport
accident, offers its victims two unpleasant alternatives. One
is to die, the other is to go incurably mad, which, as the horror of personality films show, are common options represented for Vietvets during this period. Therefore, there is a
perfectly logical reason for the soldiers to be wearing the
masks.

Once this framework is established, the narrative of the
film can be seen as running in three intersecting lines. The
first has to do with the military, who have cordoned off the
area in the hope of controlling the spread of the disease. The
second has to do with a team of scientists who are working
on an antidote. The third has to do with a small group of
Evans City residents.

This last group contains the film's Vietvets, David
(W.G. McMillan) and Clank (Harold Wayne Jones). David,
as an often resorted-to character over these years, is an ex-
Green Beret, while Clank was regular Army and a Green
Beret reject. In a brief, though rare-for-the-time overt discussion of war experiences, David disavows his military
service to Judy (Lane Carroll), who is pregnant with their
child. He tells Judy that looking back he cannot believe he
bought into the machismo surrounding his enlistment and
equates being "Evans City's only Green Beret" with his days
as a high school football hero.

When David makes this speech to Judy, they are hiding

out in a country club, a result of being pursued by the military, who want to put the whole town under quarantine and sequester all the citizens in the local high school.[11] When they meet resistance from the townspeople, one character describes what they are doing as "holding the perimeter and fighting a small scale war." Besides this one, Vietnam allusions abound in the film. One of the ways Romero does this is by frequent reference to certain icons--the self-immolation of a protesting monk, the burning of a Vietnamese's hut by an American soldier with a Zippo lighter, the execution of the Vietcong suspect in the street, and various images of helicopters--of the Vietnam War from another system, the news media.[12]

For example, a priest objecting to the way the Army is conducting affairs runs out of his church, douses himself with gasoline, and lights himself with a Zippo lighter. Some of the soldiers burn corpses with flame throwers. Clank dies by a gunshot wound to the head out of which jets a stream of blood. During a chase through the woods, a helicopter chases David's group, and he shoots it down in a scene that must have accounted for a good part of the film's small budget. For director George Romero, this concern with some of the icons of Vietnam is carried through into some of his other films, especially the middle film of the *Dead* trilogy, *Dawn of the Dead* (1979). In that film both helicopters and one character's Zippo lighter are important props, and the bullet in the head recurs enough for it to be reasonably called a motif of the movie.

Dave, one of the film's Vietvets, seems to have a natural immunity to the virus, although two other central characters, Judy and Clank, do not. Both Judy and Clank contract the disease, start going crazy, and end up shot dead by soldiers. These sequences portray, respectively, another breakdown of a family unit and another insane Vietvet, already on its way to becoming a firm stereotype through these years within and without the horror film genre.

In a unique twist, though, the film fashions an ironic world in which another Vietvet, contrary to the stereotype, is the only really sane one in town. David does not contract the disease, in fact, he seems to be the only one in Evans City with a natural immunity to Trixie. Two attempts to show that this might in fact be the case are thwarted by the military holding the town captive.

In the first, the scientist responsible for creating both the disease and an antidote is killed, cure in hand, by the Army, after being mistaken for a Crazy. Later, an Army doctor has a chance to examine the immune David, but shrugs off the suggestion after merely checking David's disheveled physical appearance. Conversely then, the Army, not the Vietvets but the ones who trained them and sent them to fight, come off as the Crazies. It is quite a while until another horror of Armageddon film features a Vietvet.

One of the salient parts of *Street Trash* (1987) is a series of very colorful, and very gory, meltdowns of human beings who have the misfortune to drink some contaminated wine. This horror film revolves around a group of junkyard dwellers, ruled by Bronson (Vic Noto). Bronson, an extremely unsavory character, has weird flashbacks to Vietnam, dreaming of the Vietcong as vampires. He's troubled by his atrocities, but not too much. A policeman describes Bronson: "The guy is a psycho. He was a hit man over in Nam, and he was selling dope over there too. Finally, he was dishonorably discharged--section eight. He's got a knife made out of a human femur bone." Bronson recalls in a flashback the time he cut up a man to get his femur, out of which he made the knife. When he later kills a different policeman with the knife and breaks it, he takes his femur to get another. This description, which leaves out some of the gorier aspects of the film, suggests that here, as in the case of the horror of personality films, the representation of the Vietvet has entered a baroque stage.

The horror of Armageddon film has been quite commercially viable into the 1970s and 1980s.[13] The trend in other horror of Armageddon films of the period has been toward representing non-Vietvet characters. The pitch for *The Thing* (1982) could have gone, "Let's redo *The Thing*, but with scientists instead of Army guys." This trend is cross-generic, as *Always* (1989) shows. Even those films containing soldier and veteran characters are distanced from their present day in time, space, or both. For example,

Escape from New York (1981) and the *The Terminator* (1984) feature veterans of World War III. *A Boy and his Dog* (1975), *Mad Max* (1980) and its sequels, *Hardware* (1990), and many others portray survivors of the apocalypse. *Aliens* (1986) contains the veterans of numerous "bug wars" in outer space, and *Total Recall* (1990) shows veterans of the wars on Mars.

Movies have sheltered the presentation of Vietvets in other wars. For example, in *Endangered Species* (1982) Ben Morgan (Hoyt Axton) is a big man in a little town in Colorado. The president of the local cattlemen's association, he gets involved with a shadowy organization that is trying out illegal chemical warfare tests around town. He is a Korean vet and flew B-52s in Vietnam. Very little is made of his service, except to suggest his right-wing escapades stem from it. Also, what starts off playing as horror of Armageddon film turns into a conspiracy thriller. The trend in the horror of the demonic film is quite similar.

Horror of the demonic films

In the horror of the demonic films Evil is represented as actually existing; it is a tangible entity, a character. In other words, characters are often supernatural or preternatural. On the other hand, innocent characters are often fated to die. Often, these character types battle violently around themes of vengeance and mystic possession. Important icons involve Christian symbols including crosses, crucifixes, and holy water.[14]

The representation of madness has an important relationship with the horror of the demonic films as well as with the horror of personality films. In horrors of the demonic, the existence of the evil thing is almost always called into question vis-a-vis the sanity of the character who spots it. A stock line in these films is "If I tell you what I saw, you'll think I'm crazy!" Horror of the demonic films that incorporate a Vietvet into a horror framework include *Deathdream* (1972) and *House* (1986).

The earlier film, like other central films noted above, is also known by more than one title. It is also known as *Dead of Night*, *Night Walk*, and *The Veteran*, again pointing to marketing trouble. The film in fact did not enjoy commercial success, although it is currently available on video as *Deathdream*.

Deathdream is a rare horror of the demonic Vietvet film, a reworking of "The Monkey's Paw." In it Charlie (John Marley) and his wife Christine (Lynn Carlin) get a telegram notifying them that their son Andy (Richard Backus) has been killed in action. Christine retreats to her bedroom and intones "You promised...," as if willing her son to make good on his word that he would be careful in Vietnam. Andy later appears at his parents' house, revealed behind a quickly opening door and then zoomed-in upon. This sequence has the net effect of his mother successfully calling him back from the dead, which indeed she has.

On his way home Andy had accepted a ride from a trucker whom he kills. Andy often needs fresh blood with which to maintain his decaying organs. His method of extraction is by hypodermic needle, which immediately sets the police off looking for drug-linked suspects. Initially, Andy avoids suspicion for, as one person in the diner where he got the ride says, "I can't believe a soldier'd do a thing like that."

Andy's odd behavior at home, however, becomes increasingly harder and harder to overlook. Finally, Charlie blurts out, "Why is he so different? I went through it too. But when I came back I didn't act like that!" This sentiment echoes an earlier mention of WWII made by the oblivious mailman, who thinks Andy's habit of scaring people is a joke, and stands as an early filmic comparison of Vietnam to other wars, the Korean as well as WWII. These references are cross-generic. For example they appear in *Welcome Home, Soldier Boys* (1972) and in *First Blood* (1982), and continue in a different way in the melodrama *Cease Fire* (1985).

When a group of neighborhood kids come over and try to revive their custom of playing football with Andy, he strangles his family's dog in order to get rid of them. Charlie has had enough and seeks help for his son, who is clearly beyond it, but his family will not admit it. The family doctor pays Andy a visit in his darkened room, and Andy scoffs at his offer of a free checkup, ironically pointing out that he does not need any medical help.

In his refusal of an offer of kindness, something Andy does repeatedly throughout the film, involving the trucker, the football-playing kids, and now the doctor, Andy seems to be saying that these things cannot begin to repay what is owed him. This is an early filmic encounter with a veteran seeking this type of satisfaction. In *Deathdream* this situation becomes overt in Andy's final encounter with the doctor.

Andy begins by taunting the doctor: "I came for my checkup." As things escalate Andy says, "I died for you, Doc. Why shouldn't you return the favor?" Finally, Andy says, "You owe me something, Doc. You owe me this!" "This" refers to the Doc's blood, which Andy greedily drinks.

The police begin to tie these events together, but not before Andy's sister arranges a double date with her boyfriend and Andy's old girlfriend. Following his pattern, Andy kills his girlfriend and his sister's date. After some random carnage at the drive-in, the police chase Andy back to his parents' house. Charley shoots himself. Andy's mom helps her son escape the police, driving Andy to a graveyard where she helps him bury himself. Andy's family has disintegrated, but it is not by his direct hand that it is done.

Andy's attacks have come on a fairly representative cross section of society. A working man, the trucker, offers him a ride and gets killed. A similar thing happens regarding a professional, the doctor. The middle-class representatives, the neighborhood kids, and the people he and his sibling date fare no better. The only people he spares are the people, directly or indirectly, who have brought the curse down upon him: his father for encouraging him to enlist and his mother for invoking his demon spirit.

Roughly in between *Deathdream* and *House* many horror of the demonic films were released, but none to my knowledge contain veteran characters. Many center around possessed children, including *The Exorcist* (1973) and its first sequel, *The Omen* (1976) and its sequels, and *Carrie* (1976) and *The Fury* (1978). There was also a renewed interest in vampire films, which fit into this category, including *Dracula A.D. 72* (1972), *Dracula's Dog* (1979), *Dracula* (1979), *The Lost Boys* (1987), *Graveyard Shift* (1987), and the comedies *Love at First Bite* (1979), *Once Bitten* (1985), and *Vamp* (1987). Somewhat similarly, the wolfman was revived in such films as *An American Werewolf in London* (1981), *The Howling* (1981) and its sequels, and the comedies *Teen Wolf* (1985) and *Teen Wolf, Too* (1987). None of these films contain a Vietvet character.

One of the central tensions in *House* can be phrased by referring to two of Derry's categories. Is this a horror of personality film or a horror of the demonic? Is Roger Cobb (William Katt) mad? Or Do Big Ben (Richard Moll) and the other demons exist outside Cobb's mind? I will argue that Roger Cobb, in a departure from the common representation depicted above, is only potentially mad and that *House* is a horror of the demonic film.

Cobb is a successful horror novelist à la Stephen King. The question of insanity is prefigured early in the film as Cobb, at a book signing, asks his agent who are all the lunatics coming up to the table. The reply is that they are his best fans. In other words he is writing books that appeal to crazy people. Also, at the beginning of the film Cobb's aunt kills herself, opening Cobb up to many questions about her insanity and whether it just might run in the family.

Cobb moves into his inheritance, the haunted house of the title, and prepares to write a book about his personal experiences in Vietnam. He does this over the objections of his agent, who tells him, "Nobody wants to read about the goddam Vietnam War anymore!" Roger feels guilty about his participation in the war and seems obsessed to get his memoir done. This is the case particularly regarding Big Ben, whom he allowed to be taken into the hands of the Vietcong, who subsequently tortured him to death. Ben had begged Roger to kill him before this could happen, but Roger went to get help instead.

Whenever he begins to write about the war, the house comes alive, making him question his sanity and linking his memories of Vietnam with the question of madness. Yard implements chase Cobb, a stuffed fish becomes reanimated, and various ghosts haunt him. As these events multiply, Cobb becomes obsessed with documenting these phenomena, just as he is obsessed about documenting his experiences in the war. The link between his experiences in Vietnam and his questionable mental health continues to grow.

Cobb himself questions his sanity to a neighbor, Harold (George Wendt). Harold tries to reassure him, reasoning that Cobb was in Vietnam and lost his son and his wife, and that anyone would "have some marbles rolling around" after all that. Cobb's son was mysteriously taken from, or by, the house some years back and his marriage collapsed because of it. Still, late in the film, Harold doubts Cobb's mental state enough to call both his estranged wife Sandy (Kay Lenz) and the local police about his behavior.

Harold's attitude about Roger changes when he witnesses some other-worldly phenomena at Cobb's side. Through a confusion in their plans to record these events, Roger gets taken into the house's haunted dimension, which turns out to be none other than the jungles of Vietnam. There, Cobb must confront Big Ben. Ben has been holding Cobb's son and wants his revenge on Roger. "I would have died for you, Ben, " Roger protests. Ben replies, "Well, now's your chance."

To defeat Ben and regain his son, Cobb has to do a similar thing he was trying to with his memoir--face up to his war experience. Here, Ben, functioning as the specter of Vietnam for Roger, resists this process. "You can't get rid of me, Roger," he proclaims. "You can't and you never will." After Roger bests Ben and the ghost re-emerges, to defeat him once and for all, Roger realizes he must look unflinchingly at the past to put it to rest. Once he acts this out, (saying things like "I beat you.... You can't scare me."), he defeats Ben and the Vietnam memories that haunt him.

What is more, this victory puts the film into the realm of the horror of the demonic. Once Ben is defeated, Roger has tangible evidence that psychic phenomena have indeed been taking place in the house. That is, his son is now freed, and he has Harold as a credible witness. The ending scene also provides something rare in a Vietvet horror film, the suggestion of the reintegration of a family. Sandy arrives at the end to see father and son walking out of the house.

It should be noted that in a very direct sense, this characterization has not been continued, as was the case above regarding the sequels to *The Texas Chainsaw Massacre* (1975). *House II: The Second Story* (1987) follows completely new characters, none of whom is a Vietvet. Also, Vietvets have not appeared in recent demonic horror films such as *The Gate* (1987), *Hellraiser* (1987), *Prince of Darkness* (1987), *Poltergeist III* (1988), and *The Guardian* (1990), among others.

Something new, however, occurs in *Graveyard Shift* (1990). Here Brad Dourif plays the Exterminator, who works around the textile mill where the main action of the film takes place. He tells the hero of rat-induced horrors (rats gnawing their way inside some of his comrades as part of Vietcong tortures) that he was aware of in Vietnam. This characterization marks a rare appearance of a Vietvet in a horror film released by a major studio, albeit in a minor role. The Exterminator here says he's not twisted, not the type of character you see Bruce Dern playing in movies all the time, but he certainly is presented that way, as something out of a David Lynch film. He looks ratty himself, still favors military garb, and is quite unhealthily obsessed with killing rats.

The film, made from a short story by Stephen King, invents this character for the screen. In this way it is similar to a short student film made based on the story "The Woman in the Room," also by King, in which a Vietvet character is invented to provide exposition. He tells the protagonist about ways to kill without being detected. In both cases filmmakers must have felt the time was right to introduce a Vietvet character in these contexts.

The genres of horror and of the outlaw biker are similar in the Vietvet filmic system in that they are the only ones the majors have almost completely avoided. *Jacob's Ladder* (1990) fits into this trend in an interesting way, for what appears at first to be a Vietvet horror film is taking place in Vietnam in Jacob's mind. The independents have also tried a similar story line in *Night Wars* (1988), and it is also cross-generic, with *Clay Pigeon* (1971). Accordingly, the major filmmakers seem to have assumed that film audiences had little interest in wanting Vietvets represented in horror films. An examination of the economic performance of these films (*House* is the only one on the *Variety* rentals list) shows that the public did not support these subsystems and indicate to filmmakers that they wanted more of the same, although most of these films are available on video.

What also emerges from this tracing of the representation of the Vietvet across genres of horror echoes something from *The Crazies*. Vietvets in these genres are usually either incurably mad or else dead. *The Crazies* itself though, and *House*, show exceptions to this trend. These are the only instances of Vietvets as heroes within this subsystem, a radical departure from the other genres of order discussed so far. Even these heroes have flaws that link them to the more common representation in horror film, that of the mad vet.

The horror of personality films carry a strong image of the human monster, the psychologically disturbed Vietvet who tries to destroy social order by killing. The idea of the invincibility of this type of human monster shown in films like *Halloween* and *Friday the 13th* and after is not picked up in the Vietvet films of this type. The mad Vietvets in *Don't Answer the Phone*, *Combat Shock*, and *The Texas Chainsaw Massacre Part 2*; seem much more easily dispatched than do Michael Miller or Jason, as if to suggest the end of the viability of this type of Vietvet character. This character type as major character has indeed apparently ended in the other genres of order before the release of the last of these horror films.

The nearly complete scarcity of Vietvet as monster of science or demon can perhaps be explained by filmmakers' reluctance to make light of what has been generally regarded as the most traumatic national experience since the Civil War. Vincent Canby's remark above is indicative of the seriousness with which the horror film has often been treated. That the major filmmakers have almost completely avoided these characterizations bears this out.

That the independents, normally not as sensitive to such concerns, have made such films, but only extremely rarely, adds credence to this claim. Comedy, like horror, is often not taken seriously by many critics. The treatment of Vietvet characters in comedy, to which I now turn, is somewhat similar to that found in the genres of horror.

Notes

[1]Larry Heinemann, *Paco's Story* (New York: Penguin, 1987); David Morrell, *Rambo: First Blood Part II* (New York: Berkley Publishing Group, 1985).

[2]Charles Derry, *Dark Dreams: The Horror Film from "Psycho" to "Jaws"* (South Brunswick, NJ, and New York: A.S. Barnes and Company, 1977); Charles Derry, "More Dark Dreams," in Gregory A. Waller, ed., *American Horrors: Essays on the Modern American Horror Film* (Urbana and Chicago: University of Illinois Press, 1987).

[3]Derry, "More Dark Dreams," p. 164.

[4]Kratsus, *AFI Guide to Motion Pictures, 1961-1970*, p. 889.

[5]*Variety Film Reviews*, vol. 13., 6-30-71.

[6]Ibid., vol. 15, 9-05-79.

[7]Ibid., vol. 15, 4-16-80.

[8]Derry, "More Dark Dreams," p. 165.

[9]Ibid., p. 171.

[10]Vincent Canby, "The Crazies," *The New York Times*, 4 March 1973, sec. 1, p. 20.

[11]Director George Romero seems nearly Frederick Wiseman-like in his preference for setting his films at American institutions--the farm, the church, the high school, the shopping center, or the retirement home.

[12]Suggested by Professor Lawrence Lichty in

"Introduction to Mass Media," class, Northwestern University, Professor Chuck Kleinhans, Fall 1985.

[13]Derry, "More Dark Dreams," p. 171.

[14]Ibid., p. 168.

W.G. McMillan (with rifle) and Harold W. Jones in *The Crazies*.

The Vietvet and the Comedy Film

Of the traditional genres of integration, one was not very common during the period under investigation, especially after the 1960s. That the musical, then, should not appear to contain many Vietvet characters should not be surprising. In one musical, *Hair* (1978), there is a suggestion of a returned dead Vietvet as the film provides the image of the grave of Berger/Claude (Treat Williams). The melodrama, on the other hand, represents many different Vietvets. The comedy, while not exactly the same case as seen in the musical, does not appear to represent very many.

In mythic terms, the Vietvet comedies introduce a character type not clearly seen before, the shaman. Campbell defines the shaman as one who in "late childhood or early youth has an overwhelming psychological experience that turns him totally inward," who undergoes "a kind of schizophrenic crack-up." To distinguish the shaman from the monster, rather than exploding social norms as the monster does, the shaman becomes "the interpreter of the heritage of mythological life."[1] This type of figure can be seen in some of the Vietvet comedies.

On the narrative level, "the lance that delivers the wound" myth can also been seen to be sometimes operative. A major difference in these films compared to those in the genres of order surrounding the idea of refighting the war comes with the introduction of compassion, in a mythic sense. Campbell decodes this concept to mean "suffering with."[2] In this sense women play a vital role in suffering along with certain returned Vietvet characters.

In general, the genres of integration do not seem as "ordered" as do the genres of order. That is, analyses concerning these genres have apparently not yielded the precise icons found in the gangster film, for example. Accordingly, the analysis of the genres of integration will be limited to the questions of character and narrative noted above.

One way to approach the comedy film is to divide it into three subgenres, the individual comedy, the screwball comedy, and the situation comedy.[3] Although all these comedy subgenres have remained in force during the period under investigation, major Vietvet characters within them do not seem at all common. In this tracing of the few Vietvet characters found in these subgenres, special attention will be given to the role of the women characters, none of them Vietnam era vets, within them.

The individual comedy

In individual comedies the main conflicts arise from the central character's "inability to get along in society." Kaminsky maintains that major comedians of their day from Keaton and Chaplin in the 1920s and 1930s to Jerry Lewis and Woody Allen in the 1960s and 1970s have often made this type of comedy.[4] Rodney Dangerfield and Whoopi Goldberg are making this type of film currently.

Individual comedies containing a Vietvet character before the 1980s are quite rare. One example is *Norwood* (1970). In it the title character (Glen Campbell) comes home to find his sister married to a "disabled" Vietvet, Bill Bird (Dom DeLuise), who has taken over the house. Norwood, tired of pumping gas, accepts a job driving a car from his home to New York City, provided the shady character who offers him the job can get him some singing auditions. Norwood also wants to collect the money that his war buddy Joe (Joe Namath) owes him. When Norwood finds out the car is stolen, he abandons it and gets to New York on his own. Once there, he tries to make a go of it within the counterculture, in scenes that have not aged very well. Failing there, he decides to take a bus home, on which he meets Rita Lee (Kim Darby). After various misadventures, Norwood reunites with Rita Lee and gets his chance to sing before a television audience.

In sum Norwood is an ex-Marine, and certainly not a great fighter in the way many characters within the genres of order are. He got a "war wound" falling off a water truck at Khesanh. Also, by that point of comparison all the vets here are incredibly well-adjusted. The film makes practically no mention of Vietnam at all, except for a few mild jokes, and characters within this subsystem are rare for the next few years.

The Crazy World of Julius Vrooder (1974), which stars Timothy Bottoms in the title role, has him escape from the VA hospital where he has been institutionalized. Unable to function properly under the restrictive situation there, Vrooder builds his own hideaway where he intends to live under a ramp of a highway near the hospital. Both of these films, released by major companies, were financially unsuccessful. Universal, though, tried again to represent a Vietvet in a comedy a few years later. *Heroes* (1978), however, can be seen as a screwball comedy and will be treated in that section.

As part of *Some Kind of Hero* (1982) is set in Vietnam, it could also be considered a Vietnam War film. I will treat it here because the thrust of the film lies elsewhere. That is, the segment in Vietnam serves to set up the longer segment stateside, which can be then treated as an individual comedy. In it Eddie Keller (Richard Pryor) is an ex-POW who returns to America to find his every opportunity to reintegrate into society thwarted.

Generally, Eddie is pursuing the money the Army owes him as back pay covering the period when he was a POW. He needs the money because his mother is behind on her payments to an expensive nursing home, and his wife, who now loves another man, lost all his savings in a business venture. The question as to whether Eddie will get the money, which he keeps saying is simply what is owed him by the Army, is never resolved.

The implication is that Eddie will not be paid because he signed a confession while a POW. While the resolution to this specific problem is not a part of the film, Eddie does turn to crime to get the needed cash. His robbery attempts are all comic. For instance, he uses a water pistol, appears to wet his pants in front of a woman bank teller, and at one point gets chased away and scolded by a woman store-owner. But when Eddie decides to rob violent men of their money, he becomes successful at it.

In his other dealings with women a mythologizing function of the film becomes apparent. Eddie, presented as a very sensitive man around women, becomes quite insensitive when it comes to money. After his wife leaves him, he begins a non-business affair with a prostitute. She offers him the money to pay for his mother's health care, but he refuses and insults her, and she associates him with her customers.

Then, still insensitive, he commits his crimes. When he then reverts to his previous pattern of behavior, his newfound woman friend is waiting for him, as if by magic. Eddie, then, refuses compassion and opts to search for money. Once he has accomplished his quest, apparently he no longer has a need for compassion, for he only suffered due to its absence. In this way, Eddie can be seen as a fairly traditional hero.

More recently several individual comedies have represented Vietvets as minor characters, which show hints of reversion to the stereotype of the insane vet. In this sense, these portrayals are similar to those at the end of the horror of personality cycle. More generally, the current trend has been towards representing Vietvets in comedies as minor character parodies of representations in other genres.

For instance, comedian Sam Kinison plays a Vietvet college teacher in *Back to School* (1986). He asks his class if anyone can explain the cause of the Vietnam War. When one student gives a historical response with a liberal bias, Kinison explodes into his screaming wildman persona: "I know that's the popular version of what went on there. I know a lot of people like to believe that. I wish I could. But I was there! I was up to my knees in rice paddies!!...."

Somewhat similarly, *Hollywood Shuffle* (1987) offers a short parody of *Rambo: First Blood Part II* (1985) and *Missing in Action* (1984). Here, a spoof trailer promotes the film *Rambro: First Youngblood.* In it Rambro (Robert Townsend) emerges from under water to spray the air with bullets from an M-60. Other films ranging from *Trading Places* (1983), which has Eddie Murphy doing a bit as a pretend Vietvet at the beginning; *The Princess Bride* (1987), which contains a joke about land wars in Asia; and *UHF*

(1989), which contains yet another parody of Rambo, continue this uneasy relationship between comedy and the Vietnam War. Reportedly, there were also songs about Vietnam that were cut from the troubled *Ishtar* (1987). Finally in this regard, *Russkies* (1987) has one of the child leads mocking another because his dad did not serve in Vietnam.

The Vietvet characters in *O.C. and Stiggs* (1987) seem a bit more mad than any to this point within the subsystem. Dennis Hopper plays a character named Sponson who acts as if he were transplanted, as the photographer character, wholly from the world of *Apocalypse Now* (1979) to the world Robert Altman has fashioned. In this world the title characters are continually tormenting an Arizona insurance king named Schwab and go to Sponson to see if he can help them. They ask him and his companion Goon (Alan Autry) if they are vets. Sponson replies with a cryptic question: "Does Ho Chi Minh eat Rice Krispies?" Later the four of them "interrogate" Schwab in Sponson's helicopter and they even "body bomb" him--at a low altitude and over water.

Finally, *Moving* (1988) contains the representation of twin brother Vietvets, Frank and Cornell Crawford (Randy Quaid). These brothers are next-door-neighbor antagonists, in two different locations, to Arlo Pear (Richard Pryor). In New Jersey, Frank torments Arlo. In an attempt to get his wife to move, Pear reminds her not to forget "the Rambo factor" that makes their New Jersey home unbearable. In their new home in Idaho, Cornell takes up his brother's activities, until Arlo puts a stop to them, donning Rambo-like costume, bearing, and equipment.

The situation comedy

In many situation comedies dealing with war themes, such as *Stripes* (1981), *Deal of the Century* (1983), *Best Defense* (1984), and *Weekend Pass* (1984), the trend has been to represent post-Vietnam soldiers in major roles, if soldiers are represented at all. *Weekend Warriors* (1986) takes a different tack, representing pre-Vietnam National Guardsmen.

Harold (Max Gail) in *D.C. Cab* (1983), on the other hand, is the rare filmic Vietvet in a situation comedy, one "who came home and made his big dreams come true." His "big dream" is to make a successful business of the rundown title company in this situational, institutional comedy. This information is conveyed to him by Albert (Adam Baldwin), the son of dead Vietvet named Deke, whose pre-story observation about Harold the above statement about dreams reflects.

The two of them view war paraphernalia with nostalgia, but this longing for the past days is highly compartmentalized. When Harold tells Albert that he is sorry to have missed his father's funeral, the implication is that he would have come, but he was too busy working. D.C. Cab is not the institution that Albert's father knew, and Harold indicates that not all of his dreams have come true. Not only is the cab company failing, so is Harold's marriage.

Myrna (Anne DeSalvo), who started off as Harold's "partner in the American Dream," is growing dissatisfied with her husband's long hours, the little profit, and the fact that she, too, has to work at the dispatcher's office to keep the business from collapsing. Along this point, one of the subplots of the film involves found money, in the form of a large reward for a violin lost in a city cab. When Harold claims the reward, Myrna thinks that they have finally begun to see some dividends from their hard work.

Harold, though, wants to reinvest the cash in the company. For Myrna this is the limit, and she takes both the reward and possession of their house. When Harold tries to reason with her, she fights him off with one of the war effects mentioned above, the flame thrower. To save this vet's dream, the other members of the company have to intervene, and do so regarding another subplot involving found money.

In this case the money is Deke's legacy to Albert, which Albert turns over to the company in order to keep it viable. Connected to this money is a subplot involving the kidnapped children of an influential diplomat. Albert, a witness to the kidnapping, rescues the children with the help of the company in order to clear his name and show that this new money has nothing to do with the crime. Once triumphant, the D.C. Cab Company is treated to a parade at the city's expense.

One inference that can be drawn from this narrative is

that the Vietvets' dreams can be answered, but we all must help. The members of the D.C. Cab Company can be seen as a group intentional hero, with a lone Vietvet as leader. But the film also suggests that this process can be reciprocal; all the members of the company are shown at the end with the suggestion that their dreams are fulfilled as well. For example, Albert is shown united with the young woman he was pursuing throughout the film. Still, for the Vietvet the dream is represented as only partially fulfilled. There is no strong indication that Myrna intends to reunite with Harold at closure.

In another situation comedy, *The Wild Life* (1984), Randy Quaid plays Charlie, a down-and-out Vietvet who is the object of the obsession of two children about to enter high school. He lives in a tumbledown shack, uses grass and heroin, looks horrible, and offers the boys beer. He gives them the message that "real" war is not G.I. Joe and Rambo, and they snap out of their obsession, starting school without military clothes or demeanor.

In addition Bruce Dern parodies some of his mad vet roles as Rumsfield in *The 'Burbs* (1989). Rumsfield still favors military clothes, has a handy infrared scope, and suggests that tapping the phone lines of the mysterious Klopeks "can be arranged." Finally, he makes use of his experience in Vietnam in a comic way as he corners one of the creepy family: "Don't you make a move, Sonny. I was eighteen months in the bush, and I could snap your neck in a heartbeat."

For a situation comedy that features Vietvets in major roles, one has to look outside the United States. In the British film *Riders of the Storm* (1988), a group of Vietvets that started as airborne "psy-ops" group in Vietnam has stayed on in their "Uncle Slam" B-29 after the war to make sure "that impulse that got us into Nam is dead." They do this by pumping an MTV-like selection of political programs through their pirate network, much to the dismay of the legitimate networks. During their expeditions they discover political secrets about a war-mongering candidate for President, which they disclose to the candidate's detriment. Their leader Cap (Dennis Hopper) himself decides he might run for the job.

The screwball comedy

According to Thomas Schatz "[p]lot and theme in the screwball comedy are essentially a function of character, with the lovers set in opposition along both sexual and socioeconomic lines."[5] Kaminsky prefers the term "man versus woman" comedies for this mode and maintains that this subgenre has maintained its viability into the 1970s and 1980s.[6] The main conflict in the screwball comedy comes in reconciling these class differences.[7]

Heroes contains the representation of another veteran with mental problems, this time within the context of a screwball comedy. Jack Dunne (Henry Winkler) escapes from a Manhattan VA mental ward to flee to the West where he hopes to fulfill his dream of owning and operating a worm farm, with money from the other institutionalized vets. In desperation he ducks into a bus station, where he meets Carol Bell (Sally Field), who is having transportation problems of her own, as she is trying to avoid her fiancé, who is making last-minute plans for their high society wedding. Thus, as these two are thrown together on a bus by fate they have a sanity as well as a class difference to reconcile.

Jack does not get off to a very promising start. When their bus gets a flat and the passengers go outside, Jack shows Carol how he can vibrate the earth to call worms to the surface. This prompts Carol to tell him he's crazy. She warms to him, though, and soon they are sharing a meal at a roadside diner. Jack will not at this point confront the war, the apparent source of his mental problems. At dinner when she wants to talk about it, all he will discuss is worms.

At the point in their journey when they are to part ways, Carol cashes in her ticket and accompanies Jack to his friend Ken's (Harrison Ford) trailer. Ken's plan is similar to Jack's; he wants to raise rabbits. When Jack gets there, however, he finds that Ken has only managed to raise three and spends most of his time in a dangerous occupation, racing cars. The irony of the failure to raise one of the traditionally fastest breeding small animals points out the frequent representation of Vietvets' failed dreams, even as innocuous ones as these.

During the Vietvets' conversation Carol is again excluded from discussion of the war. In this instance Jack and Ken are going over old war stories and Carol protests that she does not have the slightest notion of what they are talking about. Ken tells her, "Well, honey, you had to be there at the time. I'm telling you, it's four years ago and I'm still playing catch-up."

The two men, though, discuss their feelings about the war fairly openly regarding the issues of violence and companionship with women. Jack recoils against the violence that used to be a part of his life and cannot believe that Ken owns a gun: "Oh, Jesus, man, where did you get that implement of destruction? Didn't you have enough?" They commiserate that they have not seen any women since they came back from the war. Jack ends this conversation with the plaintive, "nights are the worst."

Jack moves on his way again to find another veteran friend with whom he was to start the worm farm. After he digests the information that his friend was killed four years ago, Jack walks down the street of his friend's hometown, where he imagines he is refighting the war. During this flashback, he apparently realizes that he witnessed his friend's death and has been blocking it out. Jack then meets Carol who clings to him and says, "Listen to me. You're alive.... If you're crazy, I can't have you." The strong implication is that now that Jack has confronted what he has been repressing, he will both no longer be crazy *and* get the girl, as the film literally ends in an embrace. This process, however, is not completely represented, as the film ends at this point.

Around this time screwball comedies with war themes seem to prefer to represent post-Vietnam soldiers, if any at all. *Private Benjamin* (1980), *Protocol* (1984), and *Basic Training* (1986) fall into this group. There is one other screwball comedy that contains a representation of a Vietvet.

Finders Keepers (1984) contains a dead veteran as MacGuffin, with a generic twist. The variation is that there is no corpse in the coffin. Instead, the body has been replaced with stolen cash. An Army deserter, Lane Bittlekopf (Michael O'Keefe), dons a pawned uniform and gets mixed up in the affair, himself posing as a Vietvet. This screwball comedy can be seen as a comic reworking of *Tracks* (1976), which will be discussed in a later chapter. The plots are similar and the direction of the narrative in geographic terms is similar, from west to east, which perhaps can be seen as a sort of symbolic journey of rediscovery.

These comedies, in addition to their portrayal of relationships with women, represent Vietvets directly pursuing money, which is fairly rare within the Vietvet image system. Still, this pursuit is modified in certain ways. These Vietvets chase money only because their mothers need it, or a whole company of people, either vets or non-vets, is counting on them for it.

As for the relationship with women, in these comedies the Vietvets' successes have been only partial. In *Some Kind of Hero*, the vet's suggested pairing is clearly his second choice. In *D.C. Cab*, the vet saves his company but not his marriage. In *Heroes*, the pairing is merely suggested, however strongly. In the sense of mythic compassion, "suffering with" these vets is clearly resisted in these films except in the last listed.

Carol Bell in *Heroes* is the only example of a woman clearly willing to suffer with a traumatized Vietvet in this subsystem. As noted above, even here, this process is merely suggested at the end of the film and not carried out within it to a great degree. A counter-example can be seen in the Myrna character in *D.C. Cab*, who has clearly had enough of her husband's troubles and leaves him.

The traumas here differ from those found in the Vietvet horror film. Jack Dunne in *Heroes* is positioned as insane, but as a shaman is insane. His overwhelming psychological experience, of course, is his war experience. He initially turns inward about this, and his society expels him. He rebels/escapes and attempts to interpret that experience in mythic terms, rejecting the "implements of destruction," and upholding fertility symbols, hermaphroditic worms and fertile rabbits. He also seeks and accepts compassion from Carol Bell. Julius Vrooder can be seen in a similar light.

Other mad Vietvets within this subsystem in minor roles can not necessarily be seen as shaman characters. The trend recently in major releases toward including Vietvets in minor roles, and generally, the scarcity of Vietvets in leading roles both indicate a reluctance on the part of the majors toward associating the Vietvet with comedy.[8] In this sense a sort of mirror image emerges when compared to the subsystem of Vietvets in horror films.

There, the scarcity is of Vietvets as monsters, and no major releases stand out as vehicles for examples. As for comedy there seem to be very few independent releases as carriers of examples. These two subsystems show a general reluctance to associate Vietvets with either comedy or horror. Again, critics have not traditionally taken these genres very seriously. A major inference that can be drawn is that film-makers apparently also did not think the image of the Vietvet was something to take or that would be taken lightly.

Notes

[1]Campbell, *The Power of Myth*, pp. 85 and 88.

[2]Ibid., p. 198.

[3]As in Kaminsky, *American Film Genres*.

[4]Kaminsky, *American Film Genres*, p. 135.

[5]Schatz, *Hollywood Genres*, p. 152.

[6]Kaminsky, *American Film Genres*, p. 135.

[7]Schatz, *Hollywood Genres*, p. 152.

[8]Certainly the lack of popular success, especially early, of these films has something to do with the majors' reluctance. Only *Some Kind of Hero* and *D.C. Cab* are comedies with major Vietvet characters on *Variety*'s Rental Champs list, and not high up on it at that. Some others,

such as *Back to School* and *The 'Burbs* did well, but had only minor Vietvet characters within them.

Dennis Hopper (standing) in *Riders of the Storm.*

The Vietvet and the Melodrama

The melodrama is the central carrier of the wounded Vietvet image. Other genres represent wounded Vietvets, but none as consistently as does this one. Further, the melodrama often portrays Vietvets who received their battle scars, either mental or physical, in Vietnam. Invariably, other genres follow this trend involving only mental scars. Regarding physical wounds, Vietvets in the genres of order receive them after the war is over, as in *Rolling Thunder* (1977).

The "lance that delivers the wound" myth here gets a variation. While physical refighting is common within some of the Vietvet genre of order subsystems, in the melodrama the battles are generally less physical. Within the melodrama subsystem, Vietvets often battle their own physical and emotional troubles, which are closely linked to their war experiences, in an attempt to reintegrate into society.

In a mythic sense then, these characters can be seen as heroes of a different kind than that found in the genres of order, where heroes overcome their trials by resorting to bodily deeds and remain apart from their societies. In the melodrama, the heroes, often with the help of a compassionate[1] woman, try to impart a message based upon their war experience back to their society. Campbell holds that this act is one available to a mythic hero who attempts to reintegrate into his society.[2]

Generically, one can approach the melodrama as an inverted screwball comedy[3] along the axes of character and resolution. The characters in screwball comedies often rebel against the prevailing social order, while in the melodrama the characters often appear as slaves to that order. As for resolutions, the screwball comedies often integrate the principal couple with each other, apart from that order. The

115

melodrama, on the other hand, usually integrates the central couple into the dominant, often repressive, social milieu.

Further, the characters in a melodrama can often be seen as a family,[4] either literally or figuratively. Usually, their conflict centers around one issue such as "[r]acism, drink, drugs, delinquency...and the rest: the Problem. It's an absurd view, but it does appear to be Hollywood's working assumption." These problems are generally presented as existing without antecedent causes, "nothing is anyone's fault."[5]

When Vietvet characters appear in melodramas, often the problem is the war's effect on those characters, the physical scars, mental scars, or both caused by Vietnam. The causes of these scars are only rarely represented in these films, only rarely directly addressed. No one seems to want to talk about precisely what happened. Reintegration into the society these films depict, if even presented as an option in these films, only comes after much anguish and soul-searching on the part of the Vietvet characters.

Early in the period several melodramas represented Vietvets as major characters within their texts. These vets, basically untraumatized, see their central conflict involve problems reintegrating into society, which they do with more or less difficulty. The title character (Michael Parks) in *Bus Riley's Back in Town* (1965) returns to his small Midwestern hometown and tries to cope with his vanishing dreams. Along the way he is tormented by his now rich former girlfriend, Laurel (Ann-Margret). While Riley's attempts to quit his mechanic's job are unsuccessful, his problems are not directly linked to his service experience, nor is his service directly linked to combat in Vietnam.

In a generic variation Paul (Geoff Gage) is a Marine back in San Diego on emergency leave from Vietnam in the independent film *Captain Milkshake* (1970). He comes home from Vietnam to attend his stepfather's funeral and while there has an affair with a hippie, who introduces him to the counterculture scene in Southern California. *Variety* breaks down the plot this way: "Boy meets girl, girl turns on boy, boy loses girl, boy gets killed in Vietnam," and mentions that while Paul gets along with both the right wingers and the left wingers that he meets, he seems confused and inarticulate. While his temporary reintegration therefore seems successful, the resolution of the film has it another way. After having a fight with the girlfriend, the film quickly cuts to Vietnam where Paul is killed in action.

Getting Straight (1970) has Harry Bailey (Elliot Gould) torn between finishing his work as a graduate teaching assistant and remaining faithful to his ideals, amidst period campus unrest. That this would be a tension is explained by Harry's conflict between remaining a member of the counterculture and becoming a "straight" member of the Establishment, represented in this case by the world of academia. That Harry served in Vietnam is mentioned obliquely by him during one of the seminars he attends. Harry chooses the alternative course, in the end rushing to join a student demonstration rather than completing his final oral exam.

Jud's (1970) title character (Joseph Kaufman) comes home, and according to the *Variety* review, "finds life more than he can handle psychologically." His fiancée has left him, and a close Vietvet friend at the boardinghouse where he stays commits suicide. These problems of reintegration leave Jud "a weary and psychologically shattered man."[6]

In the mid-1970s this current continues, for a series of films represents Vietvets as traumatized to varying degrees. These representations of veterans' traumas contribute to those characters' difficulties in reintegrating.

For instance, *Variety* describes the Vietvet character, Frank (Robert Forster), in *Journey Through Rosebud* (1972) as "laconic, cynical, [and] frustrated."[7] Frank is the unofficial leader of the Rosebud Indian Reservation in the Southwest, but he has a drinking problem and his marriage has broken up. After a draft dodger visits the Reservation and sleeps with Frank's ex-wife, the Vietvet gets drunk and dies in a car crash.

More traditionally within the framework of the melodrama, *Two People* (1973) represents a Vietvet, a combat deserter. After a time on the run, Evan Bonner (Peter Fonda) appears willing to return to society, despite the consequences. Following incidents in places like Casablanca and Paris, during which time Evan meets and falls in love with fashion model Deirdre McCluskey (Lindsay Wagner), he decides to return to New York to face a court-martial.

Bonner went in idealistic, and was not the type who asked any questions. But he started questioning things after he killed a Vietcong in Pleiku: "Just being in Nam was the beginning. It was like suddenly life had gone crazy. Half the guys were talking about gooks and body counts. The other half were stoned out of their minds." McCluskey knows intuitively that at the point of the Vietnamese soldier's death, Bonner felt he could not stay in Vietnam. They both feel that he was right, and the government was wrong about the war. This degree of politicization is very usual anywhere in the genres of order or in the comedy.

During this time a number of films include minor Vietvet characters interacting with a non-Vietvet major character. For example, this is the case with *Homer* (1970), a small town homefront picture. Homer (Don Scardino) has a friend named Eddie Cochran (Tim Henry) who goes off to war. When Eddie's coffin comes back from Vietnam, Homer becomes an antiwar activist, and his acts include chaining himself to a fence in front of his local VFW hall. *Outside In* (1972) centers its narrative around a draft dodger, Ollie Wilson (Darrel Larson). Ollie, returning home for his father's funeral, encounters an old friend, Bink (John Bill), a straight-laced Vietvet.

Towards the end of the 1970s and into the 1980s the representation of the vet as traumatized remains common in the melodrama. Additionally, representation of physically and mentally handicapped veterans becomes much more common within this genre.

In *Looking for Mr. Goodbar* (1977) Tony Lopanto (Richard Gere) comes back from Vietnam physically changed and appears potentially insane. In fact since the film is an adaptation of a very successful novel and enjoyed box office success, it seems safe to assume that many people knew, thought they knew, or at least suspected the outcome regarding Theresa Dunn (Diane Keaton). Taken in this light Tony can be seen as one of three possible murder suspects before the fact, although it turns out that he is not the guilty party. In this way the filmmakers can be seen as possibly making a guess about the assumptions of the audience in using a Vietvet character as a vehicle for suspense, as has often been done in the horror of personality films.

Two other films represent Vietvets in overtly sexual situations. *Stigma* (1972) has a Vietvet involved with a small town's new doctor in trying to stave off a VD epidemic, exacerbated by the townspeople's penchant for open-air orgies. Second, *The Woman Inside* (1979) revolves around a returned combat veteran's wish to have a sex change operation. Neither of these films did well at the box office, but both are available on video tape.

The box office hit *The Deer Hunter* (1978) is often treated as a war film, and not unreasonably, as one of its segments is in fact set in Vietnam during the war. Two of its segments, however, in the formally privileged positions of beginning and end, can just as reasonably be seen as melodrama. Given their positions of privilege and greater emphasis in terms of running time than that afforded the middle segment, I will consider *The Deer Hunter* a melodrama for purposes of this analysis.

This film, among other things, represents the effects of the war on three residents of a small mining town. Initially set in Clairton, Pennsylvania, the film also represents the war as alluded to above, and then returns to the mining town. Its three main Vietvet characters are Michael (Robert DeNiro), Steven (John Savage), and Nick (Christopher Walken).

At one point in the first part of the film, a returned Green Beret in uniform makes an uncharacteristic appearance. During the combination wedding/send-off part for the town's native sons, they meet this figure at the bar and ask him what to expect over there. His enigmatic reaction, echoed by other ominous signs at the affair such as the spilt wine portending bad luck, allows him to function as a specter for the war, counterpoising this representation with the many others of returned Green Berets outside the genre.

When only two of the three return, *The Deer Hunter* fits in with the pattern noted above. Nick, the one who remains in Vietnam dies there, but not as a direct result of the war. His demise is more closely connected to his insanity, a compulsion to play Russian roulette, which apparently arises from his experiences as a POW.

Steven comes back, but as an amputee. Again, this handicap relates to this veteran character's experiences as a POW, which have been dramatically condensed to involve all three characters in a single sequence. Steven destroys both his legs while attempting to escape from the POW camp that also had held Nick and Michael.

Michael is the mediating figure between these two characters, and he comes out of the war apparently unscathed. He both leads the escape from the camp and is instrumental in reintegrating Steven into their community and attempting to do so regarding Nick. While Michael fails in this last endeavor, he is not precisely the "figure in between" common to the genres of order. He apparently wants to reintegrate as well, as is shown by his presence in the film's final reunion scene.

While *The Deer Hunter* represents a simplified spectrum of physical and mental effects of the war upon veterans, *Coming Home* (1978) concentrates upon the representation of a single physically disabled veteran, Luke Martin (John Voight). Initially, Luke is institutionalized in a VA hospital. There he meets and falls in love with a service wife, Sally (Jane Fonda), who works there as a volunteer nurse out of her expressed feelings of social obligation.

Their affair can be seen as one of acculturation. They find out that their backgrounds are not so different, for they went to the same high school. She becomes more politicized by, for instance, complaining that the Marine base newsletter, which the women publish, does not address the "real issues" of the war, which suggestion the other women blithely ignore. Her change is also reflected in her appearance, especially in her change in clothes and hair. Finally, she leaves her right-wing husband for Luke.

As for Luke his affair with Sally prompts him to integrate with the society outside the VA hospital. He changes from a presumedly impotent, cynical introvert to lover and antiwar activist. Sally's love "cures" him of his impotency and, again, he has a corresponding effect on her: she has her first orgasm with Luke. Similarly, Luke's appearance changes with his new surroundings. When he moves out of the VA hospital, he gets a tan and trades in his wheelchair for a specially equipped sports car. He, too, becomes politicized. His actions in this realm include chaining himself to a fence in front of a Marine recruiting depot and going on an antiwar speaking tour to high schools.

The prowar veterans represented in the film do not fare well. In a minor role a gung-ho Marine recruiter, speaking at a high school where Luke also appears, loses the audience after Luke speaks. Even the recruiter himself appears to tear up at Luke's words. Sally's husband Bob Hyde (Bruce Dern), after being shaken in Vietnam and losing her to Luke, swims off to his apparent suicide. The two acculturative characters are integrated, with each other and within the broader community they have forged.

In this sense, a generic variation from the model Schatz describes is apparent. Luke and Sally have helped create an idealized post-Vietnam society based upon mutual understanding and suffering with each other, compassion. This is quite a change from the pre-Vietnam model Schatz delineates, which shows characters integrated into a much more repressive society that dominates them. A similar situation can also be seen in later films like *The Big Chill* (1983) and *Choose Me* (1984).

In a rare adaptation from a stage play, *When You Comin' Back, Red Ryder?* (1979) represents an extremely hostile, criminal Vietvet. Teddy (Marjoe Gortner), a near-the-border drug runner, holds an assorted group of characters hostage in a greasy spoon. The focus here is on the psychodrama. The conflicts are externalized but usually only verbally, coming from the interaction among the characters that include the cafe owner, the night cook, a waitress, a service station owner, a bickering traveling couple, and Teddy's girlfriend.

The Big Chill is another in the cycle of films that represents a Vietvet with a physical disability. Nick (William Hurt) is impotent, an aftereffect of his experience in Vietnam. Nick is a member of a group of 1960s college-educated friends who meet on the occasion of the death of one of the group's friends. Nick is portrayed as at least a partial outsider to the group, and, perhaps paradoxically, the one who has remained truest to the ideals they shared in college.

While all the others have joined the 1980s version of the Establishment, Nick still rebels against it. He sells illegal drugs for a living, and at one point in the film argues with a policeman about a traffic violation. Symptomatically of the film, Nick's friend who is a television policeman talks the "real" policeman out of giving Nick the ticket. Nick is also the only one of the group to serve in Vietnam. Still, he reintegrates, most tellingly at closure.

Here, he and Chloe (Meg Tilly), the ex-girlfriend of the group's dead friend, in what was a post-Vietnam friendship, leave together. She is not nearly as articulate as the other members of the group and beautiful, thus represented and sometimes pursued as a sexual object. Again, the implication is that this reaching out not only puts Nick in touch with the post-Vietnam society, but "cures" him of his malady as well.

With *Birdy* (1984) and *Choose Me* changes start to appear. In *Birdy*, the title character (Matthew Modine) and his close friend Al (Nicolas Cage) return from the war traumatized in different ways. Birdy, apparently due to psychosis, refuses to talk to anyone. Al comes back physically disfigured. These two major characters rely on a major social support group, each other, to "cure" themselves of their troubles and free themselves of the Army, suggested by their running off from the VA hospital at closure.

Mickey (Keith Carradine), winner of the Air Medal and later a spy for the Air Force in *Choose Me*, escapes from a mental institution and wanders into a small town where three very different women compete fairly vigorously for his attention. At first the reason he seems to be institutionalized is because he tells fantastic stories and has a tenuous grip on reality, but the film plays a game with this information.

Mickey's seemingly incredible stories about the war are literally documented in the film as a character reads the stories and sees the pictures supporting Mickey's case in a news magazine. Further, he demonstrates his amazing fighting skills on several occasions, but only when provoked and never lethally. He also is characterized as smart enough in the film to have done the other things he claims to have done.

In an ironic commentary upon the relationship of a community to a Vietvet, then, this film represents a case where a vet is literally excluded from it when his own notion of his war experience differs from theirs. When, however, members of that community interact with him and understand that he is not crazy, they accept him back. This image of the vet is very rare. Here, Mickey is sane, smart, attractive, and humane. Still, only individually do members of his community believe that a veteran can be all these things. In this sense Mickey can be seen as a shaman figure, in a variation, as one who appears crazy but has an important truth to tell. The shaman does not appear popular elsewhere within this subsystem.

Cease Fire (1985) also contains the image of a vet, Tim Murphy (Don Johnson), troubled by his war experience. The film sets up a mirroring image, another war-plagued veteran, Luke (Robert F. Lyons), who does not reintegrate successfully and commits suicide. Both vets are unemployed and have had trouble finding steady employment. They in fact meet in line at the unemployment office.

This meeting forms a friendship between the two, but seems to intensify PTSD-like symptoms in Tim. Their meetings usually involve heavy drinking, and it seems that Luke has lost his family due to his alcoholism. Tim's wife Paula (Lisa Blount), however, fights him to go to "rap groups" composed of other veterans in an attempt to curb his troubled behavior. Tim does go and seems to be making progress.

Luke's wife, on the other hand, wants to make their separation final and Luke kills himself. The loss of his friend seems to prompt the subsequent regressive behavior Tim displays. Paula persists in trying to help Tim, and it comes out that he has been racked with guilt over the fact that he shot a fellow soldier rather than let him fall into the hands of the Vietcong.

That once Tim expresses this deeply repressed thought, he will be "cured" is strongly suggested by the film's final scene. Tim, at the Vietnam War Memorial, touches the name of the soldier he killed, and another vet says, "Welcome Home." In this way the stress Tim feels is strongly associated with the problems he has had reintegrating. Conversely, Tim is able to integrate due to the support of a strong wife and Luke, without that support, cannot.

Fairly recently, melodramas have portrayed vets in minor roles who appear unaffected, in terms of physical and mental problems, by their service. *Under Fire* (1983), for instance, represents a mercenary, who did not reintegrate into American society after the war. Rather, Oates (Ed Harris) goes from war to war fighting for profit, where he often meets the journalist characters around whom the film revolves. In *Alamo Bay* (1985) Ed Harris again plays a Vietvet, Shang. He and other shrimp fishermen confront Vietnamese fishers when they feel that the refugees are interfering with their business.

Charlie (Morgan Freeman) in *That Was Then, This Is Now* (1985) is another Vietvet minor character. Charlie is a bar owner, who, in a subplot of the film dies violently, while trying to prevent a robbery. This character, in the adaptation process from S.E. Hinton novel to film, undergoes major changes.[8] Most tellingly, in the novel Charlie gets his draft notice and becomes quite upset, thinking he will have to give up the bar. The draft board, however, rejects him because of his previous criminal record. In the film, Charlie is given a soldier's burial.

In *Last Rites* (1988) Father Freddie (Paul Dooley) was a chaplain in Vietnam, one of three portrayals of a Vietvet as priest. The other two are vigilante films, *Ministry of Vengeance* (1989) and *Vietnam Texas* (1990). He saw a lot of bullet wounds there and recognizes one that the protagonist suffers during the course of the film. He normally stutters, but stops when excited. He says that he did not stutter in country. An earlier film represents a departure.

Gardens of Stone (1987) represents a Vietvet, Hazard (James Caan), who returns from Vietnam physically and apparently mentally unscathed, who has a steady job, makes some headway into reintegrating, and who returns to Vietnam. To trace these elements in this representation will illustrate a slightly different image than the ones that have come before.

Hazard returns to the States after his tour in Vietnam, but stays in the Army, as the instructor of the memorial Honor Guard. Throughout, this institution is represented as Hazard's family. Hazard as much as says this during a scene in a bar, where he is drinking, naturally enough, with Army friends. One of these friends, Willow (D.B. Sweeny), can be seen as a surrogate son as well, for Hazard only treats him kindly when he finds out that Willow's father and he were soldiers together and that Willow's father asked if he could look out for his boy. When Willow's father dies, this relationship intensifies.

Willow himself is the carrier of a myth discussed before throughout this study. At one point he states that "the right man in the right place can change the world." Hazard all along has been telling Willow that he should prepare himself for quite a shock regarding Vietnam. When Willow goes to Vietnam, starts to question this statement a bit, and dies, Hazard reacts as if he had lost a son.

Before this point, though, Hazard has started to look beyond the Army for companionship. He starts seeing an antiwar newspaper reporter and a process of acculturation not unlike the one in *Coming Home* unfolds. These two opposites end up attracting and eventually agree to marry, but Hazard wants to go to Vietnam again, apparently in direct reaction to Willow's death.

He argues that the memorial service he provides is useless. In Vietnam he can be where it really matters; he can save young men's lives. The association here with the "right man" myth is very strong. While all the melodramas relevant to the Vietvet image system concern themselves with the Vietvets' problem of reintegration, at least one can also be seen as purveyor of this myth.

This identification with a strong element of one of the genres of order, the war film, sets apart *Gardens of Stone* from films like *Coming Home*, *The Big Chill*, and *Choose Me*. Hazard apparently wants to go off and do physical deeds, to continue to be a war hero in a different sense than do the Vietvets in the earlier films. In all these films a Vietvet comes together with a compassionate woman character; only in *Gardens of Stone* is there an implied separation from that figure.

In a group variation Mark Lambert (John Lithgow), Harve (Reb Brown), and Larry (Denis Arndt) are three vets having a terrible time reintegrating in *Distant Thunder* (1988). Mark has abandoned his wife and son, Jack (Ralph Macchio), hasn't held a regular job in some time, and is ambivalent about seeing Jack again. Harve sees a purple light constantly, after killing a hundred Vietcong in a single afternoon. Larry was a LURP man who saw a young recruit die right next to him. He is charming in a bizarre sort of way, but doesn't have the sense to get up out the rain, where he is introduced sleeping one morning. One of their friends, Louis (Tom Bower), cannot take civilian life anymore and commits suicide by "kissing a train."

This trio has tried to recreate the situation of the bush by retreating to the hills of the Pacific Northwest, and the film links those two places visually. Jack visits his father there. Harve turns murderous and stabs a townsperson and then kills Larry. This skirmish at the end of the film serves both as an apparent catharsis to those who were in Vietnam, and as an object lesson to those who were not there, and by the common understanding, cannot understand the plight of the vets unless they were. Mark gets a chance to get a wounded person to safety, erasing his previous guilt about killing a comrade, and Jack sees Larry shot right in front of him, as Larry saw the raw recruit in country. The implication at the end, after Mark threatens to "kiss a train," is that father and son will remain reunited.

The representation of the vets here is mixed. Two of the Vietvets end up dead, one presumably will go to jail. A minor character, Andy (Kelly), seems to have very little trouble reintegrating, as he holds a steady job and has no outward signs of distress. Mark's family is only partially reintegrated. Also, the idea of refighting the war is fairly unusual within this subsystem, although it will reappear a bit in *Born on the Fourth of July* (1989).

The celebrated film from Ron Kovic's autobiography contains an element of refighting, during the 1972 Republican Convention scene. There, Ron Kovic (Tom Cruise) and his fellow veterans almost get arrested for storming the floor. When they get away, they regroup and talk over their new battle plan, with military language and tactics, and with flashbulbs popping and tear gas exploding all around them.

The narrative of *Born on the Fourth of July* can be seen as the process of radicalizing Ron Kovic, at least from the point where the film initially places him. At first Kovic is a right winger, staunchly Catholic, and with set ideas about winning and losing. As the film progresses, especially after he receives his devastating wounds, he begins to question each of these things. The ideas of the melodrama, that no one wants to talk of these traumas and that the repressive society will subsume the individual are resisted here, but only after a monumental struggle with both these things. Kovic can talk about his paralysis, but only at the risk of alienating his own family and the society they represent. He can, too, help forge new societal ideas about things as big as the Vietnam War itself, but only after a huge battle, repre- sented by the 1972 and 1976 Conventions, respectively, and implied by the time that came between them.

Jacknife (1989), by contrast, is a bit more conventional. The point seems to be that you have to face up to what you did over there, and to what you are, before you can start to readjust, to reintegrate.   Megs (Robert DeNiro) did it through prayer, reflection, and love; DeNiro's wonderful performance conveys these things convincingly without be- ing wishy-washy at all. He wants to try to help Dave (Ed Harris) to do the same thing, and does a good job at a hard task. Dave is upset that the infinite promise of high school has narrowed down so drastically. After being a star athlete, he cannot even play basketball anymore. Dave has associ- ated Bobby (Tom Isbell), an absent vet, with that promise and more. In Vietnam Dave tried to get Bobby to stay with him and not go after Megs, who was wounded. Bobby saved Megs, but not himself. Dave since then has lived with a terrible guilt about Bobby's death and his own cowardice.

Jackknife avoids the facile "cures" suggested by some other melodramas within this subsystem. Dave is at a vet's group at closure, wearing Bobby's hat. He admits some of the things that have been troubling him, and it is very obviously very hard for him to do so. Also, Megs's reuniting with Martha (Kathy Baker) at the end comes after a long and hard process that Megs has undergone previously; there is no impression that it is simply slapped on.

In Country (1989) also presents more than one Vietvet attempting to reintegrate, and, like *Distant Thunder*, has a young person standing in for a generation in an attempt to understand Vietnam. The film starts with Sam's (Emily Lloyd) graduation. She, at this point of passage in her life, reads through her father's letters in an attempt to find out who he was and what he did before he died in Vietnam. No one, including Emmett (Bruce Willis), will tell her. The answers vary from: she cannot know, to she cannot understand, to she does not want to know, to nobody cares anyway. When she finds out a bit she says that she does not like her dad anymore. She has a change of heart after Emmett tells her that it is not her place to criticize. He simply tells her that's what they *did*.

The film portrays a wide range of Vietvet problems, both physical, the effects of Agent Orange and of drinking, and mental to various degrees. For example, Emmett has a PTSD-like episode during an electrical storm. It also gives the general idea that people do not care about the plight of the veteran: there is low attendance at the veterans' dance. Even the Vietnam Memorial is denigrated: "It's just a hole in the ground." Still, that is just speculation on the part of people before they visit. Once Emmett, Sam, and her grandmother are there, they are obviously moved. In sum the idea remains that once a troubling thing is experienced, it can be understood and even appreciated.

Revenge (1990) represents a departure. The film has Kevin Costner playing Cochran, a fighter pilot who flew in Vietnam. While there Cochran accidentally bombed an elephant, which he had orders to do because the animals were suspected of carrying supplies for the Vietcong. He had intended to disobey the order, and the accidental death hurt him. To atone he painted an elephant on his fuselage, a symbol for him of a confusing and arbitrary war. He stayed in the service for some years after Vietnam. Love proves impossible when he tries to run off with the wife of a powerful Mexican gangster. The departure here is that Cochran is a major Vietvet character in a melodrama, almost completely unaffected by his experiences in Vietnam. This combination does not occur elsewhere in this subsystem.

In many of the other films the implication on this point is one of reintegration, not only with the woman character, but with a new, post-Vietnam society that the couple has helped form. Here, the untraumatized hero, at least by Vietnam, cannot reintegrate with either. Cochran is very alone at the end of *Revenge*. In the more typical melodrama under study, from *Coming Home* to *Gardens of Stone*, the man and woman go off together at closure, leaving an older society behind, presumably to an idealized newer one of their own creation.

Within this subsystem there are also melodramas that represent Vietvets as reintegrating into the society they find, as opposed to trying to change it, as discussed above. For example, certain films from *Bus Riley's Back in Town* to *Jacknife* can be seen to have such elements, where the vet character strives to reintegrate into the society he left for the war. In this sense Vietvets can be seen as potential bureaucrats, characters wanting to rejoin an imposed system.

The popular successes, the films in fairly high positions on the *Variety* rental list, belong to both of these groups. *The Deer Hunter*, which portrays vets returning to their old society, and *Coming Home*, *The Big Chill*, and *Born on the Fourth of July*, which do not, occupy the top positions in this regard. This genre is one, as opposed to comedy and most of the genres of order, to which the major studios have quite frequently turned when they have made films containing Vietvets. Again, one inference that can be drawn from this is that the majors have often turned to a "serious" mode of representation to deal with a sensitive topic.

Notes

[1]Used in a mythic sense, meaning to "suffer with," as in the discussion of the Vietvet and comedy film.

[2]Campbell, *The Power of Myth*, p. 129.

[3]Schatz, *Hollywood Genres*, p. 222.

[4]Ibid., p. 224.

[5]Wood, *America in the Movies*, pp. 131 and 145.

[6]*Variety Film Reviews*, vol. 13, 9-01-71.

[7]Ibid., 3-01-72.

[8]S.E. Hinton, *That Was Then, This Is Now* (New York: Viking, 1971).

Jon Voight in *Coming Home*.

The Vietvet and the Art Film

In both the genres of order and the genres of integration, filmmakers have generally treated the concerns of Vietvets as concrete as opposed to abstract problems. For example, in *Rambo: First Blood Part II* (1985), the title character, rather than talking about how in an abstract way refighting the Vietnam war might help certain vets, goes back to Vietnam and concretely helps some POWs to escape. Nick in *The Big Chill* (1983) does not actually say that acceptance by the post-Vietnam generation can help certain vets reintegrate, but his actions with Chloe suggest that this might be so. In this sense, these problems in formulaic films can be seen as "lived" as opposed to "raised."[1]

On the other hand, in non-formulaic films, films not within any of the popular genres, these types of problems can be seen as "raised" as opposed to "lived." In the Vietvet subsystem of these films, characters actually raise issues, by talking directly about them. These issues include such things as discussion of the Vietvet's loneliness upon returning from the war, conceptions of a pre-Vietnam hero, and ideas about why people fight wars and about the origin of madness.

Film texts can also be seen to raise such conceptual issues. How this can be so becomes apparent when one looks at the art film as a genre. How these films function mythically can be seen by examining the subsystem's character types and narrative patterns.

The Vietvets in the art film subsystem can be seen as shaman characters. They are represented as insane, or potentially insane, and their life-changing experience appears to be their war experience. While they initially attempt to bring their message back to society by talking about it (treating it as a raised issue), by closure they treat it as a lived issue, by acting it out. Sometimes this acting-out is suggested; sometimes it is depicted. Within the Vietvet art film subsystem, the usual action-first emphasis of popular genre film is here reversed.

In generic terms one can describe a narrative film as an "art film" when that film breaks in specific and significant ways with the conventions of the rest of the body of narrative films. William Charles Siska points out that one central way art film can be seen to break with the conventions of formulaic film is in terms of subject matter, and narrative feature films in which ideas, as opposed to actions, become subject matter can be considered art films.[2] In a sense, then, theme becomes plot. That is, these films can be said to be "about" these conceptual issues.

In the process of foregrounding these conceptual issues, these contemplative films display certain "modernist characteristics,"[3] formal derivatives of the precepts of modernist perception itself. These include narrative intransitivity from subjectivity, estrangement from point-of-view, fragmentation from reflexivity, and intertextuality and aperture from open texture. These can be seen as the conventions of the art film, as opposed to the precise icons that can be seen in some of the genres of order.[4]

Filmmakers can foreground these issues in many ways. For instance, the problems can be treated in the abstract as opposed to in the concrete, the way these problems are generally treated in the formulaic films, as mentioned above. One primary way this can be done is to have characters talk about such issues as issues.

Also, filmmakers can call attention to images in certain ways such as by making use of unusual camera angles, "unusual" from the point of view of those often used in the formulaic films. Another way a filmmaker can call attention to an image is to position it apparently apart from the film's narrative cause-and-effect chain. Filmmakers can also foreground conceptual issues by including images that can be read as metaphors for a character's internal state.[5]

In *Taxi Driver* (1976) Travis Bickle (Robert DeNiro), driven mad by both his loneliness and his disgust for the street life of New York City, goes mad and shoots up a whorehouse. From merely this description the film would not be wholly incompatible with the horror of personality films discussed earlier. The main difference is the film's treatment of these plot events. Where that group of films foregrounds some elements, as mentioned above, *Taxi Driver* barely addresses them. Conversely, *Taxi Driver* makes as its text certain conceptual issues, such as loneliness and disgust, that are more deeply buried in the formulaic films.

Travis speaks about his disgust concerning the state of the streets to the other cabbies and to Palantine (Leonard Harris), a Presidential candidate, when asked "the one thing that bugs you the most." Further, he often writes about the problem in his diary, which is in turn read in his voice over images. He often mentions the rain that he hopes will come to "wash the trash off the sidewalk."

When Betsy (Cybill Shepherd) emerges as one set apart from these streets, one that "they cannot touch," Travis immediately becomes obsessed with her. He watches her from afar and finally summons the strength to ask her out. On each date their relationship seems more doomed to fail. First, Betsy talks of social phenomena of which Travis is only dimly aware. For instance, he does not know who Kris Kristofferson is, although he later makes an effort to find out.

By then it is too late for their relationship. Over her objections Travis takes Betsy to a pornographic film. When she walks out Travis complains that he does not know too much about movies, that they could do other things, that he does not know too much about them either, but he would be willing to make an effort to find out.

This lack of social intelligence then leads Travis to complain, in voice-over through his diary, that loneliness has followed him, his whole life, everywhere. After he loses the affections of Betsy, though, he associates his loneliness with his other problem, his hate of the city street life. For instance, after they have parted company Travis tells Betsy that she is "in a hell. You're just like the rest of them."

Also, dissimilar objects start to have similar psychological effects upon Travis. The flowers that Betsy keeps sending back to Travis accumulate in his apartment, rot, and make him sick to his stomach, just as he told Palantine that the streets sometimes do. When these two problems merge for Travis, he starts becoming more and more observably insane.

His inarticulateness prevents him from talking his way through his problems. He tells Wizard (Peter Boyle), another cabbie, that "things got me really down. I just wanna go out and really do something.... I got some bad ideas in my head." Wizard is no help. His advice ends, "Get laid, get drunk.... Don't worry so much." Even Travis realizes ("That's about the dumbest thing I ever heard.") the futility of turning to his peer group for help with his mental problems.

He first attempts to battle back by shooting Palantine, indirectly attacking Betsy. When that attempt is unsuccessful, he attacks the inhabitants of the whorehouse. With that act of violence against the type of street life he finds repugnant, Travis seems purged of his demons, at least temporarily.

But this foregrounding of conceptual problems is only part of what makes *Taxi Driver* an art film. Certain instances of unusual camera placement can be seen as a strategy of attracting attention to image and not action, and some of these images can be seen as metaphors for Travis' inner state. There is a series of shots in the film taken from an unusual angle, a bird's-eye view. These include images of glasses of cola and antacid, guns, bullets, and the aftermath of Travis' using the latter two objects. Thus, these dissimilar objects are associated by means of their similar but unusual presentation. The first two, both bubbling over, may suggest Travis' inner state. Taken as a series these images can be seen as an allegory for what transpires in Travis' life: when he cannot keep his frustration inside him, he "bubbles over," goes mad.

The film seems reluctant to present symbolic images that might be read as signs. For instance, images of two statues that could otherwise be read as symbolic signs are framed in such a way as to keep the narrative flow firmly in tact. In one instance, Travis is trying to socialize with a counter worker in a porno house and a copy of the Venus de Milo is framed in the foreground throughout. Later, when Palantine is making a speech a statue with widely outstretched arms is framed behind him, as if underlining his communication skills and counterpoising the armless statue and Travis' troubles talking to people.

Camera movement figures in one break in the narrative flow as Travis tries to talk Betsy into seeing him again. He is in the corridor of a building talking to her on a public phone. At one point the camera pans right and presents no strict narrative information. The image is of a long empty hallway, which can perhaps be read as a signifier of the void their relationship has become. In other cases, such as the mysterious fight two old men have in the street, it turns out later that this is what Travis was observing.

The film can also be seen as somewhat fragmented due to reflexivity and intertextuality. The diarist in Travis indicates some reflection on his own life, and can be, with other images of Travis, seen as an allusion to Bresson. There are many other references to film, such as the scenes set at porno houses. Also, Martin Scorsese appears in the film and is identified in the credits for his role. The film also refers to other texts such as rock music and television. All of these instances are narratively motivated to greater or lesser degrees.

Travis' war experience is something, however, that is not foregrounded. The only direct reference to it is minimal. This occurs during his interview with the personnel director (Joe Spinell) at the cab company. When the interviewer mentions that he, too, was in the Marines, Travis neglects to make anything out of what other genres have traditionally represented as at least a minimal fraternal bond. As such this scene just serves to point up Travis' problems of communication. Thus it can be seen as subsumed into the larger problem of his loneliness.

Also--something that is very common in the Vietvet art films--in *Taxi Driver* the raised problems tend to become lived problems. While this seems to be the case, in these films they are only lived problems for a small part of these films. Thus the thrust seems to lie elsewhere, in the realm of problems that are mostly raised, but then apparently have to be lived out. Generally, in the art films as well as the formulaic films, Vietvets are represented, at least partially, as men of action.

Similarly, in *Tracks* (1976) a raised problem that will become lived is raised before the credits in a direct address. "Do you think about your childhood often?" asks Jack (Dennis Hopper), who confides that he does when things get hard for him to manage. Jack, a returning combat veteran, is ostensibly escorting by train the body of a hero back to his hometown for "a parade, a marching band, and a funeral."

The film is quite intertextual in a fairly specific way. It makes reference to a collection of songs popular during WWII. These are played by Jack on his cassette player and include "Praise the Lord and Pass the Ammunition," "These Foolish Things," "Don't Sit Under the Apple Tree," and other WWII standbys. It later becomes apparent that when Jack was a child his self-image was at least partly created by reference to a WWII-era Army hero and that these songs can be seen as a desperate harkening-back to that era.

Many images occurring within the narrative flow might also suggest Jack's interior state. For instance, the image of Jack in an ill-fitting blue jeans outfit suggests his internal awkwardness in first meeting Stephanie (Taryn Powers) on the train. He looks stiff and ill-at-ease out of his uniform. More overtly Jack has several hallucinations which apparently mirror his interior state precisely. He hallucinates, among other things, that Stephanie gets raped in and his mother gets kidnapped from the club car of the train, and that he and Stephanie make love in the countryside which the train rushes past.

During these hallucinations it seems that Jack witnessed an atrocity in Vietnam and felt compelled to shoot the men involved in its commission. Apparently this action was so out of keeping with his self-image that Jack went insane. When he gets to what is his own hometown, it is revealed that the coffin contains battle gear with which he plans to bring the war back home to his old neighbors, again making what was only a raised problem before a lived problem.

In this way Jack can be seen as a shaman becoming a

potential monster. This process is oblique, for the film ends with a freeze frame of Jack storming out of the coffin. Before the point that the coffin becomes involved in the narrative in this way, it can be seen as a symbolic image used as a sign for the death of Jack's WWII dreams of glory.

The trend of minimizing those images that could be seen as breaking up the narrative, while foregrounding conceptual issues continues in *The Ninth Configuration* (1980). This film represents a whole group of Vietvets, all officers, many decorated for bravery in the face of the enemy, who are stricken with some form of mental illness involving an obsession of one type or another. When a new psychiatrist, Colonel Kane (Stacy Keach), comes to the castle where the Army has put the men, he and the leader of the institutionalized soldiers, Cutshaw (Scott Wilson), spend most of the movie discussing issues such as the evil/madness dichotomy and proofs for the existence of God.

Though this film, too, is intertextual, rupture with the narrative is generally avoided. For instance, the references to Hamlet's madness come in the context of an inmate putting on that play, with an all-canine cast, no less. Similarly, paintings in the film, which could be seen as reflections of the inmates' mental states, are represented as being the work of those same inmates.

Also typical of the genre when representing Vietvets, the raised problem becomes a lived problem at closure. In this process, Kane becomes a clear shaman figure. Cutshaw challenges Kane's argument that evil stems from madness and not the other way around by asking Kane to come up with one example of a person knowingly giving up his or her life for another. Kane cannot do so. Later, Cutshaw finds out that Kane is not really a psychiatrist, but rather "Killer" Kane, a mentally troubled expert warrior posing as one. Cutshaw escapes and encounters a gang of bikers. Kane finds him and gives up his life to prove his thesis.

The Stunt Man (1980) directly raises the issue of why we fight wars. Highly self-reflexive, it is a movie about making movies. While this does serve to fragment the narrative to some degree, in a sense all of the seeming disjunctures are narratively motivated. The film plays a game with viewers, asking them to pay close attention to find out What Next?

The madness/evil dichotomy is also raised, directly in the case of Eli (Peter O'Toole), when Cameron (Steve Railsback) posits that he is the former rather than the latter, and indirectly in the case of Cameron. Cameron, a Vietvet, had enlisted and fought in Vietnam for over two years. He comes onto Eli's film set in desperation, being pursued by the police.

It transpires that the police are pursuing him for a minor matter, and that his apparent breakdown in relating his minor criminal activity is just playacting. Cameron turns out as neither evil nor crazy, though throughout the film he is presented as potentially both. In mythic terms his character changes from apparent shaman to intentional hero. This representation taken as a whole is quite unusual for a Vietvet major character, especially in 1980, although the doubts that the characterization raises are not unusual.

Eli is another matter entirely. He, too, is presented at times as being potentially crazy or evil or both. Keeping with a central theme of the film, that nothing is as it appears, it turns out that he is neither of those as well. But getting back to one of the film's directly addressed issues, why we fight, Eli also attempts to "answer" that at closure.

Initially, Eli maintains that war is but a symptom of a disease whose underlying carrier is man. The disease, Eli finally holds, is "screwing other people." This is what the manipulative Eli has been doing throughout the whole film. The act of spreading the "disease" that causes wars while merely making a movie problematizes Eli's characterization.

In this regard the central issue of the film is neither directly raised by the Vietvet character, nor does he attempt to answer it. Cameron remains a mythic hero, with an association of madness. The other characters in this subsystem, also associated with madness, are not so portrayed. Travis, Jack, and Kane can be seen as shaman characters who struggle against becoming monsters.

In a new development, *Wild at Heart* (1990) contains an evil Vietvet in a minor but striking role. Bobby Peru (Willem Dafoe) was involved in a Mylai-like massacre while a Marine in Vietnam. He even mocks another vet who was "only" in the Navy, and did not make "contact" with the people as he did. After his encounters with Lula (Laura Dern) and Sailor (Nicolas Cage), one can only imagine what that contact meant in Vietnam.

The most complex of these characters is probably Travis Bickle. Whether he remains a shaman character or becomes a human monster seems dependent upon his choice of targets in his shooting spree. Travis avoids the political target and chooses the whorehouse. The ironic epilogue to *Taxi Driver* indicates that society regards him as a hero, although he does not seem much changed from his pre lived-crisis days. This process can perhaps be seen as indicative as the process the surrounding culture has in positioning characters as mythic types.

The blending of shaman/monster characters does not appear to be common outside of this subsystem. The human monster characters of the Vietvet horror of personality films seem motivated only by their twisted psyches and cannot reasonably be seen as shaman types. Conversely, the shaman characters of the Vietvet comedy films are clearly not human monsters. The Vietvet art films seem to be the prime carriers of the more ambiguous character type.

The Vietvet characters in these films do not resist the violent processes that move these raised problems into the realm of lived problems. Also, while these films picture Vietvets talking, sometimes they represent the Vietvets doing it ineffectively, as in Travis Bickle's case. In all cases, articulate or not, talking is not enough for these Vietvets. This seems to be consistent in the recent American art film tradition, where it also seems that talking is not enough and that mere talk is usually supplemented by physical action. This certainly seems to be the case in art films outside the Vietvet system directed by Robert Altman, Dennis Hopper, David Lynch, and Martin Scorsese.

The Vietvet art film system has had some measure of popular success. *Taxi Driver* and *Wild at Heart* are on the *Variety* "Rentals Champs" list, ranking them as very successful art films in general. Within the Vietvet system *Taxi Driver* ranks in about the middle of the popularly successful

Vietvet films. While filmmakers do not often seem to be making this type of film containing a Vietvet currently, all these films are available on video tape. In all cases except *Wild at Heart*, this would involve more active selection than would video release of films of later theatrical release dates.

Major studios released three of these five films. Again, an inference can be drawn about this release pattern. Certainly, no group of films has traditionally been given more "serious" attention than has the art film. This observation seems to apply not only to critics but to audiences as well. In this sense, major filmmakers can be seen to give a "serious" treatment to a sensitive topic. Accordingly, the art film can be seen as a somewhat similar, slightly "elevated" vehicle for the Vietvet character when compared to the melodrama.

Notes

[1]This division and the following discussion of the conventions of the art film are suggested in large part by William Charles Siska, "Modernism in the Narrative Cinema: The Art Film as a Genre" (Ph.D. diss., Northwestern University, 1976).

[2]Siska, "The Art Film as a Genre," p. 6.

[3]Ibid., p. 32.

[4]Ibid., pp. 2-3.

[5]Ibid., p. 6.

Conclusion

The preceding generic/mythic/systemic analysis was undertaken to examine the role the image of the returned Vietvet has played in American narrative film history. Before reexamining how the filmic Vietvet image system has changed over time, I would like to mention briefly some things not often represented within this image system.

Representation of black veterans is fairly rare, especially in the period of the late 1970s to the early 1980s, although out of that period it is cross-generic within the genres of order. Only recently have black vets been represented in the genres of integration with *Some Kind of Hero* (1982), *That Was Then, This Is Now* (1985), *Hollywood Shuffle* (1987), and *Jacknife* (1989). The later of these films represent blacks in minor roles. In the genres of order recently, as in *Lethal Weapon* (1987), black vet characters have had major roles. Representation of Native American Vietvets is also very rare, apart from the appearances of Billy Jack. There is another instance of this in *Fleshburn* (1984), which contains a disturbed Navajo. As far as I can tell there has not yet been a representation of a black vet with apparent serious mental problems, nor a representation of a Hispanic vet in a release from a major studio. *Latino* (1985), which represents two Hispanic Vietvets, comes from an independent.

Representations of Vietnamese veterans of the war, or those there during the war, are almost totally absent from these films. In the few instances that they are represented, they appear as villains as in *Search and Destroy* (1981), *Steele Justice* (1987), and *Gleaming the Cube* (1989), although in the later films the treatment is somewhat more balanced. The other exceptions are the refugees represented in *Alamo Bay* (1985) and the characters in *Rambo: First Blood Part II* (1985) and *Braddock: Missing in Action III*

(1988), both Vietnamese women, both never to leave Vietnam. Again, towards the later part of this range, the picture is a bit more optimistic, as in *White Ghost* (1988).

Regarding American women returned veterans, as far as I can tell, there are none represented in film. *Nowhere to Hide* (1987), however, contains a woman character who is a Marine veteran, but not clearly a Vietnam era vet. The same can be said for *Opposing Force* (1987). There is some reason to think that this situation might change, though, as Sally Field, Cher, and Jane Fonda have purportedly expressed interest in making films about women Vietnam-era vets, playing roles similar to the one Cheryl Ladd plays in *Purple Hearts* (1984), but concentrating the film around when those characters come home.

Otherwise, women within this system seem to play roles similar to those represented outside the system in film. For example, women in the Vietvet films have taken on strong, non-traditional roles, often in media professions, in the 1980s in films like *Eyewitness* (1981), *The Big Chill* (1983), *Under Fire* (1983), *Choose Me* (1984), *Alamo Bay*, *Year of the Dragon* (1985), *Gardens of Stone* (1987), *Jacknife*, and *Revenge* (1990), which mirror the roles that their counterparts outside the Vietvet image have played.

As to the role the Vietvet image system has played regarding the film industry, I will now briefly check the output of the major and minor studios, the films' performance in rentals, and the amount and kinds of adaptations. Most of the non-formulaic films are from major studios. By far the majority of the genres of order come from independent studios, with exceptions in the mid-1980s and later in the police, caper, and war genres.

The majority of the genres of integration come from major studios, especially from the mid-1970s to the present. The major studios have been quite reluctant over the relevant time period to release films containing major Vietvet characters in anything but melodramas and art films. Apparently, studio decision-makers felt these "serious" forms were best suited to deal with Vietvets, although this trend seems to be changing a bit.

All of the top ten rental films from this system were distributed by a major studio; of those, eight (*Lethal Weapon 2* (1989), *Top Gun* (1986), *Rambo: First Blood Part II*, *Lethal Weapon*, *Firefox* (1982), *The Big Chill*, *First Blood* (1982), and *Blue Thunder* (1983)) were released in the 1980s. The highest on the rental list from an independent company is Cannon's *Missing in Action* (1984), which is within the top twenty for the group. The genres of order have out-performed the genres of integration by far in this respect, with nearly four times as many films in the top rentals group.

Again, appearance on *Variety*'s list is here taken as just a thumbnail sketch of a film's popularity with the audience. Also, it cannot be shown that these films were popular sim-ply because a Vietvet character appears within them. Major studio stars Clint Eastwood, Sylvester Stallone, and inde-pendent studio star Chuck Norris appear in many of these films, for example, and these popular films surely gained part of their audience due to their presence. What can be said, however, is that films representing Vietvets have been popular and continue to be popular into the 1990s.

Adaptations can provide an insight into how the film in-dustry has interacted with another system representing Viet-nam veterans. Adaptations from fiction in the Vietvet system were more common in the genres of order than in the genres of integration, although this fact can possibly be explained by the fact that veterans seem to appear in those genres much more often than in genres of integration or non-formulaic films.

It seems that only recently has there been a trend of cross adaptation in this area, in which non-veteran characters in fiction become veterans in film as in *That Was Then, This Is Now*, *O.C. and Stiggs* (1987), and *Graveyard Shift* (1990). Conversely, some veterans in fiction have not stayed veter-ans as in the film adaptations of *Fletch* (1985), *Fletch Lives* (1989), and *Cobra* (1986). The two comedies show again the majors' reluctance to place a Vietvet into that genre.

Adaptations from stage plays appear only rarely in the films *When You Coming Back, Red Ryder?* (1979), *Cease Fire* (1985), and *Jacknife*. Elmore Leonard often includes a veteran character in his novels, some of which have been filmed, such as *The Big Bounce* (1969) and *Mr. Majestyk* (1974). Sequels, adaptations from other films, have been discussed as they have come up in the main body of the text and have been treated as another indicator of an initial film's popularity.

Within the films' texts themselves, often the conflicts can be seen as the veteran character pitted against some form of bureaucracy. Many times this bureaucracy can take the form of the police, as discussed previously. Often, vets can be seen as confronting either the Army itself or the VA and examples of both types, *The Crazies* (1973) and *Some Kind of Hero*; *Black Sunday* (1976) and *The Crazy World of Julius Vrooder* (1974), appear in both genres of integration and of order.

More commonly in the genres of order, from *The Domino Principle* (1977) to *The Package* (1989), a vet character will come into conflict with more vaguely defined representatives of the American government. In a very rare representation, *Getting Straight* (1970) has its vet character battle the academic establishment. In mythic terms, the figure of the Vietvet as bureaucrat is not often represented, even in minor roles.

In recent American narrative film, central characters living under imposed systems are not all that common. The trend Schatz describes seems limited to the family melodrama in the 1950s. In a generic/mythic sense, Vietvet characters as in *Cease Fire* can be seen as significant, albeit unusual. In that film Tim Murphy's troubles are such that he longs to "move up" even to an imposed society.

This educated-veteran image is quite rare as is mentioned in the chapter on the art film. If an articulate, informed character can be seen in some sense as "educated," then its rare appearance is cross-generic, as extremely articulate, informed veteran characters appear in *Twilight's Last Gleaming* (1976), *Choose Me*, and *Born on the Fourth of July* (1989). Much more typical is the representation of the vet who chooses not to talk, or cannot talk, about the war except with those with whom he served. This trend can be explained by the general emphasis shown in American narrative film of action over talk, even in the art film. Vietvet characters are certainly no exception to this trend.

Outside the Vietvet image system, the 1979 and 1980 Harris polls do not list "education problems" as one of the top "most serious ones" facing the returning vets in the opinion of the public, although it is listed as one of problems that the vets themselves feel they commonly face. Also, the survey indicates that "Vietnam era veterans have attained a higher level of education than has the public,"[1] something the films certainly do not reflect.

Important icons are the tools of war used as props mainly in the genres of order, not just within the war genre as in *The Dogs of War* (1980) and *Uncommon Valor* (1983), but without it as well in such films as both *Chrome and Hot Leather* (1971) and *Welcome Home, Soldier Boy*s (1972), which display diverse weapons, and the *The Exterminator* (1980), in which the title character uses a flame thrower. In the non-formulaic *The Stunt Man* (1980), tools of war are also used as props. Representations of characters displaying skills learned in wartime appear in films as diverse as *Taxi Driver* (1976) and *The Annihilators* (1985). Recently similar props have appeared in a genre of integration, in such comedy films as *D.C. Cab* (1983), *O.C. and Stiggs*, and *Moving* (1988).

In terms of archetypal significance in the Vietvet image systems, these icons are more closely aligned with their use in pre-Vietnam films than are the "monstrosities" of the post-Vietnam war film that Smith talks about. Vietvet heroes do not associate with such uses of weapons. Vietvet human monsters use weapons more akin to those characters in the horror of personality films than those used by Vietvets elsewhere in the system.

Of the icons derived from the television news representation of Vietnam--the monk, the lighter, the bullet in the head, and the helicopter--only one film, *The Crazies*, incorporates them systematically. Very many of these films include helicopters as props, and John Rambo in particular seems to be the special enemy of this icon. Rambo has, so far, destroyed helicopters with a rock, an arrow, an anti-aircraft gun, a tank, and another helicopter's air-to-air missile.

The helicopter can be seen to function as a chief symbol of the ambiguity of the Vietnam war itself. In archetypal terms, the helicopter can be seen as a variation of the airplane, which, as previously discussed, Campbell holds as another important symbol for modern man, a machine variant of the eagle. Rather than providing unambiguous escape from the constraints of the world, the helicopter is more earthbound and omnidirectional. Closer to the action than are the fighter planes, a helicopter can promise life, in evacuations, as well as deliver death, by machine gun or "body bomb." It is no wonder that the WWII-type hero Rambo represents wants to destroy these objects.

Many of these films contain characters getting shot in the head, although many outside the Vietvet image system do as well during the period. Allusions to the self-immolation seem to be rare within the system, although "full body burns" have appeared in horror films outside the system such as *Swamp Thing* (1982), *The Thing* (1982), and *Friday the Thirteenth, Part 7* (1988). Other icons of the news representation of Vietnam can be seen in *Firefox*, the napalmed Vietnamese girl, and in *The Deer Hunter* (1978) and *Braddock: Missing in Action III*, the roof of the American Embassy during the fall of Saigon.

The settings for the Vietvet image system are unmistakably rural and small-town until the mid to early 1970s, as the biker film was the central way the image was carried in these years. Then, with the rise of the caper, the vigilante, and the horror of personality films portraying the vet, urban settings predominated, often with the portrayal of an "urban jungle," from *Gordon's War* (1973) to *Don't Answer the Phone* (1980). The idea of the urban jungle is one that is commonly associated with refighting and by extension with the myth of "the lance that delivers the wound."

During the same period the genres of integration from *Homer* (1970) to *When You Comin' Back Red Ryder?* were generally set in small towns and rural areas. Into the 1980s the Vietvet image system has seen a mixture of these two settings.

Many of the Vietvet films also contain brief images of the Vietnam War itself, either as a prologue to the film or as the veteran character's flashback, dream, or hallucination. Fitting into this first category are *Deathdream* (1972), *Two People* (1973), *The Domino Principle*, *The Deer Hunter*, *Good Guys Wear Black* (1978), *Who'll Stop the Rain?* (1978), *The Dogs of War*, *Search and Destroy*, *Some Kind of Hero*, *The Violent Breed*, *The Annihilators*, *Steele Justice*, and *Above the Law* (1988). Films in this second category include *Rolling Thunder* (1977), *Tracks* (1976), *Heroes* (1977), *The Ninth Configuration* (1980), *Firefox*, *First Blood*, *Blue Thunder*, *Missing In Action*, *Armed Response* (1985), *House* (1986), *Backfire* (1989), and *Vietnam Texas* (1990). These films are overwhelmingly genres of order and do not show much overlap between the two types noted.

That is, the films starting with a Vietnam War prologue only rarely have the vet character experiencing dreams or hallucinations about the war, unless dreams at the outset of a film, such as in *Cease Fire* and *Combat Shock* (1986), are considered prologues. These representations did not become common until the mid to late 1970s, which puts them a bit ahead of the first explosion of Vietnam War films. Those films which portray a Vietvet returning to Vietnam after the war seem limited to the mid-1980s and sometimes cross over into the dream category.

These dreams, nightmares, and hallucinations can be seen as the most common way PTSD-like symptoms of Vietvets are represented, as this is one of the aspects of the stress response isolated by Herbert Hendin and Ann Pollinger Haas.[2] It should be noted that historically veterans of other wars and other traumas have been diagnosed as having PTSD. For example, Audie Murphy developed many PTSD symptoms.[3] Within the Vietvet image system, though, veterans of other wars are nearly always set apart from Vietvets.

Also, certain wartime activities--especially seeing combat and being involved in atrocities--seem to predispose Vietvets outside the common myth systems to PTSD.[4] The Vietvet films draw their characters overwhelmingly from this group, although it is usual for a Vietvet protagonist to be portrayed as having committed an atrocity. Many other films can be seen to represent other symptoms of a PTSD-like disease, in paranoid manifestations, in which "the veteran perceives civilian life as an extension of the war"[5] and depressive manifestations, which are marked by unemployment, marital difficulties, and drug and alcohol abuse.[6]

Representations of characters with what can be seen as paranoid manifestations of a PTSD-like disease are found in nearly every genre of order, in the non-formulaic films, and sometimes in the genres of integration, in comedies such as *Heroes*, *Some Kind of Hero*, and *O.C. and Stiggs*. While many examples of depressive manifestations of a PTSD-like disease can be found in the genres of integration, many of the characters in the genres of order display some of these symptoms along with paranoid ones. In other words, the characters' symptoms here are often mixed; these characters, such as John Rambo, are often unemployed.

Films representing a Vietvet's homecoming are common throughout the period and cross-generic. Very early veterans are represented as having trouble adjusting to home again, as in *Bus Riley's Back in Town* (1965). These problems--broken families, substance abuse, madness, physical impairment, various crises of masculinity, and even death--are nearly always concrete problems as opposed to abstract problems and are not linked directly to Vietnam until the early 1970s.

The ultimate "problem" is death, and images of returning dead vets are common and cross-generic. Monster veterans appear in *Deathdream* and *House*, and are suggested by the zombie squad in *Extreme Prejudice* (1987). Representations of vets in coffins returning home include those in *Homer*, *The Hard Ride* (1971), *Tracks*, *The Deer Hunter*, *Hair* (1979), *Finders Keepers* (1984), and *Gardens of Stone*.

Another common problem represented is a Vietvet returning home to find support systems destroyed or weak. Often, as in the vigilante films, this destruction has nothing to do with the war itself; the destruction comes from outside agencies at home, for example from the Mafia. Later in the cycle, families split up due to the amount of time a vet has spent abroad as a POW as in *Rolling Thunder*, *Some Kind of Hero*, and *Vietnam Texas*.

These support groups are later in the cycle represented as being broken by the problems of Vietvets, which in turn are linked to their experience in Vietnam. For example, in *Cease Fire* a vet character loses his family due to a drinking problem he did not have before the war. In the genres of order, when drinking is even treated as a lived problem, it is done so lightly, as in *Steele Justice.*

These instances are rare, but more common than representations of returned vets with drug problems, which seem practically non-existent, as discussed in the context of the biker and vigilante genres. One exception to this trend can be found in *The Wild Life* (1984), and briefly in some melodramas, but only among minor characters. In another check of an outside system, the Harris surveys in 1979 and 1980 show that while the public thought these substance abuse problems were very common, the vets interviewed did not think them nearly as common.[7]

Other families are represented as weakened after a Vietvet character in that family exhibits physical disabilities suffered in Vietnam such as in *The Deer Hunter* and *Born on the Fourth of July*. In *Birdy* (1984) a social support group suffers as a result of both physical and mental trauma suffered in combat, but the members of that group are apparently able to overcome their problems.

Other support groups are represented as weakened or destroyed due to a Vietvet character's madness or potential madness, which are in turn associated with his experiences in Vietnam, such as in *Black Sunday*, although this does not occur commonly until the mid-1980s with *Cease Fire*, *Combat Shock*, *House*, *Tough Guys Don't Dance* (1987), and *Jacknife*. In some of these films, however, the family unit is reintegrated.

The character of the mad vet apart from any support groups appears most commonly in the horror of personality films, although there are instances of this character type in other genres and situations as well from *Motor Psycho* (1965) to *Heroes* to *The Texas Chainsaw Massacre Part 2* (1986), where, ironically, it is the vet character's madness that *allows* him to remain with his insane family. A distinction is apparent in the comedies that feature a mad vet in a major role, as that vet often appears as a shaman figure, interpreting his war experience in mythic terms.

Only very recently have there been Vietvet representations in which the vet character loses his family due to something he himself did, that something not being directly involved with his experiences in Vietnam. For example, a vet character in *Alamo Bay* loses his wife due to his philandering. In *Heartbreak Ridge* (1986) a vet character temporarily loses his wife because he devotes too much attention to his other family, the Marines.

Vietvet problems of masculinity are only very rarely treated as raised issues, as in *Tracks* where the vet character's idea of himself as pre-Vietnam hero could not survive his experiences in Vietnam. Something similar can be found in *Born on the Fourth of July*. In *Taxi Driver* this problem is shifted over to one of loneliness, which is directly addressed. In the formulaic films, the genres of order do not often represent this problem as a lived one. Rather, castration metaphors such as cut-off hands and arms in *Rolling Thunder* and *House* occur infrequently. In the genres of integration, impotence and other crises of masculinity are often represented as lived problems of Vietvets.

Vietvet characters apparently only very rarely directly address the question of what they feel they are owed by the country when they return from war.[8] This concept, as far as I can tell, is never raised as a concept in the art films containing Vietvets. It can be seen as a lived problem in a way in some of the genres of order, such as in the case of *Deathdream* and the films in which vet characters, frustrated by lack of success in the normal endeavors, turn to crime such as *Welcome Home, Soldier Boys*, although actual depiction of this frustration seems rare.

By the early 1980s this issue is lived by the Vietvet characters in *First Blood* and *Some Kind of Hero*, both of whom want simple things, a steady job and money owed by the Army, respectively. Rambo raises the issue briefly in *Rambo: First Blood Part II* by saying all the vets want is for America to "love...[them] as much as they love it."

Starting in the early 1970s direct reference to World War II is infrequently made by non-Vietvet characters, usually in a context to differentiate the behavior displayed by Vietvet characters from that of those returning from the earlier war. Instances of this can be found in *Deathdream* and *Welcome Home, Soldier Boys*. In the mid-1980s other wars are evoked, as in *Armed Response*, *Heartbreak Ridge*, and *Extreme Prejudice*, and the new implication is that Vietvets act no differently than do veterans of those other wars.

At about this same time both the Vietvet intentional hero and the Vietvet adventurer began to get associated with traditional WWII heroes. As more Vietvet characters can be classified as heroes than as any other archetype, this is a central change. At this time the Vietvet representation started to move away from a portrayal of an anti-hero and towards one of a law-abiding and law-upholding intentional hero. Transitional figures can be seen both in genres of order, in *Firefox*, *First Blood*, and *Blue Thunder*, and in genres of integration, in *Some Kind of Hero*, *The Big Chill*, and *D.C. Cab*.

Vietvet characters as bureaucrat, monster, and shaman characters have been relegated to the fringes of American narrative film. This trend can be seen in the reluctance of filmmakers to position Vietvet main characters as bureaucrats and in the minor bureaucrat characters that exist in the fringes of film narratives. This trend can also be seen in the horror films, which present Vietvets as monsters, but which exist only on the fringes of the industry, as independent films. Finally, this trend can be seen in the comedies, which major studios seem reluctant to make and have done so only infrequently.

The heroic image of the Vietvet that emerges is one that varies from, but does not break from, archetypes that appear to be timeless. The hero archetype has been modified over time to suit audiences, but the image of Vietvet as hero is clearly and strongly present in the system of Vietvet films.

Notes

[1]*Myths and Realities: A Study of Attitudes Toward Vietnam Era Veterans* (Washington, DC: Government Printing Office, 1980), pp. 108 -110 and xlii.

[2]Herbert Hendin and Ann Pollinger Haas, *Wounds of War: The Psychological Aftermath of Combat in Vietnam* (New York: Basic Books, 1984), p. 26.

[3]Hendin and Haas, *Wounds of War*, p. 6.

[4]Boulanger and Kadushin, eds., *The Vietvet Redefined*, p. 7; Hendin and Haas, *Wounds of War*, p. 28.

[5]Hendin and Haas, *Wounds of War*, p. 88.

[6]Ibid., p. 109.

[7]*Myths and Realities*, p. 110. Boulanger and Kadushin eds., in *The Vietvet Redefined* agree with this finding; The sample in Hendin and Haas, *Wounds of War*, is limited to vets with PTSD, which is not comparable to the Harris Poll's sample.

[8]*Myths and Realities*, p. 104, holds that "a majority of Vietnam era veterans feel that they, as a group, have not received all the benefits they deserve," and that the public tends to agree with them, in the case of especially troubled vets, p. xlvi.

A Vietvet Filmography

This filmography contains the year of release, the major credits, a brief plot summary, and the Vietvet characters within the films. A filmography of Vietnam War films follows.

Above the Law (1988)
DIRECTOR: Andrew Davis WRITERS: Steven Pressfield, Ronald Shusett, Andrew Davis; Story by Andrew Davis, Steven Seagal EDITOR: Michael Brown CAMERA: Robert Steadman (Technicolor) MUSIC: David M. Frank PRODUCERS: Steven Seagal, Andrew Davis DISTRIBUTOR: Warner Bros. VIDEO: Yes

Nico Toscani (Steven Seagal), Zagon (Henry Silva), Fox (Chelcie Ross). A Chicago cop, Toscani, takes on CIA drug runners trying to finance a covert invasion of Nicaragua, whom he first encountered in Vietnam/Cambodia.

Alamo Bay (1985)
DIRECTOR: Louis Malle WRITER: Alice Arlen EDITOR: James Bruce CAMERA: Curtis Clark (Du-Art color) MUSIC: Ry Cooder PRODUCERS: Louis and Vincent Malle DISTRIBUTOR: Tri-Star VIDEO: Yes

Shang (Ed Harris). Vietnamese-American fishers encounter resentment, and escalating violence, in a small Texas town.

Americana (1981)
DIRECTOR: David Carradine WRITER: Richard Carr EDITOR: David Kern CAMERA: Michael Stringer (color) MUSIC: Craig Hundley, David Carradine PRODUCERS: David Carradine, Skip Sherwood DISTRIBUTOR: Carradine/Sherwood VIDEO: Yes

Soldier (David Carradine). A Vietvet drifter goes to a small town in Kansas and becomes obsessed with fixing a merry-go-round there, which was once the object of civic pride in the community. The town resists his efforts.

Angels From Hell (1968)
DIRECTOR: Bruce Kessler WRITER: Jerome Wish EDITOR: William Martin CAMERA: Herman Knox (Perfect color) MUSIC: Stu Phillips

PRODUCER: Kurt Neumann DISTRIBUTOR: American International Pictures VIDEO: No

Mike (Tom Stern). A returned Vietvet starts a new gang as a protest against the Establishment and battles rival gangs and police.

Angry Breed, The (1968)
DIRECTOR: David Commons WRITERS: David Commons; Story by Rex Carlton EDITOR: David Saxon CAMERA: Gregory Sandor (color) MUSIC: Lawrence Brown, Mike Curb PRODUCER: David Commons DISTRIBUTOR: Commonwealth United VIDEO: No

Johnny Taylor (Murray McLeod). A Vietvet gets involved in the movie business in Hollywood, with some bikers, and with the drug trade.

Annihilators, The (1985)
DIRECTOR: Charles E. Sellier, Jr. WRITER: Brian Russell EDITOR: Dan Gross CAMERA: Henning Schellerup (color) MUSIC: Bob Summers PRODUCERS: Allan C. Pedersen, Tom Chapman DISTRIBUTOR: New World VIDEO: Yes

Sarge (Christopher Stone), Ray Ray (Gerrit Graham), Flash (Lawrence-Hilton Jacobs), Woody (Andy Wood), Joey (Dennis Redfield). Vietvets outside Atlanta rejoin their unit to battle street crime in this very violent reworking of *The Magnificent Seven.*

Armed Response (1986)
DIRECTOR: Fred Olen Ray WRITERS: T.L. Lankford; Story by Paul Hertzberg, Fred Olen Ray, T.L. Lankford EDITOR: Miriam L. Preissel CAMERA: Paul Elliott (United color) MUSIC: Thomas Chase, Steve Rucker PRODUCER: Paul Hertzberg DISTRIBUTOR: Cinetel Films VIDEO: Yes

Jim Roth (David Carradine), Clay Roth (David Goss), Tommy Roth (Brent Huff). A whole family of veterans become involved in a Chinatown battle over valuable jade.

Back to School (1986)
DIRECTOR: Alan Metter WRITERS: Steven Kampmann, Will Porter, Peter Torokvei, Harold Ramis; Story by Rodney Dangerfield, Greg Fields, Dennis Snee EDITOR: David Rawlins CAMERA: Thomas E. Ackerman (Panavision, Deluxe color) MUSIC: Danny Elfman PRODUCER: Chuck Russell DISTRIBUTOR: Orion VIDEO: Yes

Professor Terguson (Sam Kinison). Kinison does a funny turn as a maniacal Vietvet history professor, whose right-wing sympathies the Rodney Dangerfield character shares.

Backfire (1989)
DIRECTOR: Gilbert Cates WRITERS: Larry Brand, Rebecca Reynolds EDITOR: Melvin Shapiro CAMERA: Tak Fujimoto (color) MUSIC: David Shire PRODUCER: Danton Rissner DISTRIBUTOR: ITC VIDEO: Yes

Donny (Jeff Fahey), Reed (Keith Carradine). A wife tries to do in the rich Vietvet Donny, in a story very reminiscent of *Diabolique*.

Band of the Hand (1986)
DIRECTOR: Paul Michael Glaser WRITERS: Leo Garen, Jack Baran EDITOR: Jack Hofstra CAMERA: Reynaldo Villalobos (Metrocolor) MUSIC: Bob Dylan, The Reds PRODUCER: Michael Rauch DISTRIBUTOR: Tri-Star VIDEO: Yes

Joe (Stephen Lang). A Vietvet trains Miami street gang and leads them in a war against drug dealers there.

Bears and I, The (1974)
DIRECTOR: Bernard McEveety WRITERS: John Whedon; Book by Robert Franklin Leslie EDITOR: Gregg McLaughlin CAMERA: Ted D. Landon (Technicolor) MUSIC: Buddy Baker PRODUCER: Winston Hibler DISTRIBUTOR: Buena Vista VIDEO: Yes

Bob Leslie (Patrick Wayne). This Disney family programmer has a Vietvet adopt three abandoned bear cubs, while helping out some Indians with a land dispute.

Betrayed (1988)
DIRECTOR: Constantin Costa-Gavras WRITER: Joe Eszterhaus EDITOR: Joelle Van Effenterre CAMERA: Patrick Blossier (Astro color, Alpha Cine color) MUSIC: Bill Conti PRODUCER: Irwin Winkler DISTRIBUTOR: MGM/UA VIDEO: Yes

Gary Simmons (Tom Berenger), Bobby Flynn (Jeffrey DeMunn). Simmons is a decorated vet who is involved with a murderous white supremacy group.

Big Bounce, The (1969)
DIRECTOR: Alex March WRITERS: Robert Dozier, Novel by Elmore Leonard EDITOR: William Ziegler CAMERA: Howard R. Schwartz (Technicolor) MUSIC: Michael Curb PRODUCER: William Dozier DISTRIBUTOR: Warner Bros./Seven Arts VIDEO: No

Jack Ryan (Ryan O'Neal). A Vietvet gets involved with a strange and dangerous young woman.

Big Chill, The (1983)
DIRECTOR: Lawrence Kasdan WRITERS: Lawrence Kasdan, Barbara

Benedek EDITOR: Carol Littleton CAMERA: John Bailey (Metrocolor) PRODUCER: Michael Shamberg DISTRIBUTOR: Columbia VIDEO: Yes

Nick (William Hurt). Nick, a drug dealer, meets his old friends from Michigan University on the occasion of the death of their friend.

Billy Jack (1971)
DIRECTOR: T. C. Frank (Tom Laughlin) WRITERS: T.C. Frank, Teresa Christina (Delores Taylor) EDITORS: Larry Heath, Marion Rothman CAMERA: Fred Koenekamp, John Stephens (Technicolor) MUSIC: Mundell Lowe PRODUCER: Mary Rose Solti DISTRIBUTOR: Warner Bros. VIDEO: Yes

Billy Jack (Tom Laughlin). The title character in the second of a successful series battles town bullies and saves an alternative school.

Billy Jack Goes to Washington (1977)
DIRECTOR: T. C. Frank (Tom Laughlin) WRITERS: T.C. Frank, Teresa Christina (Delores Taylor); Original screenplay by Sidney Buchman; Story, Lewis R. Foster CAMERA: Jack Merta (color) MUSIC: Elmer Bernstein PRODUCER: Frank Capra, Jr. DISTRIBUTOR: Taylor-Laughlin Distribution VIDEO: No

Billy Jack (Tom Laughlin). Billy Jack battles corruption in Congress in the fourth of the series.

Birdy (1984)
DIRECTOR: Alan Parker WRITERS: Sandy Kroopf, Jack Behr; Novel by William Wharton EDITOR: Gerry Hambling CAMERA: Michael Seresin (Metrocolor) MUSIC: Peter Gabriel PRODUCER: Alan Marshall DISTRIBUTOR: Tri-Star VIDEO: Yes

Birdy (Matthew Modine), Al Columbato (Nicolas Cage). A traumatized Vietvet refuses to speak upon his return and his war buddy tries to help him.

Black Gunn (1972)
DIRECTOR: Robert Hartford-Davis WRITERS: Franklin Coen, Robert Shearer; Idea by Robert Hartford-Davis EDITORS: David DeWilde, Pat Somerset CAMERA: Richard H. Kline (color) MUSIC: Tony Osborne PRODUCERS: John Heyman, Norman Priggen DISTRIBUTOR: Columbia VIDEO: No

Scott Gunn (Herbert Jefferson, Jr.), Hopper (Jim Watkins). A nightclub owner goes after the mob when they kill his brother, a Vietvet.

Black Six, The (1974)
DIRECTOR: Matt Cimber WRITER: George Theakos EDITOR: William Swenning CAMERA: William Swenning (color) MUSIC: David Moscoe PRODUCER: Matt Cimber DISTRIBUTOR: Cinemation Industries VIDEO: Yes

Bubba (Gene Washington), Junior Bro (Carl Eller), Frenchy (Lem Barney), Bookie (Mercury Morris), Tommy (Willie Lanier), Kevin ("Mean" Joe Green). Title Vietvets fight racist murders in a small California town.

Black Sunday (1977)
DIRECTOR: John Frankenheimer WRITERS: Ernest Lehman, Kenneth Ross, Ivan Moffat ; Novel by Thomas Harris EDITOR: Tom Rolf CAMERA: John A. Alonzo (Movielab color) MUSIC: John Williams PRODUCER: Robert Evans DISTRIBUTOR: Paramount VIDEO: Yes

Lander (Bruce Dern). Terrorists enlist the crazed Lander, a Vietvet pilot, to help them bomb the Orange Bowl on Super Sunday.

Blue Thunder (1983)
DIRECTOR: John Badham WRITERS: Dan O'Bannon, Don Jakoby EDITORS: Frank Morriss, Edward Abroms CAMERA: John A. Alonzo (Panavision, Deluxe color) MUSIC: Arthur B. Rubinstein PRODUCER: Gordon Carroll DISTRIBUTOR: Columbia VIDEO: Yes

Murphy (Roy Scheider), Cochrane (Malcom McDowell). Good vet Murphy fights bad vet Cochrane above the skies of L.A., as the latter is part of a group trying to start a riot in order to sell their high-tech "Blue Thunder" helicopters.

Borderline (1980)
DIRECTOR: Jerrold Freedman WRITERS: Steve Kline, Jerrold Freedman EDITOR: John Link CAMERA: Tak Fujimoto (Eastmancolor) MUSIC: Gil Melle PRODUCER: James Nelson DISTRIBUTOR: ITC VIDEO: Yes

Hotchkiss (Ed Harris). Hotchkiss, in a small role, runs illegal immigrants over the border into the U.S.

Born Losers (1967)
DIRECTOR: T. C. Frank (Tom Laughlin) WRITER: E. James Lloyd EDITOR: John Winfield CAMERA: Gregory Sander (Pathe color) PRODUCER: Donald Henderson DISTRIBUTOR: American International Pictures VIDEO: Yes

Billy Jack (Tom Laughlin). The first appearance of Billy Jack has him fighting a bike gang and a corrupt justice system.

Born on the Fourth of July (1989)
DIRECTOR: Oliver Stone WRITERS: Oliver Stone, Ron Kovic;
Autobiography by Ron Kovic EDITOR: David Brenner CAMERA:
Robert Richardson (Deluxe color) MUSIC: John Williams
PRODUCERS: A. Kitman Ho, Oliver Stone DISTRIBUTOR:
Universal VIDEO: Yes
     Ron Kovic (Tom Cruise), Charlie (Willem Dafoe). Kovic
attempts to reintegrate amidst the changing times and circumstances in
America in the early 1970s.

Braddock: Missing in Action III (1988)
DIRECTOR: Aaron Norris WRITERS: James Bruner, Chuck Norris;
characters by Arthur Silver, Larry Levinson, Steve Bing EDITOR:
Michael J. Duthie CAMERA: Joao Fernandes (Rank color) MUSIC:
Jay Chattaway PRODUCERS: Menahem Golan, Yoram Globus
DISTRIBUTOR: Cannon VIDEO: Yes
     Braddock (Chuck Norris). Braddock returns to Vietnam to try to
reclaim his Vietnamese wife, whom he thought dead, and his son from
their marriage.

Brotherhood, The (1969)
DIRECTOR: Martin Ritt WRITER: Lewis John Carlino EDITOR:
Frank Bracht CAMERA: Boris Kaufman (Technicolor) MUSIC: Lalo
Schifrin PRODUCER: Kirk Douglas DISTRIBUTOR: Paramount
VIDEO: Yes
     Vince Ginetta (Alex Cord). Vince returns from Vietnam and
rejoins the family gangster business.

'Burbs, The (1989)
DIRECTOR: Joe Dante WRITER: Dana Olsen EDITOR: Marshall
Harvey CAMERA: Robert Stevens (Deluxe color) MUSIC: Jerry
Goldsmith PRODUCERS: Michael Finnell, Larry Brezner
DISTRIBUTOR: Universal VIDEO: Yes
     Mark Rumsfield (Bruce Dern). Rumsfield has a supporting role in
goings-on in a suburban neighborhood where the new neighbors just
might be cannibals. A funny twist on Dern's troubled vet roles.

Bus is Coming,The (1971)
DIRECTOR: Wendell James Franklin WRITERS: Horace Jackson,
Robert H. Raff, Mike Rhodes EDITOR: Donald R. Rode CAMERA:
Mike Rhodes (Deluxe color) MUSIC: Tom McIntosh PRODUCER:
Horace Jackson DISTRIBUTOR: William Thompson International
VIDEO: Yes
     Billy Mitchell (Mike Simms). Mitchell takes matters into his

own hands when he returns home to find his activist brother murdered.

Bus Riley's Back in Town (1965)
DIRECTOR: Harvey Hart WRITERS: Walter Gage; Story by William
Inge EDITOR: Folmar Blangsted CAMERA: Russell Metty
(Eastmancolor) MUSIC: Richard Markowitz PRODUCER: Elliott
Kastner DISTRIBUTOR: Universal VIDEO: No
Bus Riley (Michael Parks). The title character attempts to
reintegrate upon return to his small hometown.

Cage (1989)
DIRECTOR: Lang Elliott WRITER: Hugh Kelley EDITOR: Mark S.
Westmore CAMERA: Jacques Haitkin (Deluxe color) MUSIC: Michael
Wetherwax PRODUCER: Lang Elliott DISTRIBUTOR: New Century-
Vista VIDEO: Yes
Billy (Lou Ferrigno), Scott (Reb Brown). Billy and Scott get
tangled up with the Italian and Chinese mobs, who are staging illegal
"cage" fights in Chinatown.

Captain Milkshake (1970)
DIRECTOR: Richard Crawford WRITERS: Richard Crawford, Barry
Leichtling EDITOR: David Korn CAMERA: Robert A. Sherry
(Technicolor) MUSIC: Various artists PRODUCERS: Richard
Crawford, Lloyd Marchus, Harvey Levitt DISTRIBUTOR: Richmark
VIDEO: No
Paul (Geoff Gage). Paul comes home to San Diego on an
emergency leave and examines the late 1960s scene there.

Casualties of War (1989)
DIRECTOR: Brian DePalma WRITERS: David Rabe; Book by Daniel
Lang EDITOR: Bill Pankow CAMERA: Stephen H. Burum
(Panavision, Deluxe color) MUSIC: Ennio Morricone PRODUCER:
Art Linson DISTRIBUTOR: Columbia VIDEO: Yes
Erikson (Michael J. Fox). Erikson has an extended flashback to
Vietnam, where he tried to report fellow soldiers for their part in an
atrocity, but no one wanted to listen.

Cease Fire (1985)
DIRECTOR: David Nutter WRITER: George Fernandez from his play
Vietnam Trilogy EDITOR: Julio Chaves CAMERA: Henning
Schellerup (Continental color) MUSIC: Gary Fry PRODUCER:
William Grefe DISTRIBUTOR: Cineworld Enterprises VIDEO: Yes
Tim Murphy (Don Johnson), Luke (Robert F. Lyons). Murphy's
wife tries to get him to join a vet's group, and Murphy does, but only

after the suicide of Luke.

Charley Varrick (1973)
DIRECTOR: Don Siegel WRITERS: Dean Riesner, Howard Rodman; Novel, *The Looters* by John Reese EDITOR: Frank Morriss CAMERA: Michael Butler (Technicolor) MUSIC: Lalo Schifrin PRODUCER: Don Siegel DISTRIBUTOR: Universal VIDEO: Yes

Harman (Andy Robinson). Caper film has Harman helping bank robbers using demolition skills learned in Vietnam.

Choirboys, The (1977)
DIRECTOR: Robert Aldrich WRITERS: Christopher Knopf; Novel by Joseph Wambaugh EDITORS: Maury Winetrobe, William Martin, Irving Rosenblum CAMERA: Joseph Biroc (Technicolor) MUSIC: Frank DeVol PRODUCERS: Merv Adelson, Lee Rich DISTRIBUTOR: Universal VIDEO: Yes

Lyles (Don Stroud), Bloomguard (James Woods). Vietvet pals who become cops figure into this episodic film.

Choose Me (1984)
DIRECTOR: Alan Rudolph WRITER: Alan Rudolph EDITOR: Mia Goldman CAMERA: Jan Kiesser (Movielab color) MUSIC: Teddy Pendergrass PRODUCERS: Carolyn Pfeiffer, David Blocker DISTRIBUTOR: Island Alive VIDEO: Yes

Mickey (Keith Carradine). Mickey is a mysterious vet with tall tales to tell, all of which turn out to be true.

Chrome and Hot Leather (1971)
DIRECTOR: Lee Frost WRITERS: Michael Haynes, David Neibel, Don Tait; Story by Michael Haynes, David Neibel EDITORS: Alfonso P. La Mastra, Edward Shryver CAMERA: Lee Frost (Movielab color) MUSIC: Porter Jordan PRODUCER: Wes Bishop DISTRIBUTOR: American International Pictures VIDEO: No

Mitch (Tony Young), T. J. (William Smith), Al (Peter Brown), Jim (Marvin Gaye), Hank (Michael Sterns). A Green Beret learns that a bike gang caused the accident that took his girlfriend's life, and he enlists his old troop to get even.

Code Name: Zebra (1987)
DIRECTOR: Joe Tornatore WRITERS: Robert Leon; Characters by Joe Tornatore EDITOR: Ed Hansen CAMERA: Bill Dickson, Tom Denove (Foto-Kem color) MUSIC: Louis Febre, Peter Rotter PRODUCER: Joseph Lucchese DISTRIBUTOR: Trans World VIDEO: Yes (Direct to video)

Cougar (Timmy Brown), Noble (Robert Dryer), Alonzo (Robert Apisa), Larson (Dennis Rucker), Temple (Steve Thompson). An elite group of Vietvets take on the mob.

Colors (1988)
DIRECTOR: Dennis Hopper WRITERS: Michael Schiffer; Story by Michael Schiffer, Richard DiLello EDITOR: Robert Estrin CAMERA: Haskell Wexler (Metrocolor) MUSIC: Herbie Hancock PRODUCER: Robert H. Solo DISTRIBUTOR: Orion VIDEO: Yes

Vietnam Veteran (Tom Todd). A concerned Vietvet, in a very small role, speaks out at a public meeting about gang violence.

Combat Shock (1986)
DIRECTOR: Buddy Giovinazzo WRITER: Buddy Giovinazzo EDITOR: Buddy Giovinazzo CAMERA: Stella Varveris (color) MUSIC: Ricky Giovinazzo PRODUCER: Buddy Giovinazzo DISTRIBUTOR: Troma VIDEO: Yes

Frankie (Ricky Giovinazzo). An extremely troubled vet cannot make his loan shark's demands and turns graphically violent.

Coming Home (1978)
DIRECTOR: Hal Ashby WRITERS: Waldo Salt, Robert C. Jones; Story by Nancy Dowd EDITOR: Don Zimmerman CAMERA: Haskell Wexler (Deluxe color) MUSIC: Various period artists. PRODUCER: Jerome Hellman DISTRIBUTOR: United Artists VIDEO: Yes

Luke Martin (John Voight), Bob Hyde (Bruce Dern), Bill (Robert Carradine). This drama chronicles different effects the war has on a number of different vets.

Cool Breeze (1972)
DIRECTOR: Barry Pollack WRITERS: Barry Pollack; Novel, *The Asphalt Jungle* by W.R. Burnett. EDITOR: Morton Tubor CAMERA: Andy Davis (Metrocolor) MUSIC: Solomon Burke PRODUCER: Gene Corman DISTRIBUTOR: Metro Goldwyn Mayer VIDEO: No

Roy Harris (Rudy Challenger). This bank-caper picture has a Vietvet involved in a big heist.

Crazies, The (1973)
DIRECTOR: George A. Romero WRITERS: Paul McCollough; Story by George A. Romero EDITOR: George A. Romero CAMERA: S. William Hinzman (color) MUSIC: Bruce Roberts PRODUCER: Alvin C. Croft DISTRIBUTOR: Cambist VIDEO: Yes

David (W. G. McMillan), Clank (Harold Wayne Jones). A bio-toxin plagues a small town, and two army buddies try to avoid the fascistic quarantine imposed by the government.

Crazy World of Julius Vrooder, The (1974)
DIRECTOR: Arthur Hiller WRITER: Daryl Henry EDITOR: Robert C. Jones CAMERA: David Walsh (Panavision, Deluxe color) MUSIC: Bob Alcivar PRODUCERS: Edward Rissien, Arthur Hiller DISTRIBUTOR: Twentieth Century Fox VIDEO: No
     Julius Vrooder (Timothy Bottoms). This comedy explores the world an escaped mental patient creates.

Cutter's Way (1981) AKA: *Cutter and Bone*
DIRECTOR: Ivan Passer WRITERS: Jeffrey Alan Fiskin; Novel, *Cutter and Bone* by Newton Thornburg EDITOR: Caroline Ferriol CAMERA: Jordan Cronenweth (Technicolor) MUSIC: Jack Nitzsche PRODUCER: Paul R. Gurian DISTRIBUTOR: United Artists VIDEO: Yes
     Alex Cutter (John Heard). A bitter Vietvet becomes obsessed with solving a murder.

D.C. Cab (1983)
DIRECTOR: Joel Schumacher WRITERS: Joel Schumacher; Story by Topper Carew, Joel Schumacher EDITOR: David Blewitt CAMERA: Dean Cundey (Technicolor) MUSIC: Giorgio Moroder PRODUCER: Topper Carew DISTRIBUTOR: Universal VIDEO: Yes
     Harold (Max Gail). Comic complications arise when Harold's cab company competes with another in order to win a big prize.

Dangerously Close (1986)
DIRECTOR: Albert Pyun WRITERS: Scott Fields, John Stockwell, Marty Ross; Story by Marty Ross EDITOR: Dennis O'Connor CAMERA: Walt Lloyd (TVC color) MUSIC: Michael McCarty PRODUCER: Harold Sobel DISTRIBUTOR: Cannon VIDEO: Yes
     Corrigan (Madison Mason). A high school vigilante group gets involved in a murder, and their Vietvet adviser is accused of the crime.

Death Before Dishonor (1987)
DIRECTOR: Terry J. Leonard WRITERS: John Gatliff, Lawrence Kubik; Story by John Gatliff, Lawrence Kubik EDITOR: Steve Mirkovich CAMERA: Don Burgess (Deluxe color) MUSIC: Brian May PRODUCER: Lawrence Kubik DISTRIBUTOR: New World VIDEO: Yes
     Burns (Fred Dryer). A gung-ho marine battles Arab terrorists to free his kidnapped colonel. Quite bloody.

Deathdream (1972) AKA: *Dead of Night, Night Walk, The Veteran*
DIRECTOR: Bob Clark WRITER: Alan Ormsby EDITOR: Ron
Sinclair CAMERA: Jack McGowan (color) MUSIC: Carl Zittrer
PRODUCERS: Bob Clark, Benjamin Clark, Tom Karr
DISTRIBUTOR: Europix VIDEO: Yes
Andy (Richard Backus). A dead vet comes back to seek revenge on
the society that got him into the war.

Deer Hunter, The (1978)
DIRECTOR: Michael Cimino WRITERS: Deric Washburn; Story by
Michael Cimino, Deric Washburn, Louis Garfinkle, Quinn K. Redeker
EDITOR: Peter Zinner CAMERA: Vilmos Zsigmond (Panavision,
Technicolor) MUSIC: Stanley Myers PRODUCERS: Barry Spikings,
Michael Deeley, Michael Cimino, John Peverall DISTRIBUTOR:
Universal/EMI VIDEO: Yes
Michael (Robert DeNiro), Steven (John Savage), Nick (Christopher
Walken). This highly acclaimed and heavily criticized drama concerns
three boyhood friends whose lives are shattered by the war.

Delirium (1979)
DIRECTOR: Peter Maris WRITERS: Richard Yalem; Story by Richard
Yalem, Eddie Krell, Jim Loew EDITOR: Dan Perry CAMERA: John
Huston, Bill Mensch MUSIC: David Williams PRODUCERS: Sunny
Vest, Peter Maris DISTRIBUTOR: Odyssey VIDEO: Yes
Eric Stern (Barron Winchester), Charlie Gunther (Nick Panouzis).
Stern is the leader of a group of vigilantes who kill criminals who slip
through the cracks of the justice system. Gunther, one of the group,
goes insane and goes free-lance.

Delta Force, The (1986)
DIRECTOR: Menahem Golan WRITERS: James Bruner, Menahem
Golan EDITOR: Alain Jakubowicz CAMERA: David Gurfinkel (color)
MUSIC: Alan Silvestri PRODUCERS: Menahem Golan, Yoram
Globus DISTRIBUTOR: Cannon VIDEO: Yes
Scott McKay (Chuck Norris). An elite fighting troop, led by
McKay, tries to free hostages from terrorists in the Middle East.

Desperate Hours, The (1990)
DIRECTOR: Michael Cimino WRITERS: Lawrence Konner, Mark
Rosenthal, Joseph Hayes; Novel and play by Joseph Hayes EDITOR:
Peter Hunt CAMERA: Doug Milsome (Technicolor) MUSIC: David
Mansfield PRODUCERS: Dino DeLaurentiis, Michael Cimino
DISTRIBUTOR: MGM/UA VIDEO: Yes
Tim Cornell (Anthony Hopkins). Cornell's family is taken

hostage in their own home by an escaped convict and his gang. Not much is made of Cornell's service.

Die Hard (1988)
DIRECTOR: John McTiernan WRITERS: Jeb Stuart, Steven E. de Souza; Novel, *Nothing Lasts Forever* by Roderick Thorp EDITORS: Frank J. Urioste, John F. Link CAMERA: Jan De Bont (Panavision, Deluxe color) MUSIC: Michael Kamen PRODUCERS: Lawrence Gordon, Joel Silver DISTRIBUTOR: Twentieth Century Fox VIDEO: Yes
     Big Johnson (Robert Davi), Little Johnson (Grand L. Bush). Johnson and Johnson are two FBI agents assigned to a terrorism case who have little regard for the lives of the hostages.

Distant Thunder (1988)
DIRECTOR: Rick Rosenthal WRITERS: Robert Stitzel; Story by Robert Stitzel, Deedee Wehle EDITOR: Dennis Virkler CAMERA: Ralf D. Bode (Technicolor) MUSIC: Maurice Jarre PRODUCER: Robert Schaffel DISTRIBUTOR: Paramount VIDEO: Yes
     Mark Lambert (John Lithgow), Harve (Reb Brown), Larry (Dennis Arndt), Louis (Tom Bower), Andy (John Kelly). Lambert, after deserting his family, attempts a reconciliation with his son years later. Complications include PTSD and murder.

Doberman Gang, The (1972)
DIRECTOR: Byron Ross Chudnow WRITERS: Louis Garfinkle, Frank Ray Perilli EDITOR: Herman Freedman CAMERA: Robert Caramico (CFI color) MUSIC: Bradford Craig, Alan Silvestri PRODUCER: David Chudnow DISTRIBUTOR: Warner Bros. VIDEO: Yes
     Barney (Hal Reed). A Vietvet gets tricked by bank robbers into training title animals for a bank robbery.

Dogs of War, The (1980, British)
DIRECTOR: John Irvin WRITERS: Gary DeVore, George Malko; Novel by Frederick Forsythe EDITOR: Antony Gibbs CAMERA: Jack Cardiff (Panavision, Technicolor) MUSIC: Geoffry Burgon PRODUCER: Larry DeWaay DISTRIBUTOR: United Artists VIDEO: Yes
     Shannon (Christopher Walken), Drew (Tom Berenger), North (Colin Blakely), Endean (Hugh Millais), Derek (Paul Freeman). This war film has a platoon re-forming to become mercenaries in Africa and elsewhere.

Domino Principle, The (1977)
DIRECTOR: Stanley Kramer WRITER: Adam Kennedy, from his novel EDITOR: John Burnett CAMERA: Fred Koenekamp, Ernest Laszlo (Panavision, CFI color) MUSIC: Billy Goldenberg PRODUCER: Stanley Kramer DISTRIBUTOR: Avco Embassy VIDEO: Yes

Roy Tucker (Gene Hackman). Tucker gets involved in a conspiracy to kill a political figure.

Don't Answer the Phone (1980)
DIRECTOR: Robert Hammer WRITERS: Robert Hammer, Mike Castle EDITOR: Joseph Fineman CAMERA: James Carter (Metrocolor) MUSIC: Bryon Allerd PRODUCERS: Robert Hammer, Mike Castle DISTRIBUTOR: Crown International Pictures VIDEO: Yes

Kirk (Nicholas Worth). A deranged Vietvet turns to strangling to vent his frustrations.

Easy Wheels (1989)
DIRECTOR: David O'Malley WRITERS: Juan Raimi, Celia Abrams, David O'Malley EDITOR: John Currin CAMERA: James Lemmo (Technicolor) MUSIC: John Ross PRODUCERS: Dimitri Villard, Robby Wald DISTRIBUTOR: Fries Entertainment VIDEO: Yes

Bruce (Paul LeMat), Animal (Mark Holton), Paco (Carlos Compean). The Born Losers tangle with the Women of the Wolf in this parody of biker films.

Electra Glide in Blue (1973)
DIRECTOR: James William Guerico WRITERS: Robert Boris, Michael Butler; Story by Robert Boris, Rupert Hitzig EDITORS: Jim Benson, Jerry Greenburg, John F. Fink III CAMERA: Conrad Hall (Panavision, Deluxe color) MUSIC: Various artists PRODUCER: James William Guerico DISTRIBUTOR: United Artists VIDEO: Yes

John Wintergreen (Robert Blake), Zemko (Peter Cetera), Trucker (Michael Butler). This police drama has Wintergreen trying to solve a murder and become a plainclothes detective.

Endangered Species (1982)
DIRECTOR: Alan Rudolph WRITERS: Alan Rudolph, John Binder; Story by Judson Klinger, Richard Woods EDITOR: Tom Walls CAMERA: Paul Lohmann (Metrocolor) MUSIC: Gary Wright PRODUCER: Carolyn Pfeiffer DISTRIBUTOR: MGM/UA VIDEO: Yes

Ben Morgan (Hoyt Axton). Morgan becomes involved in this

conspiracy thriller revolving around cattle mutilations.

Enemy Territory (1987)
DIRECTOR: Peter Manoogian WRITERS: Stuart M. Kaminsky,
Bobby Liddell; Story by Stuart M. Kaminsky EDITOR: Peter Teschner
CAMERA: Ernest Dickerson (Precision color) MUSIC: Sam Winans,
Richard Koz Kosinaki PRODUCERS: Cynthia De Paula, Tim Kincaid
DISTRIBUTOR: Empire VIDEO: Yes
    Parker (Jan-Michael Vincent). An assorted group of people trapped
in a high-rise apartment battle back when besieged by a street gang.

Executioner Part II , The (1984)
DIRECTOR: James Bryant CAMERA: (Pacific color) PRODUCER:
Renee Harmon DISTRIBUTOR: 21st Century VIDEO: Yes
    Lt. O'Malley (Christopher Mitchum), Mike (Antoine John
Mottet). A cop searches for a grenade-lobbing vigilante, who, it turns
out, saved his life in Vietnam. Part I does not exist.

Exterminator, The (1980)
DIRECTOR: James Glickenhaus WRITER: James Glickenhaus
EDITOR: Corky O'Hara CAMERA: Robert M. Baldwin (color)
MUSIC: Joe Renzetti PRODUCER: Mark Buntzman DISTRIBUTOR:
Avco Embassy VIDEO: Yes
    John Eastland (Robert Ginty). Eastland takes up a flame thrower
to rid the streets of crime in this vigilante tale.

Exterminator II (1984)
DIRECTORS: Mark Buntzman, William Sachs WRITERS: Mark
Buntzman, William Sachs EDITORS: George Norris, Marcus Manton
CAMERA: Bob Baldwin, Joseph Mangine (TVC color) MUSIC: David
Spear PRODUCERS: Mark Buntzman, William Sachs
DISTRIBUTOR: Cannon VIDEO: Yes
    Johnny Eastland (Robert Ginty), Be Gee (Frankie Faison).
Eastland continues his activities from the first movie in this series, this
time taking on a deadly street gang.

Extreme Prejudice (1987)
DIRECTOR: Walter Hill WRITERS: Deric Washburn, Harry Kleiner;
Story by John Milius, Fred Rexer EDITOR: Freeman Davis
CAMERA: Matthew F. Leonetti (Technicolor) MUSIC: Jerry
Goldsmith PRODUCER: Buzz Feitshans DISTRIBUTOR: Tri-Star
VIDEO: Yes
    Hackett (Michael Ironside), McRose (Clancy Brown). Vietvets
become a clandestine unit ostensibly working for the government.

Eye of the Tiger (1986)
DIRECTOR: Richard Sarafian WRITER: Michael Montgomery
EDITOR: Greg Prange CAMERA: Peter Collister (United color)
PRODUCER: Tony Scotti DISTRIBUTOR: Scotti Brothers VIDEO:
Yes
Buck Matthews (Gary Busey). Matthews, out of prison for a crime
he didn't commit, tries to reintegrate, but drug-running bikers prevent
him from doing so.

Eyewitness (1981)
DIRECTOR: Peter Yates WRITER: Steve Tesich EDITOR: Cynthia
Schneider CAMERA: Matthew F. Leonetti (Technicolor) MUSIC:
Stanley Silverman PRODUCER: Peter Yates DISTRIBUTOR:
Twentieth Century Fox VIDEO: Yes
Daryll Deever (William Hurt). A decorated vet gets involved in a
murder that turns out to be part of a conspiracy.

F/X (1986)
DIRECTOR: Robert Mandel WRITERS: Robert T. Megginson,
Gregory Fleeman EDITOR: Terry Rawlings CAMERA: Miroslav
Ondricek (Technicolor) MUSIC: Bill Conti PRODUCERS: Dodi
Fayed, Jack Wiener DISTRIBUTOR: Orion VIDEO: Yes
Adams (Tim Gallin). Adams is at least a Vietnam-era vet and has a
bit part as an assassin sent to kill the protagonist.

Fear (1988)
DIRECTOR: Robert A. Ferretti WRITERS: Rick Scarry, Kathryn
Connell; Story by Robert A. Ferretti EDITOR: Michael Eliot
CAMERA: Dana Christiaansen (Foto-Kem color) MUSIC: Alfi
Kabiljo PRODUCER: Lisa M. Hansen DISTRIBUTOR: Cinetel
VIDEO: Yes
Jack Gracie (Robert Factor), Don Haden (Cliff DeYoung). A
family on a road trip encounters a group of escaped prisoners. Gracie
and Haden fight it out at the end.

Firefox (1982)
DIRECTOR: Clint Eastwood WRITERS: Alex Lasker, Wendell
Wellman; Novel by Craig Thomas EDITORS: Ferris Webster, Ron
Spang CAMERA: Bruce Surtees (Panavision, Deluxe color) MUSIC:
Maurice Jarre PRODUCER: Clint Eastwood DISTRIBUTOR: Warner
Bros. VIDEO: Yes
Mitchell Gant (Eastwood). A hermit-like Vietvet is called out of
retirement so he can steal a high-tech Russian MIG.

First Blood (1982)
DIRECTOR: Ted Kotcheff WRITERS: Michael Kozoll, William Sackheim, Q. Moonblood; Novel by David Morrell EDITOR: Tom Noble CAMERA: Andrew Lazlo (Panavision, Technicolor) MUSIC: Jerry Goldsmith PRODUCER: Buzz Feitshans DISTRIBUTOR: Orion VIDEO: Yes
    John Rambo (Sylvester Stallone), Trautman (Richard Crenna). Rambo destroys a good part of a small town in the first of a series.

Flashpoint (1984)
DIRECTOR: William Tannen WRITERS: Dennis Syhrack, Michael Butler; Novel by George La Fountaine EDITOR: David Garfield CAMERA: Peter Moss (Metrocolor) MUSIC: Tangerine Dream PRODUCER: Skip Short DISTRIBUTOR: Tri-Star VIDEO: Yes
    Bog Logan (Kris Kristofferson). A lawman vet gets tangled up in what turns out to be the Kennedy assassination cover-up.

Fleshburn (1984)
DIRECTOR: George Gage WRITERS: Beth Gage, George Gage; Novel, *Fear in a Handful of Dust* by Brian Garfield EDITOR: Sonya Sones CAMERA: Bill Pecchi (Deluxe color) MUSIC: Arthur Kempel, Don Felder PRODUCER: Beth Gage DISTRIBUTOR: Crown International Pictures VIDEO: Yes
    Calvin Duggai (Sonny Landham), Jim Brody (Robert Alan Browne). A Navajo Vietvet seeks revenge against the four psychiatrists who testified against him and sent him to a mental hospital.

Force of One, A (1979)
DIRECTOR: Paul Aaron WRITERS: Ernest Tidyman; Story by Ernest Tidyman, Pat Johnson EDITOR: Bert Lovitt CAMERA: Roger Shearman (CFI color) MUSIC: Dick Halligan PRODUCER: Alan Belkin DISTRIBUTOR: American Cinema Releasing VIDEO: Yes
    Matt Logan (Chuck Norris). A small-town narcotics squad enlists Logan to fight drug traffickers.

Forced Vengeance (1982)
DIRECTOR: James Fargo WRITER: Franklin Thompson EDITOR: Irving C. Rosenblum CAMERA: Rexford Metz (Metrocolor) MUSIC: William Goldstein PRODUCER: John B. Bennett DISTRIBUTOR: MGM/UA VIDEO: Yes
    Josh Randall (Chuck Norris). Randall tries to get back the kidnapped daughter of his boss, who was killed by the mob.

Fourth War, The (1990)
DIRECTOR: John Frankenheimer WRITERS: Stephen Peters, Kenneth Ross; Novel by Stephen Peters EDITOR: Robert F. Shugrue CAMERA: Gerry Fisher (Alpha Cine color) MUSIC: Bill Conti PRODUCER: Wolf Schmidt DISTRIBUTOR: Kodiak Films VIDEO: Yes

Col. Jack Knowles (Roy Scheider), Gen. Hackworth (Harry Dean Stanton). Knowles, a hero in Vietnam, has desperate troubles adjusting to peacetime.

G.I. Executioner, The (1971-1985) AKA: *Wit's End*
DIRECTOR: Joel M. Reed WRITERS: Joel M. Reed; Story by Keith Lorenz, Ian Ward EDITOR: Victor Kanefsky CAMERA: Marvin Farkas (Cineffects color) MUSIC: Elliot Chiprut, Jason Garfield PRODUCER: Marvin Farkas DISTRIBUTOR: Troma VIDEO: Yes

Dave Dearborn (Tom Keena). A Vietvet cannot escape the effects of the war and gets pulled into a spy intrigue in the Orient.

Gardens of Stone (1987)
DIRECTOR: Francis Coppola WRITERS: Ronald Bass; Novel by Nicholas Proffitt EDITOR: Barry Malkin CAMERA: Jordan Cronenweth (Deluxe color) MUSIC: Carmine Coppola PRODUCERS: Michael I. Levy, Francis Coppola DISTRIBUTOR: Tri-Star VIDEO: Yes

Hazard (James Caan), Willow (D.B. Sweeny). Hazard is deeply affected by the death of his young charge, Willow, and returns to a combat role.

Getting Straight (1970)
DIRECTOR: Richard Rush WRITERS: Robert Kaufman; Novel by Ken Kolb EDITOR: Maury Winetrobe CAMERA: Laszlo Kovacs (Eastmancolor) MUSIC: Ronald Stein PRODUCER: Richard Rush DISTRIBUTOR: Columbia VIDEO: Yes

Harry Bailey (Elliot Gould). A Vietvet fights the rules of the Establishment while trying to finish his teaching degree.

Ghettoblaster (1989)
DIRECTOR: Alan Stewart WRITER: Clay McBride EDITOR: Tony Malanowski CAMERA: Thomas Callaway (color) MUSIC: Reg Powell, Sam Winans PRODUCERS: David Decoteau, John Schouweiler DISTRIBUTOR: Prism VIDEO: Yes

Travis (Richard Hatch). Travis fights a vicious gang, the Hammers, who are threatening to take over his old neighborhood.

Gleaming the Cube (1989)
DIRECTOR: Graeme Clifford WRITER: Michael Tolkin EDITOR: John Wright CAMERA: Reed Smoot (Deluxe color) MUSIC: Jay Ferguson PRODUCERS: Lawrence Turman, David Foster DISTRIBUTOR: Twentieth Century Fox VIDEO: Yes
Colonel Trac (Le Tuan), Nick Oliver (Joe Gosha). Skateboarding kids fight Vietnam relief-fund-based conspiracy.

Glory Boy (1971) AKA: *My Old Man's Place, The Old Man's Place*
DIRECTOR: Edwin Sherin WRITERS: Stanford Whitemore; Novel, *The Old Man's Place* by John Sanford EDITOR: Ferris Webster CAMERA: Richard C. Glouner (Technicolor) MUSIC: Charles Gross (Norma Green) PRODUCER: Phillip A. Waxman DISTRIBUTOR: Cinerama VIDEO: No
Martin Flood (Mitchell Ryan), Jimmy Pilgrim (William Devane), Trubee Pell (Michael Moriarty). Vietvets visiting Pell's father's farm have to fight the murderous Flood.

Good Guys Wear Black (1978)
DIRECTOR: Ted Post WRITERS: Bruce Cohn, Mark Medoff; Story by Joseph Fraley MUSIC: Craig Safan PRODUCER: Allan F. Bodoh DISTRIBUTOR: MarVista VIDEO: Yes
John T. Booker (Chuck Norris). Booker, a college professor, has to return to his ways of action when he uncovers a conspiracy from high up in the United States government.

Gordon's War (1973)
DIRECTOR: Ossie Davis WRITERS: Howard Friedlander, Ed Spielman EDITOR: Eric Albertson CAMERA: Victor J. Kemper (Panavision, Deluxe color) MUSIC: Horace Ott PRODUCER: Robert L. Schaffel DISTRIBUTOR: Twentieth Century Fox VIDEO: Yes
Gordon (Paul Winfield), Bee (Carl Lee), Otis (David Downing), Roy (Tony King). Gordon and his army buddies reform the unit to battle the drug mobsters who are ruining their old neighborhood.

Graveyard Shift (1990)
DIRECTOR: Ralph S. Singleton WRITERS: John Esposito; Short story by Stephen King EDITORS: Jim Gross, Randy John Morgan CAMERA: Peter Stein (color) MUSIC: Anthony Marinelli, Brian Banks PRODUCERS: William J. Dunn, Ralph S. Singleton DISTRIBUTOR: Paramount VIDEO: Yes
The Exterminator (Brad Dourif). The Exterminator here has a small role amid creepy goings-on centered around an old textile mill.

Hard Ride, The (1971)
DIRECTOR: Burt Topper WRITER: Burt Topper EDITOR: Kenneth Crane CAMERA: Robert Sparks (Movielab color) MUSIC: Harley Hatcher PRODUCER: Charles Hanawalt DISTRIBUTOR: American International Pictures VIDEO: No

Phil (Robert Fuller). Phil returns with his buddy's coffin and tries to get the members of his old gang to attend the funeral, but gets caught between two gangs instead.

Hardcase and Fist (1989)
DIRECTOR: Tony Zarindast WRITERS: Bud Fleischer, Tony Zarindast; Story by Tony Zarindast EDITOR: Bill Cunningham CAMERA: Robert Hayes (Foto-Kem color) MUSIC: Tom Tucciarone, Matthew Tucciarone PRODUCER: Tony Zarindast DISTRIBUTOR: United Entertainment VIDEO: Yes

Bud McCall (Ted Prior), Tony Marino (Tony Zarindast). Marino, a hit man, gets orders to kill McCall, a cop, from his drug overlord. Marino has a change of heart when he discovers that McCall is the very person who saved his life in Vietnam.

Have a Nice Weekend (1975)
DIRECTOR: Michael Walters WRITERS: Michael Walters, John Byrum, Marsha Sheiness EDITOR: Irwin Krechaf CAMERA: Robert Ipcar (Eastmancolor) MUSIC: Charles Gross DISTRIBUTOR: Weekend Production Company VIDEO: No

Paul (M.B. Miller). Paul invites a group over to an island for a getaway, but dead bodies start appearing.

Heartbreak Ridge (1986)
DIRECTOR: Clint Eastwood WRITER: James Carabatsos EDITOR: Joel Cox CAMERA: Jack N. Green (Technicolor) MUSIC: Lennie Niehaus PRODUCER: Clint Eastwood DISTRIBUTOR: Warner Bros. VIDEO: Yes

Highway (Clint Eastwood), Choozo (Arlen Dean Synder). Highway trains raw recruits and leads them on the invasion of Grenada.

Heated Vengeance (1985)
DIRECTOR: Edward Murphy WRITER: Edward Murphy EDITOR: Richard Halsey CAMERA: Frank Johnson (Deluxe color) MUSIC: Jim Price PRODUCER: Edward Murphy DISTRIBUTOR: Fries Entertainment VIDEO: Yes

Hoffman (Richard Hatch), Bingo (Ron Max), Michelle (Jolina Mitchell-Collins), Snake (Michael J. Pollard), Tucker (Mills Watson), Jacobs (Bruce Baron). Hoffman battles Bingo, a sex-offender he reported in Vietnam, currently involved with drugs in Thailand.

Heroes (1977)
DIRECTOR: Jeremy Paul Kagan WRITER: James Carabatsos
EDITOR: Patrick Kennedy CAMERA: Frank Stanley (Technicolor)
MUSIC: Jack Nitzsche, Richard Hazard PRODUCERS: David Foster,
Lawrence Turman DISTRIBUTOR: Universal VIDEO: Yes

Jack (Henry Winkler), Ken (Harrison Ford), Peanuts (Michael
Cavanaugh), Adcock (Bennie Moore). Jack wants to get together with
his old war pals and start a worm farm, but reality intervenes.

Hi, Mom! (1970)
DIRECTOR: Brian DePalma WRITERS: Brian DePalma; Story by
Brian DePalma, Charles Hirsch EDITOR: Paul Hirsch CAMERA:
Robert Elfstrom (Eastmancolor) MUSIC: Eric Katz PRODUCER:
Charles Hirsch DISTRIBUTOR: Sigma III VIDEO: No

John Rubin (Robert DeNiro). Rubin, recently returned from the
war, goes through a series of comic adventures while trying to become
a filmmaker.

High Velocity (1977)
DIRECTOR: Remi Kramer WRITERS: Michael J. Parsons, Remi
Kramer MUSIC: Jerry Goldsmith PRODUCER: Takashi Ohashi
DISTRIBUTOR: First Asian Films of California VIDEO: Yes

Clifford Baumgartner (Ben Gazzara), Watson (Paul Winfield).
Baumgartner and Watson use their war skills to free a wealthy
businessman, but get caught in a double-cross.

Hollywood Shuffle (1987)
DIRECTOR: Robert Townsend WRITERS: Robert Townsend, Keenan
Ivory Wayans EDITOR: W.O. Garrett CAMERA: Peter Deming (color)
MUSIC: Patrice Rushen, Udi Harpaz PRODUCER: Robert Townsend
DISTRIBUTOR: Samuel Goldwyn Co.VIDEO: Yes

Rambro (Robert Townsend). Rambro appears as a black version of
the famous character in this very funny series of skits.

Home Free All (1983)
DIRECTOR: Stewart Bird WRITER: Stewart Bird EDITOR: Daniel
Lowenthal CAMERA: Robert Levi (color) MUSIC: Jay Chattaway
PRODUCERS: Stewart Bird, Peter Belsito VIDEO: Yes

Barry Simon (Allan Nicholls), Marvin (Lorry Goldman), Al
(Roland Caccavo). A radical writer looks up his old pals after his
girlfriend moves out.

Homer (1970)
DIRECTOR: John Trent WRITERS: Claude Harz; Story by Claude Harz, Matt Clark EDITOR: Michael Menne CAMERA: Lazlo George (Technicolor) MUSIC: Don Scardino PRODUCERS: Terrence Dene, Steven North DISTRIBUTOR: National General VIDEO: No
 Eddie Cochran (Tim Henry). This drama is set in a small town and has title character in conflict with Eddie.

House (1986)
DIRECTOR: Steve Miner WRITERS: Ethan Wiley; Story by Fred Dekker EDITOR: Michael N. Knue CAMERA: Mac Ahlberg (Metrocolor) MUSIC: Harry Manfredini PRODUCER: Sean S. Cunningham DISTRIBUTOR: New World VIDEO: Yes
 Cobb (William Katt), Big Ben (Richard Moll). Cobb is literally haunted by a ghost of Vietnam, the apparition of Big Ben.

In Country (1989)
DIRECTOR: Norman Jewison WRITERS: Frank Pierson, Cynthia Cidre; Novel by Bobbie Ann Mason EDITORS: Anthony Gibbs, Lou Lombardo CAMERA: Russell Boyd (Technicolor) MUSIC: James Horner PRODUCERS: Norman Jewison, Richard Roth DISTRIBUTOR: Warner Bros. VIDEO: Yes
 Emmett Smith (Bruce Willis), Pete (Stephen Tobolowsky), Earl (Jim Beaver), Tom (John Terry), Jim (Ken Jenkins). Emmett attempts to reintegrate, while his niece tries to understand the war that took her father's life.

In Dangerous Company (1987)
DIRECTOR: Ruben Preuss WRITER: Mitch Brown EDITOR: W.O. Garrett CAMERA: James Carter (Foto-Kem color) MUSIC: Berington Van Campen PRODUCERS: Ruben Preuss, Robert Newell DISTRIBUTOR: Manson VIDEO: Yes
 Blake (Cliff DeYoung), Chris (Chris Mulkey), Truong (Dana Lee). Blake, a hit man, gets involved in an art forgery scheme in this fairly taut adventure.

Initiation,The (1968)
DIRECTOR: William Wellburn WRITERS: Ron Sands, Tom Parker CAMERA: Roberto Caramico PRODUCER: Tom Parker DISTRIBUTOR: Original Films VIDEO: No
 Kelly (Rick Strausser). Kelly, in a 1960s drug-trip film, ultimately gets arrested for distributing heroin.

Iron Eagle (1986)
DIRECTOR: Sidney J. Furie WRITERS: Kevin Elders, Sidney J. Furie
EDITOR: George Grenville CAMERA: Adam Greenberg (Metrocolor)
MUSIC: Basil Poledouris PRODUCERS: Ron Samuels, Joe Wizan
DISTRIBUTOR: Tri-Star VIDEO: Yes
    Chappy (Louis Gossett Jr.). Kids band together to fly one of their
fathers out of the Middle East, and Chappy helps them.

Iron Eagle II (1988)
DIRECTOR: Sidney J. Furie WRITERS: Kevin Elders, Sidney J. Furie
EDITOR: Rit Wallis CAMERA: Alain Dostie (Bellevue Pathe color)
MUSIC: Amin Bhatia PRODUCERS: Jacob Kotzky, Sharon Harel,
John Kemeny DISTRIBUTOR: Tri-Star VIDEO: Yes
    Chappy (Louis Gossett, Jr.). Chappy leads a ragtag
Russian/American group on another bombing run.

Jacknife (1989)
DIRECTOR: David Jones WRITER: Stephen Metcalfe; Play, *Strange
Snow* by Stephen Metcalfe EDITOR: John Bloom CAMERA: Brian
West (Technicolor) MUSIC: Bruce Broughton PRODUCERS: Robert
Schaffel, Carol Baum DISTRIBUTOR: Cineplex Odeon VIDEO:Yes
    Megs (Robert DeNiro), Dave (Ed Harris), Jake (Charles Dutton).
Megs tries to help Dave overcome his guilt at being afraid during
combat.

Journey Through Rosebud (1972)
DIRECTOR: Tom Gries WRITER: Albert Ruben EDITOR: Patricia
Finn Lewis CAMERA: Minervino Rojas (Panavision, Movielab)
MUSIC: Johnny Mandel PRODUCER: David Gil DISTRIBUTOR:
GSF VIDEO: No
    Frank (Robert Forster). This drama has Frank trying to reintegrate
on a Sioux Indian reservation.

Jud (1971)
DIRECTOR: Gunther Collins WRITER: Gunther Collins EDITOR:
Gunther Collins CAMERA: Isidore Mankofsky (Movielab color)
MUSIC: Stu Phillips PRODUCER: Igo Kantor DISTRIBUTOR:
Maron VIDEO: No
    Jud Carney (Joseph Kaufman), Ben (Jo Levitt Cato). This drama is
set in a boarding house, revolving around the title character and his
attempts to readjust to life after Vietnam.

Karate Kid, The (1984)
DIRECTOR: John G. Avildsen WRITER: Robert Mark Kamen

EDITORS: Bud Smith, Walt Mulconery, John G. Avildsen CAMERA: James Crabe (Metrocolor) MUSIC: Bill Conti PRODUCER: Jerry Weintraub DISTRIBUTOR: Columbia VIDEO: Yes

Kreese (Martin Kove). Kreese plays an evil Vietvet karate teacher in the first of a series.

Karate Kid II, The (1986)
DIRECTOR: John G. Avildsen WRITER: Robert Mark Kamen; Characters by Robert Mark Kamen EDITORS: David Garfield, Jane Kurson, John G. Avildsen CAMERA: James Crabe (Deluxe color) MUSIC: Bill Conti PRODUCER: Jerry Weintraub DISTRIBUTOR: Columbia VIDEO: Yes

Kreese (Martin Kove). Kreese has a bit part as the venomous Vietvet karate teacher from the first picture in the series.

Karate Kid III, The (1989)
DIRECTOR: John G. Avildsen WRITER: Robert Mark Kamen EDITORS: John Carter, John G. Avildsen CAMERA: Stephen Yaconelli (Deluxe color) MUSIC: Bill Conti PRODUCER: Jerry Weintraub DISTRIBUTOR: Columbia VIDEO: Yes

John Kreese (Martin L. Kove), Terry Silver (Thomas Ian Griffith). Kreese and Silver conspire to ruin the karate champ of the last two pictures in this series.

Kill Squad (1982)
DIRECTOR: Patrick G. Donahue WRITER: Patrick G. Donahue EDITOR: Rick Yacco CAMERA: Christopher W. Strattan MUSIC: Joseph Conlan PRODUCERS: Michael D. Lee, Patrick G. Donahue DISTRIBUTOR: Summa Vista Pictures VIDEO: Yes

Six former Vietvets get back together to save their old commander from a bad guy trying to take over his electronics firm.

Kill Zone (1985)
DIRECTOR: David A. Prior WRITERS: David A. Prior, Jack Marino EDITOR: Victor Alexander CAMERA: Alexander (Eastmancolor) MUSIC: Robert A. Higgins PRODUCER: Jack Marino DISTRIBUTOR: Shapiro Entertainment VIDEO: Yes

McKenna (Fritz Matthews), Mitchell (Ted Prior). A war-games exercise turns to murder when the participants take it literally.

Last Rites (1988)
DIRECTOR: Donald P. Bellisario WRITER: Donald P. Bellisario EDITOR: Pembroke J. Herring CAMERA: David Watkin (Deluxe color) MUSIC: Bruce Broughton PRODUCERS: Donald P. Bellisario,

Patrick McCormick DISTRIBUTOR: MGM/UA VIDEO: Yes
    Father Freddie (Paul Dooley). Father Freddie was a chaplain in
Vietnam before the story of the film begins. A supporting part, he saw
a lot of victims of combat there.

Late Liz, The (1971)
DIRECTOR: Dick Ross WRITERS: Bill Rega; Book, Gert Behanna
EDITOR: Mike Pozen CAMERA: Harry Stradling, Jr. (Metrocolor)
MUSIC: Ralph Carmichael PRODUCER: Dick Ross DISTRIBUTOR:
Gateway Films VIDEO: Yes
    James Hatch (Steve Forrest), Peter (Bill Katt), Alan (Reid Smith).
This drama portrays three vets of different backgrounds and interests : a
doctor and two of Liz's sons.

Latino (1985)
DIRECTOR: Haskell Wexler WRITER: Haskell Wexler EDITOR:
Robert Dalva CAMERA: Tom Sigel (Du-Art color) MUSIC: Diane
Louie PRODUCER: Benjamin Berg DISTRIBUTOR: Cinecom
International VIDEO: Yes
    Eddie Guerrero (Robert Beltran), Ruben (Tony Plana). Vietvet
officers become involved with the civil war in Nicaragua.

Let's Get Harry (1987)
DIRECTOR: Alan Smithee (Stuart Rosenberg) WRITERS: Charles
Robert Carner; Story by Mark Feldberg, Samuel Fuller EDITORS:
Ralph E. Winters, Rick R. Sparr CAMERA: James A. Contner
(Metrocolor) MUSIC: Brad Fiedel PRODUCERS: Daniel H. Blatt,
Robert Singer DISTRIBUTOR: Tri-Star VIDEO: Yes
    Norman Shrike (Robert Duvall). Shrike, a Congressional Medal of
Honor winner, leads a group of novices to Central America to rescue
their kidnapped friend.

Lethal Weapon (1987)
DIRECTOR: Richard Donner WRITER: Shane Black EDITOR: Stuart
Baird CAMERA: Stephen Goldblatt (Technicolor) MUSIC: Michael
Kamen, Eric Clapton PRODUCERS: Richard Donner, Joel Silver
DISTRIBUTOR: Warner Bros. VIDEO: Yes
    Martin Riggs (Mel Gibson), Roger Murtaugh (Danny Glover),
Joshua (Gary Busey), Mike (Tom Atkins). Murtaugh has to cope with
a suicidal partner as they fight drug runners.

Lethal Weapon 2 (1989)
DIRECTOR: Richard Donner WRITERS: Jeffery Boam; Story by
Shane Black, Warren Murphy; Characters by Shane Black EDITOR:

Stuart Baird CAMERA: Stephen Goldblatt (Panavision, Technicolor)
MUSIC: Michael Kamen, Eric Clapton, David Sanborn
PRODUCERS: Richard Donner, Joel Silver, Steve Perry, Jennie Lew
Tugend DISTRIBUTOR: Warner Bros. VIDEO: Yes
    Martin Riggs (Mel Gibson), Roger Murtaugh (Danny Glover).
Riggs and Murtaugh battle South African drug smugglers.

Limbo (1972)
DIRECTOR: Mark Robson WRITERS: Joan (Micklin) Silver, James
Bridges; Story, Joan (Micklin) Silver EDITOR: Dorothy Spencer
CAMERA: Charles Wheeler (Technicolor) MUSIC: Anita Kerr
PRODUCER: Linda Gottlieb DISTRIBUTOR: Universal VIDEO: No
    Lt. Roy Lawton. A group of women try to help each other cope
with the problems that have arisen during the war.

Lively Set, The (1964)
DIRECTOR: Jack Arnold WRITERS: Mel Goldberg, William Wood;
Story by Mel Goldberg, William Alland EDITOR: Archie Marshek
CAMERA: Carl Guthrie (Eastmancolor) MUSIC: Bobby Darin
PRODUCER: William Alland DISTRIBUTOR: Universal VIDEO: No
    Casey Owens (James Darren). Owens decides to quit school in
order to try to become a race car driver.

Looking For Mr. Goodbar (1977)
DIRECTOR: Richard Brooks WRITERS: Richard Brooks; Novel by
Judith Rossner EDITOR: George Grenville CAMERA: William A.
Fraker (Panavision, Metrocolor) MUSIC: Artie Kane PRODUCER:
Freddie Fields DISTRIBUTOR: Paramount VIDEO: Yes
    Tony Lopanto (Richard Gere). Lopanto is one of the pick-ups in
this look at the late 1970s dating scene.

Magnum Force (1973)
DIRECTOR: Ted Post WRITERS: John Milius, Michael Cimino;
Story by Michael Cimino; Characters created by Harry Julian Fink,
R.M. Fink EDITOR: Ferris Webster CAMERA: Frank Stanley
(Panavision, Technicolor) MUSIC: Lalo Schifrin PRODUCER: Robert
Daley DISTRIBUTOR: Warner Bros. VIDEO: Yes
    Davis (David Soul), Sweet (Tim Matheson), Grimes (Robert
Urich), Astrachan (Kip Niven). Special Forces vets form the core of a
vigilante gang which Dirty Harry has to stop.

Malone (1987)
DIRECTOR: Harley Cokliss WRITERS: Christopher Frank; Novel,
Shotgun by William Wingate EDITOR: Todd Ramsay CAMERA:

Gerald Hirschfeld (Deluxe color) MUSIC: David Newman
PRODUCER: Leo L. Fuchs DISTRIBUTOR: Orion VIDEO: Yes
    Malone (Burt Reynolds), Barlow (Scott Wilson). The title
character helps out Barlow and his daughter as an evil developer tries to
take over their land.

Marked for Death (1990)
DIRECTOR: Dwight H. Little WRITERS: Michael Grais, Mark Victor
EDITOR: O. Nicholas Brown CAMERA: Ric Waite (Deluxe color)
MUSIC: James Newton Howard PRODUCERS: Michael Grais, Mark
Victor, Steven Seagal DISTRIBUTOR: Twentieth Century Fox
VIDEO: Yes
    Hatcher (Steven Seagal), Max (Keith David). An ex-DEA man and
old war buddy fight a Jamaican drug posse.

Masterblaster (1987)
DIRECTOR: Glenn R. Wilder WRITERS: Randy Grinter, Glenn R.
Wilder, Jeff Moldovan; Story by Randy Grinter EDITOR: Angelo Ross
CAMERA: Frank Pershing Flynn (color) MUSIC: Alain Salvati
PRODUCER: Randy Grinter DISTRIBUTOR: Artist Entertainment
Group VIDEO: Yes
    Jeremy Hawk (Jeff Moldovan). During a survival game, someone
is stalking the players with real bullets instead of red paint.

Mean Johnny Barrows (1976)
DIRECTOR: Fred Williamson WRITER: Charles Walker CAMERA:
Bob Caramico (Panavision, Movielab color) PRODUCER: Fred
Williamson DISTRIBUTOR: Atlas VIDEO: Yes
    Johnny Barrows (Fred Williamson). The title character takes on
the mob.

Mean Streets (1973)
DIRECTOR: Martin Scorsese WRITERS: Martin Scorsese, Mardik
Martin EDITOR: Sid Levin CAMERA: Kent Wakeford (Technicolor)
MUSIC: Various artists PRODUCER: Jonathan T. Taplin
DISTRIBUTOR: Warner Bros. VIDEO: Yes
    Jerry (Harry Northup). Jerry, a minor character, comes home to the
party the guys in the neighborhood throw for him and breaks down.

Ministry of Vengeance (1989)
DIRECTOR: Peter Maris WRITERS: Mervyn Emryys, Brian D.
Jeffries, Ann Narus; Story by Randal Patrick EDITOR: Michael Haight
CAMERA: Mark Morris (color) MUSIC: Scott Roewe PRODUCERS:
Brad Krevoy, Steven Stabler DISTRIBUTOR: Concorde VIDEO: Yes

David Miller (John Schneider), Freeman (James Tolkan). Miller, a minister, sees his family wiped out by terrorists and takes off after them.

Missing in Action (1984)
DIRECTOR: Joseph Zito WRITERS: James Bruner; story by John Crowther, Lance Hool EDITORS: Joel Goodman, Daniel Loewenthal CAMERA: Joao Fernandes (Metrocolor) MUSIC: Jay Chattaway PRODUCERS: Menahem Golan, Yoram Globus DISTRIBUTOR: Cannon VIDEO: Yes

Braddock (Chuck Norris), Tuck (M. Emmet Walsh). Braddock returns to Vietnam, along with the help of munitions man Tuck, to free MIAs.

Mission Kill (1987)
DIRECTOR: David Winters WRITERS: David Winters, Maria Dante EDITOR: Ned Humphreys CAMERA: Tom Denove (Deluxe color) MUSIC: Jesse Frederick, Jeff Koz PRODUCER: David Winters DISTRIBUTOR: Media Home Entertainment VIDEO: Yes

Coop (Robert Ginty), Harry (Cameron Mitchell). Coop, a demolitions expert, becomes involved with a revolution in Central America.

Mr. Majestyk (1974)
DIRECTOR: Richard Fleischer WRITER: Elmore Leonard from his novel EDITOR: Ralph E. Winters CAMERA: Richard H. Kline (Deluxe color) MUSIC: Charles Bernstein PRODUCER: Walter Mirisch DISTRIBUTOR: United Artists VIDEO: Yes

Vince Majestyk (Charles Bronson). Majestyk uses his combat skills to better a mob hit man who has it in for him.

Moon in Scorpio (1987)
DIRECTOR: Gary Graver WRITER: Robert S. Aiken EDITOR: Omer Tal CAMERA: Gary Graver (Foto-Kem color) MUSIC: Robert Ragland PRODUCER: Alan Amiel DISTRIBUTOR: Trans World VIDEO: Yes

Allen (John Phillip Law), Burt (William Smith), Mark (Louis Van Bergen). A trio of vets are plagued by memories of the war and hunted by a mysterious killer on board a yacht.

Motor Psycho (1965)
DIRECTOR: Russ Meyer WRITERS: William E. Sprauge, Russ Meyer; Story by Russ Meyer, James Griffith, Hal Hopper EDITOR: Charles G. Schelling CAMERA: Russ Meyer (black and white)

MUSIC: Igo Kantor PRODUCER: Russ Meyer DISTRIBUTOR: Eve Productions VIDEO: No

Brahmin (Stephen Oliver). A veterinarian gets revenge against a group of motorcyclists, one of whom is a deranged Vietvet, after they rape his wife.

Moving (1988)
DIRECTOR: Alan Metter WRITER: Andy Beckman EDITOR: Alan Balsalm CAMERA: Donald McAlpine (Technicolor) MUSIC: Howard Shore PRODUCER: Stuart Cornfeld DISTRIBUTOR: Warner Bros. VIDEO: Yes

Frank/Cornell Crawford (Randy Quaid). The Crawfords terrorize Arlo Pear (Richard Pryor) in this comedy about relocating.

Night Flowers (1979)
DIRECTOR: Luis San Andres WRITER: Gabriel Walsh EDITOR: Luis San Andres CAMERA: Larry Pizer MUSIC: Harry Manfredini PRODUCER: Sally Faile DISTRIBUTOR: Willow Production Company VIDEO: No

Vietnam Veterans (Jose Perez, Gabriel Walsh). Vietvets get involved in rape and murder.

Nightforce (1987)
DIRECTOR: Lawrence D. Foldes WRITERS: Lawrence D. Foldes, Russell W. Colgin, Michael Engel, Don O'Melveny; Story by Lawrence D. Foldes EDITOR: Ed Hansen CAMERA: Roy H. Wagner, Billy Dickson (Foto-Kem color) MUSIC: Nigel Harrison, Bob Rose PRODUCERS: Victoria Paige Meyerink, Lawrence D. Foldes, Russell W. Colgin, William S. Weiner DISTRIBUTOR: Vestron VIDEO: Yes

Bishop (Richard Lynch). Bishop leads a group of novices to Central America to rescue their kidnapped friend.

Ninth Configuration, The (1980)
DIRECTOR: William Peter Blatty WRITER: William Peter Blatty from his novel EDITORS: T. Battle Davis, Peter Lee-Thompson, Roberto Silvi CAMERA: Gerry Fisher (color) MUSIC: Barry DeVorzon PRODUCER: William Peter Blatty DISTRIBUTOR: Warner Bros. VIDEO: Yes

Kane (Stacy Keach), Cutshaw (Scott Wilson), Reno (Jason Miller), Fell (Ed Flanders), Groper (Neville Brand), Fairbanks (George DiCenzo), Nammack (Moses Gunn), Bennish (Robert Loggia), Spinell (Joe Spinell), Gomez (Alejandro Rey), Krebs (Tom Atkins). Kane, a disturbed Vietvet, impersonates a psychiatrist and approves radical treatment in this reworking of *Spellbound*.

No Dead Heroes (1987)
DIRECTOR: J.C. Miller WRITERS: J.C. Miller, Arthur N. Gelfield
EDITOR: Edgar Vine CAMERA: Freddie C. Grant (color) MUSIC:
Marita M. Wellman PRODUCER: J.C. Miller DISTRIBUTOR:
Cineventures VIDEO: Yes

Ric Sanders (Max Thayer), Harry Cotter (John Dresden), Baylor
(Mike Monty), General Craig (Dave Anderson). In a plot similar to
The Manchurian Candidate, a vet gets a bio-electric chip implanted in
his brain in a Russian-backed scheme to kill the Pope. Very gory.

No Mercy Man, The (1975) AKA: *Trained to Kill*
DIRECTOR: Daniel Vance WRITERS: Daniel Vance, Mike Nolin
PRODUCER: Paul Rubey Johnson VIDEO: No

Vietvet explodes when punks try to take over his town.

Norwood (1970)
DIRECTOR: Jack Haley, Jr. WRITERS: Marguerite Roberts; Novel by
Charles Portis EDITORS: Warren Low, John W. Wheeler CAMERA:
Robert B. Hauser (Technicolor) MUSIC: Al DeLory PRODUCER: Hal
B. Wallis DISTRIBUTOR: Paramount VIDEO: No

Norwood Pratt (Glen Campbell), Joe William Reese (Joe Namath),
Bill Bird (Dom De Luise). The title character travels cross-country to
get a shot singing on television, while battling his brother-in-law, Bird,
and trying to get the money back he lent Reese.

Nowhere to Hide (1987)
DIRECTOR: Mario Azzopardi WRITERS: Alex Rebar, George
Goldsmith; Story by Alex Rebar EDITOR: Rit Wallis CAMERA: Vic
Sarin (Film House color) MUSIC: Brad Fiedel PRODUCER: Andras
Hamori DISTRIBUTOR: New Century VIDEO: Yes

Rob Cutter (Daniel Hugh Kelly), Ben (Michael Ironside). Vietvets
become involved in a conspiracy to sell defective armaments.

O.C. and Stiggs (1987)
DIRECTOR: Robert Altman WRITERS: Donald Cantrell, Ted Mann;
Story by Tod Carroll, Ted Mann EDITOR: Elizabeth Kling CAMERA:
Pierre Mignot (Metrocolor) MUSIC: King Sunny Ade PRODUCERS:
Robert Altman, Peter Newman DISTRIBUTOR: Metro Goldwyn
Mayer VIDEO: Yes

Sponson (Dennis Hopper), Goon (Alan Autry). Sponson and
Goon aid O.C. and Stiggs in the quest to terrorize their neighbors in
this little-seen comedy.

Omega Syndrome (1987)
DIRECTOR: Joseph Manduke WRITER: John Sharkey EDITOR:
Stephen A. Isaacs CAMERA: Harvey Genkins (United color) MUSIC:
Nicholas Carras, Jack Cookerly PRODUCER: Luigi G. Cingolani
DISTRIBUTOR: New World Pictures VIDEO:Yes
    Jack Corbett (Ken Wahl), Phil Horton (George DiCenzo). A
reporter and old Vietvet buddy try to get back his daughter from
kidnapping neo-Nazis.

Opposing Force (1987)
DIRECTOR: Eric Karson WRITER: Gil Cowan EDITOR: Mark Conte
CAMERA: Michael A. Jones (Deluxe color) MUSIC: Marc Donohue
PRODUCERS: Daniel Jay Berk, Tamar E. Glaser DISTRIBUTOR:
Orion VIDEO: Yes
    Maj. Logan (Tom Skeritt), Becker (Anthony Zerbe), Tuan (George
Kee Chung). A military survival exercise turns deadly.

Outside In (1972)
DIRECTOR: Allen Baron WRITERS: Robert Hutchinson; Story by
Robert Hutchinson, Allen Baron CAMERA: Mario Tosi (Deluxe color)
MUSIC: Randy Edelman PRODUCER: George Edwards
DISTRIBUTOR: Harold Robbins International VIDEO: No
    Bink Schroeder (John Bill). A draft dodger comes home and gets
involved with Bink and a war resister.

Package, The (1989)
DIRECTOR: Andrew Davis WRITERS: John Bishop; Story by John
Bishop, Dennis Haggerty EDITORS: Don Zimmerman, Bill Weber
CAMERA: Frank Tidy (Astro color) MUSIC: James Newton Howard
PRODUCERS: Beverly J. Camhe, Tobie Haggerty DISTRIBUTOR:
Orion VIDEO: Yes
    Johnny Gallagher (Gene Hackman), Boyette (Tommy Lee Jones),
Milan Delich (Dennis Franz). Gallagher, a career army man, runs into
a conspiracy trying to deliver his "package," Boyette, from Germany to
the States.

Patriot, The (1986)
DIRECTOR: Frank Harris WRITERS: Andy Ruben, Katt Shea Ruben
EDITOR: Richard E. Westover CAMERA: Frank Harris (Foto-Kem
color) MUSIC: Jay Ferguson PRODUCER: Michael Bennett
DISTRIBUTOR: Crown International VIDEO: Yes
    Matt Ryder (Gregg Henry). Ryder, dishonorably discharged, fights
a band of nuclear-equipped terrorists.

Perfect Strangers (1984)
DIRECTOR: Larry Cohen WRITER: Larry Cohen EDITOR: Armond Lebowitz CAMERA: Paul Glickman (color) MUSIC: Dwight Dixon PRODUCER: Paul Kurta DISTRIBUTOR: Hemdale Pictures VIDEO: Yes

Johnny (Brad Rijn). Johnny is torn when his mob boss tells him he must kill a woman and her young son when he finds out that they witnessed one of Johnny's earlier killings.

Presidio, The (1988)
DIRECTOR: Peter Hyams WRITER: Larry Ferguson EDITOR: James Mitchell CAMERA: Peter Hyams (Panavision, Technicolor) MUSIC: Bruce Broughton PRODUCER: D. Constantine Conte DISTRIBUTOR: Paramount VIDEO: Yes

Lt. Col. Alan Caldwell (Sean Connery), St. Maj. Ross "Top" Maclure (Jack Warden). Maclure is involved with drug smuggling that leads to a murder Caldwell is determined to solve.

Private Duty Nurses (1972)
DIRECTOR: George Armitage WRITER: George Armitage EDITOR: Alan Collins CAMERA: John McNichol (color) MUSIC: Sky PRODUCER: George Armitage DISTRIBUTOR: New World VIDEO: Yes

Domino (Dennis Redfield). A Vietvet biker meets one of the title characters after a head trauma in the war.

Protector, The (1985)
DIRECTOR: James Glickenhaus WRITER: James Glickenhaus EDITOR: Evan Lottman CAMERA: Mark Irwin (Technicolor) MUSIC: Ken Thorne PRODUCER: David Chan DISTRIBUTOR: Warner Bros. VIDEO: Yes

Garoni (Danny Aiello). Garoni and title character travel to Hong Kong to fight a drug cartel.

Psycho A Go-Go! (1965) AKA: *Blood of Ghastly Horror, The Fiend with the Electric Brain, The Love Maniac, The Man with the Synthetic Brain*
DIRECTOR: Al Adamson WRITERS: Chris Martino, Mark Eden; Story by Al Adamson CAMERA: Vilmos Zsigmond (Techniscope, Technicolor) MUSIC: Don McGinnis, Billy Storm PRODUCER: Al Adamson DISTRIBUTOR: American General VIDEO: No

Joe Corey (Roy Morton). Corey, with a device implanted in his brain, goes mad and commits murder and kidnappings.

Pursuit of D.B. Cooper (1981)
DIRECTOR: Roger Spottiswoode WRITERS: Jeffrey Alan Fiskin;
Novel, *Freefall* by J.D. Reed EDITORS: Allan Jacobs, Robbe Roberts
CAMERA: Harry Stradling (Metrocolor) MUSIC: James Horner
PRODUCERS: Daniel Wigutow, Michael Taylor DISTRIBUTOR:
Universal VIDEO: Yes
     Meade (Treat Williams), Gruen (Robert Duvall). Gruen tracks
Meade, a hijacker, whom he trained to do just the kind of survival
exercises they find themselves doing.

Rambo: First Blood Part II (1985)
DIRECTOR: George Pan Cosmatos WRITERS: Sylvester Stallone,
James Cameron; Story by Kevin Jarre EDITORS: Mark Goldblatt,
Mark Helfrich CAMERA: Jack Cardiff (Panavision, Technicolor)
MUSIC: Jerry Goldsmith PRODUCER: Buzz Feitshans
DISTRIBUTOR: Tri-Star VIDEO: Yes
     John Rambo (Sylvester Stallone), Trautman (Richard Crenna).
Rambo returns to Vietnam to free American POWs.

Rambo III (1988)
DIRECTOR: Peter MacDonald WRITERS: Sylvester Stallone, Sheldon
Lettich; Characters by David Morrell EDITORS: James Symons,
Andrew London CAMERA: John Stanier (Technicolor) MUSIC: Jerry
Goldsmith PRODUCER: Buzz Feitshans DISTRIBUTOR: Tri-Star
VIDEO: Yes
     John Rambo (Sylvester Stallone), Trautman (Richard Crenna).
Rambo becomes involved in the Afghan/Russian war when Trautman is
taken prisoner by the Russians.

Ransom (1977) AKA: *Maniac!*
DIRECTOR: Richard Compton WRITERS: John C. Broderick, Ron
Silkosky; Story by John C. Broderick EDITOR: Tina Hirsch
CAMERA: Charles Correll (Metrocolor) MUSIC: Don Ellis
PRODUCERS: Patrick Ferrell, Jim Hart DISTRIBUTOR: New World
VIDEO: Yes
     Victor (Paul Koslo), Tracker (Jim Mitchum), Davey (Arch
Archambault). Vietvet Victor, disguised as an Indian, threatens to kill
people in a resort town unless paid millions. A hit man is called in to
deal with him.

Ravager, The (1970)
DIRECTOR: Charles Nizet CAMERA: Carl Johnston (Eastmancolor)
PRODUCER: Dave Ackerman DISTRIBUTOR: Manson VIDEO: No
     Joe Salkow (Pierre Gostin, Gaston). Salkow, a demolitions

expert, witnesses an atrocity in Vietnam and becomes a murderer stateside when sexually aroused.

Revenge (1990)
DIRECTOR: Tony Scott WRITERS: Jim Harrison, Jeffrey Fiskin; Novella by Jim Harrison EDITOR: Chris Lebenzon CAMERA: Jeffrey Kimball (Deluxe color) MUSIC: Jack Nitzsche PRODUCERS: Hunt Lowry, Stanley Rubin DISTRIBUTOR: Columbia VIDEO: Yes
Cochran (Kevin Costner). An ace pilot quits the service and gets involved in romantic intrigue in Mexico.

Riders of the Storm (1988, British)
DIRECTOR: Maurice Phillips WRITER: Scott Roberts EDITOR: Tony Lawson CAMERA: John Metcalfe (color) MUSIC: Brian Bennett PRODUCERS: Laurie Keller, Paul Cowan DISTRIBUTOR: Miramax VIDEO: Yes
Cap (Dennis Hopper), Doc (Michael J. Pollard), Bennedict (Al Matthews), Claude (James Aubrey), Ace (Eugene Lipinski), Sam (Derek Hoxby), Jerry (William Armstrong), Minh (Michael Ho). A group of vets in a stolen B-29 monitor the American political scene.

Rolling Thunder (1977)
DIRECTOR: John Flynn WRITERS: Paul Schrader, Heywood Gould EDITOR: Frank P. Keller CAMERA: Jordan Cronenweth (Deluxe color) MUSIC: Barry DeVorzon PRODUCER: Norman T. Herman DISTRIBUTOR: American International Pictures VIDEO: Yes
Charles Rane (William Devane), Johnny Vohden (Tommy Lee Jones). Rane and Vohden seek revenge on the gang that killed Rane's family.

Ruckus (1981) AKA: *The Loner*
DIRECTOR: Max Kleven WRITER: Max Kleven EDITOR: Angelo Bernarducci CAMERA: Don Michael Burgess (CFI color) MUSIC: Willie Nelson, Hank Cochran PRODUCER: Paul Maslansky DISTRIBUTOR: New World VIDEO: Yes
Kyle Hanson (Dirk Benedict). There is a good cast in this pre-Rambo story very similar to *First Blood*.

Russkies (1987)
DIRECTOR: Rick Rosenthal WRITERS: Alan Jay Glueckman, Sheldon Lettich, Michael Nankin; Story by Sheldon Lettich, Alan Jay Glueckman EDITOR: Antony Gibbs CAMERA: Reed Smoot (Continental color, Technicolor) MUSIC: James Newton Howard PRODUCERS:Mark Levinson, Scott Rosenfelt DISTRIBUTOR: New

Century/Vista VIDEO: Yes

Kovac (Benjamin Hendrickson). A Vietvet's son gets involved with a stranded Russian sailor.

Satan's Sadists (1969)
DIRECTOR: Al Adamson WRITER: Dennis Wayne EDITOR: Gary Graver CAMERA: Gary Graver (Deluxe color) MUSIC: Harley Hatcher PRODUCER: Al Adamson DISTRIBUTOR: Independent-International VIDEO: Yes

Johnny Martin (Gary Kent). Martin battles the title bike gang in the desert, using the combat skills he learned in Vietnam.

Savage Dawn (1985)
DIRECTOR: Simon Nuchtern WRITER: William P. Milling EDITOR: Jerry Greenberg CAMERA: Gerald Feil (Eastmancolor) PRODUCER: Gregory Earls DISTRIBUTOR: Mag Enterprises VIDEO: Yes

Ben Stryker (Lance Henriksen). A special forces vet helps out a town terrorized by bikers.

Scum of the Earth (1976) AKA: *Poor White Trash II*
DIRECTOR: S.F. Brownrigg WRITERS: Mary Davis, Gene Ross EDITOR: Brian H. Hooper CAMERA: Robert Alcott (color) MUSIC: Robert Farrar PRODUCER: S.F. Brownrigg DISTRIBUTOR: Dimension VIDEO: Yes

Jim (Hugh Feagin). A crazed Vietvet slasher murders most of a backwoods family.

Search and Destroy (1981)
DIRECTOR: William Fruet WRITER: Don Enright EDITOR: Donald Ginsberg CAMERA: Rene Verziger (Deluxe color) MUSIC: FM PRODUCER: James Margellos DISTRIBUTOR: Eabee/Film Ventures International VIDEO: Yes

Kip Moore (Perry King), Buddy Grant (Don Stroud), Assassin (Park Jong Soo). Moore battles his former Vietnamese adviser in a stateside resort town.

Skyjacked (1972)
DIRECTOR: John Guillermin WRITERS: Stanley R. Greenberg; Novel, *Hijacked* by David Harper EDITOR: Robert Swink CAMERA: Harry Stradling, Jr. (Panavision, Metrocolor) MUSIC: Perry Botkin, Jr. PRODUCER: Walter Seltzer DISTRIBUTOR: Metro Goldwyn Mayer VIDEO: No

Weber (James Brolin). A disturbed vet hijacks an airplane.

Slaughter (1972)
DIRECTOR: Jack Starrett WRITERS: Mark Hanna, Don Williams
EDITOR: Clarence C. "Renn" Reynolds CAMERA: Rosalio Solano
(Deluxe color) MUSIC: Luchi DeJesus PRODUCER: Monroe Sachson
DISTRIBUTOR: American International Pictures VIDEO: No
     Slaughter (Jim Brown). A former Green Beret battles the mob,
who killed his parents.

Slaughter's Big Rip-Off (1973)
DIRECTOR: Gordon Douglas WRITERS: Charles Johnson; Characters
by Don Williams EDITOR: Christopher Holmes CAMERA: Charles
Wheeler (Movielab color) MUSIC: James Brown, Fred Wesley
PRODUCER: Monroe Sachson DISTRIBUTOR: American
International Pictures VIDEO: No
     Slaughter (Jim Brown), Reynolds (Brock Peters). Slaughter battles
the mob again, in the second of a short series.

Soldier's Revenge (1986)
DIRECTOR: David Worth WRITERS: Lee Stull, David Worth; Story
by Eduard Sarlui EDITOR: Raja Gosnell CAMERA: Leonard Solis,
Stephen Sealy (color) MUSIC: Don Great, Gary Rist PRODUCER:
J.C. Crespo DISTRIBUTOR: Continental Motion Pictures VIDEO:
Yes
     Frank Morgan (John Savage). An antiwar vet returns home to hard
feelings, and later gets mixed up in a revolution in Central America.

Solomon King (1974)
DIRECTOR: Sal Watts, Jack Bomay WRITERS: Sal Watts; Story by
Jim Alston EDITORS: Sal Watts, Chuck Colwell CAMERA: Chuck
Colwell, Phil Caplan (CFI color) MUSIC: Jimmy Lewis
PRODUCER: Sal Watts DISTRIBUTOR: Sal-Wa, Stage Struck, Inc.
VIDEO: No
     Solomon King (Sal Watts), Maney ("Little Jamie" Watts). A
former Green Beret leads an attack against a Middle East sheik who has
murdered his old girlfriend.

Some Kind of Hero (1982)
DIRECTOR: Michael Pressman WRITERS: James Kirkwood, Robert
Boris; Novel by James Kirkwood EDITOR: Christopher Greenbury
CAMERA: King Baggot (Movielab color) MUSIC: Patrick Williams
PRODUCER: Howard W. Koch DISTRIBUTOR: Paramount VIDEO:
Yes
     Eddie Keller (Richard Pryor). Keller has troubles adjusting when
returned home and turns to crime in this comedy/drama.

Special Delivery (1976)
DIRECTOR: Paul Wendkos WRITER: Don Gazzaniga EDITOR:
Houseley Stevenson CAMERA: Harry Stradling, Jr. (Deluxe color)
MUSIC: Lalo Schifrin PRODUCER: Richard Berg DISTRIBUTOR:
American International Pictures VIDEO: Yes

Jack Murdock (Bo Svenson), Lopez (Alex Colon), Anderson (Mel
Scott), Browne (Phillip R. Allen). Murdock leads a group of vets in
this bank heist caper.

Stanley (1977)
DIRECTOR: William Grefe WRITERS: Gary Crutcher; Story by
William Grefe EDITOR: Julio Chavez CAMERA: Cliff Poland
(Deluxe color) MUSIC: Post Production Associates PRODUCER:
William Grefe DISTRIBUTOR: Crown International Pictures VIDEO:
Yes

Tim Ochopee (Chris Robinson). An unbalanced vet turns to
murder, using his pet snakes. The title character is one of his pets.

Steele Justice (1987)
DIRECTOR: Robert Boris WRITER: Robert Boris EDITORS: John
O'Connor, Steve Rosenblum CAMERA: John M. Stephens (United
color) MUSIC: Misha Segal PRODUCER: John Strong
DISTRIBUTOR: Atlantic VIDEO: Yes

John Steele (Martin Kove), Harry (Joseph Campanella), Kwan
(Soon-Teck Oh), Lee (Robert Kim). Steele battles the Vietnamese
Mafia in Southern California.

Stigma (1972)
DIRECTOR: David E. Durston WRITER: David E. Durston EDITOR:
Murray Solomon CAMERA: Robert M. Baldwin (color) MUSIC:
Jacques Urbant PRODUCER: Charles B. Moss, Jr. DISTRIBUTOR:
Cinerama VIDEO: Yes

Bill Waco (Harlan Poe). A Vietvet and young doctor try to get
people in a small island town to stop having orgies until a Typhoid
Mary-type who is spreading VD around can be identified.

Stone Killer, The (1973)
DIRECTOR: Michael Winner WRITERS: Gerald Wilson; Novel, *A
Complete State of Death* by John Gardner EDITOR: Frederick Wilson
CAMERA: Richard Moore (Technicolor) MUSIC: Roy Budd
PRODUCER: Michael Winner DISTRIBUTOR: Columbia VIDEO:
Yes

Lawrence (Stuart Margolin), Lipper (David Moody), Langley (Paul

Koslo). A renegade policeman tries to stop a paramilitary group of killers.

Street Trash (1987)
DIRECTOR: Jim Muro WRITER: Roy Frumkes EDITOR: Dennis Werner CAMERA: David Sperling (Technicolor) MUSIC: Rick Ulfik PRODUCER: Roy Frumkes DISTRIBUTOR: Chaos/Lightning VIDEO: Yes
Bronson (Vic Noto). This scatological cult film centers around a murderous Vietvet who commands a legion of junkyard bums who have discovered a case of contaminated wine.

Stunt Man, The (1980)
DIRECTOR: Richard Rush WRITERS: Lawrence B. Marcus, Richard Rush; Novel by Paul Brodeur EDITORS: Jack Hofstra, Caroline Ferriol CAMERA: Mario Tosi (Metrocolor) MUSIC: Dominic Frontiere PRODUCER: Richard Rush DISTRIBUTOR: Twentieth Century Fox VIDEO: Yes
Cameron (Steve Railsback). Cameron, on the run from the law, becomes a stunt man and has to deal with a maniacal director.

Suspect (1987)
DIRECTOR: Peter Yates WRITER: Eric Roth EDITOR: Ray Lovejoy CAMERA: Billy Williams (Technicolor) MUSIC: Michael Kamen PRODUCER: Daniel A. Sherkow DISTRIBUTOR: Tri-Star VIDEO: Yes
Carl Wayne Anderson (Liam Neeson). A deaf-mute, homeless Vietvet goes on trial for murder.

Taxi Driver (1976)
DIRECTOR: Martin Scorsese WRITER: Paul Schrader EDITORS: Marcia Lucas, Tom Rolf, Melvin Shapiro CAMERA: Michael Chapman (Panavision, Metrocolor) MUSIC: Bernard Herrmann PRODUCERS: Michael and Julia Phillips DISTRIBUTOR: Columbia VIDEO: Yes
Travis Bickle (Robert De Niro), Personnel Officer (Joe Spinell). The title character cannot take any more of the crime he sees in New York and goes on a rampage.

Texas Chainsaw Massacre Part 2, The (1986)
DIRECTOR: Tobe Hooper WRITER: L.M. Kit Carson EDITOR: Alain Jakubowicz CAMERA: Richard Kooris (TVC color) MUSIC: Tobe Hooper, Jerry Lambert PRODUCERS: Menahem Golan, Yoram Globus DISTRIBUTOR: Cannon VIDEO: Yes

Chop Top (Bill Moseley). Chop Top is one of the cannibalistic family in this, the sequel to one of the most influential horror movies of the last twenty-five years.

That Was Then, This Is Now (1985)
DIRECTOR: Christopher Cain WRITERS: Emilio Estevez; Novel by S.E. Hinton EDITOR: Ken Johnson CAMERA: Juan Ruiz-Anchia (TVC color) MUSIC: Keith Olsen, Bill Cuomo PRODUCERS: Gary R. Lindberg, John M. Ondov DISTRIBUTOR: Paramount VIDEO: Yes
    Charlie Woods (Morgan Freeman). Woods is a minor character in this youth-oriented drama about crime and friendship.

Thou Shalt Not Kill...Except (1987)
DIRECTOR: Josh Becker WRITERS: Josh Becker, Scott Spiegel; Story by Josh Becker, Sheldon Lettich, Bruce Campbell MUSIC: Joseph Lo Duca PRODUCER: Scott Spiegel DISTRIBUTOR: Filmworld VIDEO: Yes
    Jack Stryker (Brian Schulz), Miller (John Manfredi), Jackson (Robert Rickman), Tyler (Tim Quill). Stryker regroups old army buddies to save a girlfriend from the clutches of a deadly cult.

Tiger By The Tail (1970)
DIRECTOR: R.G. Springsteen WRITER: Charles A. Wallace EDITOR: Terry O. Morse CAMERA: Alan Stensvold (color) MUSIC: Joe Greene PRODUCER: Francis D. Lyon DISTRIBUTOR: Commonwealth VIDEO: No
    Steve Michaelis (Christopher George). Michaelis fights a battle over ownership of a race track in California.

To Kill a Clown (1972)
DIRECTOR: George Bloomfield WRITERS: George Bloomfield, I.C. Rapoport; Story, "Master of the Hounds," Algis Budrys EDITOR: Ralph Kemplen CAMERA: Walter Lassally (color) MUSIC: Richard Hill, John Hawkins PRODUCER: Teddy Sills DISTRIBUTOR: Twentieth Century Fox VIDEO: Yes
    Major Ritchie (Alan Alda). A Vietvet terrorizes a couple staying at his beach house.

Tom (1973)
DIRECTOR: Greydon Clark WRITERS: Greydon Clark, Alvin L. Fast EDITOR: Earl Watson, Jr. CAMERA: Louis Horvath (Eastmancolor) MUSIC: Sheldon Lee PRODUCER: Alvin L. Fast DISTRIBUTOR: Four Star International VIDEO: No
    Jim (Greydon Clark). Jim tries to reintegrate amid personal and

societal troubles, especially among the races.

Top Gun (1986)
DIRECTOR: Tony Scott WRITERS: Jim Cash, Jack Epps, Jr. EDITORS: Billy Weber, Chris Lebenzon CAMERA: Jeffrey Kimball (Metrocolor) MUSIC: Harold Faltermeyer PRODUCERS: Don Simpson, Jerry Bruckheimer DISTRIBUTOR: Paramount VIDEO: Yes
    Viper (Tom Skeritt). Viper is Maverick's (Tom Cruise) mentor, as he tells him the real story of his father and prepares him for combat.

Tough Guys Don't Dance (1987)
DIRECTOR: Norman Mailer WRITER: Norman Mailer from his novel EDITOR: Debra McDermott CAMERA: John Bailey (TVC color) MUSIC: Angelo Badalamenti PRODUCERS: Menahem Golan, Yoram Globus DISTRIBUTOR: Cannon VIDEO: Yes
    Regency (Wings Hauser). Regency is an ex-Green Beret policeman involved in a murder.

Tracks (1976)
DIRECTOR: Henry Jaglom WRITER: Henry Jaglom EDITOR: George Folsey, Jr. CAMERA: Paul Glickman (color) MUSIC: Various artists PRODUCERS: Howard Zucker, Irving Cohen, Ted Shapiro DISTRIBUTOR: Rainbow Pictures VIDEO: Yes
    Jack (Dennis Hopper). Jack, a troubled Vietvet, experiences disillusionment with his prewar ideals, and decides to bring the war back home.

Trial of Billy Jack, The (1974)
DIRECTOR: Frank Laughlin WRITERS: Frank and Teresa Christina Laughlin EDITORS: Tom Rolf, Michael Economou, George Grenville, Michael Karr Jules Wayfack CAMERA: Jack A. Marta (Panavision, Metrocolor) MUSIC: Elmer Bernstein PRODUCER: Joe Cramer DISTRIBUTOR: Taylor-Laughlin VIDEO: Yes
    Billy Jack (Tom Laughlin). Billy Jack, in the third of the series, again battles injustice and corruption.

Twilight Zone--The Movie [First Segment] (1983)
DIRECTOR: John Landis WRITER: John Landis EDITOR: Malcolm Campbell CAMERA: Steve Larner (Technicolor) MUSIC: Jerry Goldsmith PRODUCERS: Steven Spielberg, John Landis DISTRIBUTOR: Warner Bros. VIDEO: Yes
    Bill (Vic Morrow). Bill travels through time from the present day, to WWII, to Vietnam, and back.

Twilight's Last Gleaming (1977)
DIRECTOR: Robert Aldrich WRITERS: Ronald M. Cohen, Edward Huebsch; Novel, *Viper Three* by Walter Wager EDITORS: Michael Luciano, Maury Winetrobe CAMERA: Robert Hauser (Technicolor) MUSIC: Jerry Goldsmith PRODUCER: Merv Adelson DISTRIBUTOR: Allied Artists VIDEO: Yes

Lawrence Dell (Burt Lancaster), Powell (Paul Winfield). Ex-con Vietvets hold a nuclear missile, and the whole world, hostage.

Two (1974)
DIRECTOR: Charles Trieschmann WRITER: Charles Trieschmann EDITOR: David McKenna CAMERA: Vilis Lapenieks (Movielab color) MUSIC: Akiva Talmi PRODUCER: Charles Trieschmann DISTRIBUTOR: Colmar VIDEO: No

Steven (Douglas Travis). An obscure drama in which a Vietvet kidnaps a young woman. It ends in tragedy, after a bank robbery.

Two People (1973)
DIRECTOR: Robert Wise WRITER: Richard DeRoy EDITOR: William Reynolds CAMERA: Henri Decae, Gerald Hirschfeld (Technicolor) MUSIC: David Shire PRODUCER: Robert Wise DISTRIBUTOR: Universal VIDEO: No

Evan Bonner (Peter Fonda). A field deserter has a fling with a fashion model he meets on a train abroad before turning himself in.

UHF (1989)
DIRECTOR: Jay Levey WRITERS: Al Yankovic, Jay Levey EDITOR: Dennis O'Connor CAMERA: David Lewis (Alpha Cine color) MUSIC: John Du Prez PRODUCERS: Gene Kirkwood, John Hyde DISTRIBUTOR: Orion VIDEO: Yes

George Newman (Al Yankovic). Newman does a Rambo parody in one of a number of loosely connected skits.

Uncommon Valor (1983)
DIRECTOR: Ted Kotcheff WRITER: Joe Gayton EDITOR: Mark Melnick CAMERA: Stephen H. Burum (Movielab color) MUSIC: James Horner PRODUCERS: John Milius, Buzz Feitshans DISTRIBUTOR: Paramount VIDEO: Yes

Rhodes (Gene Hackman), Wilkes (Fred Ward), Sailor (Randall "Tex" Cobb), Blaster (Reb Brown), Johnson (Harold Sylvester), Charts (Tim Thomerson), Frank Rhodes (Todd Allen). Rhodes forms a fighting unit to return to Vietnam and retrieve a POW.

Under Fire (1983)
DIRECTOR: Roger Spottiswoode WRITERS: Ron Shelton, Clayton Frohman; Story by Clayton Frohman EDITOR: Mark Conte CAMERA: John Alcott (Technicolor) MUSIC: Jerry Goldsmith PRODUCER: Jonathan Taplin DISTRIBUTOR: Orion VIDEO: Yes
    Oates (Ed Harris). Oates is minor character, a mercenary now fighting in Nicaragua.

Vanishing Point (1971)
DIRECTOR: Richard C. Sarafian WRITERS: Guillermo Cain; Story by Malcolm Hart EDITOR: Stefan Arnsten CAMERA: John A. Alonzo (Deluxe color) MUSIC: Jimmy Bowen PRODUCER: Norman Spencer DISTRIBUTOR: Twentieth Century Fox VIDEO: Yes
    Kowalski (Barry Newman). A decorated vet battles himself and the Establishment in an illegal road race.

Vietnam Texas (1990)
DIRECTOR: Robert Ginty WRITERS: Tom Badal, C. Courtney Joyner EDITOR: Jonathan P. Shaw CAMERA: Robert M. Baldwin, Jr. (Deluxe color) MUSIC: Richard Stone PRODUCERS: Robert Ginty, Ron Joy DISTRIBUTOR: Epic VIDEO: Yes
    McCain (Robert Ginty), Max (Tim Thomerson). McCain, a Catholic priest, goes to Houston's Little Saigon to visit his estranged Vietnamese wife and daughter, whom he has never seen.

Vigilante Force (1976)
DIRECTOR: George Armitage WRITER: George Armitage EDITOR: Morton Tubor CAMERA: William Cronjager (Deluxe color) MUSIC: Gerald Fried PRODUCER: Gene Corman DISTRIBUTOR: United Artists VIDEO: No
    Aaron Arnold (Kris Kristofferson). A town hires a vet to clean things up and then cannot rid themselves of him.

Visitors, The (1972)
DIRECTOR: Elia Kazan WRITER: Chris Kazan EDITOR: Nick Proferes CAMERA: Nick Proferes (color) MUSIC: Bach, William Matthews PRODUCERS: Chris Kazan, Nick Proferes DISTRIBUTOR: United Artists VIDEO: No
    Bill Schmidt (James Woods), Mike Nickerson (Steve Railsback), Tony Rodriguez (Chico Martinez). Two vets "visit" the home of Schmidt, who testified against them and sent them to jail for rape.

War Birds (1989)
DIRECTOR: Ulli Lommel WRITERS: Clifford B. Wellman, Ulli

Lommel EDITOR: Joe Negron CAMERA: Deland Nuse (Foto-Kem color) MUSIC: Jerry Lambert PRODUCERS: Kurt Eggert, Joanne Watkins DISTRIBUTOR: Vidmark VIDEO: Yes

Lt. Col. Ronson (Bill Brinsfield). An obscure attempt to cash in on the success of *Top Gun*, the story concerns fliers bombing a Middle East country.

Welcome Home (1989)
DIRECTOR: Franklin J. Schaffner WRITER: Maggie Kleinman EDITOR: Bob Swink CAMERA: Fred J. Koenekamp (Eastmancolor) PRODUCER: Martin Ransohoff DISTRIBUTOR: Columbia VIDEO: Yes

Lt. Jake Robbins (Kris Kristofferson). Robbins is an Air Force POW who cannot fit in when he returns home years after the war.

Welcome Home, Soldier Boys (1972)
DIRECTOR: Richard Compton WRITER: Guerdon Trueblood EDITOR: Patrick Kennedy CAMERA: Don Birnkrant (Deluxe color) MUSIC: Ken Wannberg, Ronee Blakely, The Country Gazette PRODUCER: Marvin Schwartz DISTRIBUTOR: Twentieth Century Fox VIDEO: No

Danny (Joe Don Baker), Shooter (Paul Koslo), Kid (Alan Vint), Fatback (Elliot Street). A grim, depressing study of a group of vets who get easily fed up with what society has to offer them upon their return, and level a whole town.

Whatever It Takes (1986)
DIRECTOR: Bob Demchuck WRITERS: Chris Weatherhead, Bob Demchuck EDITOR: Bob Demchuck CAMERA: John Drake MUSIC: Garry Sherman PRODUCERS: Bob Demchuck, Walter J. Scherr DISTRIBUTOR: Aquarius Films VIDEO: No

Jeff Perchick (Tom Mason). A cabdriving Vietvet helps out at his dad's diner, and dreams of being a cartoonist.

When You Comin Back, Red Ryder? (1979)
DIRECTOR: Milton Katselas WRITER: Mark Medoff from his play EDITOR: Richard Chew CAMERA: Jules Brenner (color) MUSIC: Jack Nitzsche PRODUCER: Marjoe Gortner DISTRIBUTOR: Columbia VIDEO: No

Teddy (Marjoe Gortner). Teddy, a drug-dealing Vietvet, terrorizes a group of people trapped in a diner.

White Ghost (1988)
DIRECTOR: B.J. Davis WRITER: Gary Thompson EDITOR: Ettie

Feldman CAMERA: Hans Kuhle (Kodak color) MUSIC: Parmer Fuller PRODUCERS: Jay Davidson, William Fay DISTRIBUTOR: Gibraltar VIDEO: Yes

Steve Shepard (William Katt), Walker (Wayne Crawford) A Vietvet in white makeup stays in Vietnam and keeps up the fight. Some other vets are sent over to take him out.

White Line Fever (1975)
DIRECTOR: Jonathan Kaplan WRITERS: Ken Friedman, Jonathan Kaplan EDITOR: O. Nicholas Brown CAMERA: Fred Koenekamp (Metrocolor) MUSIC: David Nichtern PRODUCER: John Kemeny DISTRIBUTOR: Columbia VIDEO: Yes

Hummer (Jan Michael Vincent). Hummer, an Air Force hero, will not buckle under to corruption in the trucking industry.

Who'll Stop the Rain? (1978)
DIRECTOR: Karel Reisz WRITERS: Judith Rascoe, Robert Stone; Novel, *Dog Soldiers* by Robert Stone EDITOR: John Bloom CAMERA: Richard H. Kline (Technicolor) MUSIC: Laurence Rosenthal PRODUCERS: Herb Jaffe, Gabriel Katzka DISTRIBUTOR: United Artists VIDEO: Yes

Ray (Nick Nolte). Ray gets involved in drug smuggling which leads to deadly complications for all involved.

Wild at Heart (1990)
DIRECTOR: David Lynch WRITERS: David Lynch; Novel by Barry Gifford EDITOR: Duwayne Dunham CAMERA: Frederick Elmes (color) MUSIC: Angelo Badalamenti PRODUCERS: Monty Montgomery, Steve Golin, Sigurjon Sighvatsson DISTRIBUTOR: Samuel Goldwyn Co. VIDEO: Yes

Bobby Peru (Willem Dafoe). Weird goings-on on a trip from Cape Fear to New Orleans to Big Tuna, Texas, and back to Cape Fear.

Wild Life, The (1984)
DIRECTOR: Art Linson WRITER: Cameron Crowe EDITOR: Michael Jablow CAMERA: James Glennon (Technicolor) MUSIC: Edward Van Halen, Donn Landee PRODUCERS: Art Linson, Cameron Crowe DISTRIBUTOR: Universal VIDEO: Yes

Charlie (Randy Quaid). Charlie is the object of obsession of a high school underclassman, who finds out from him that war is not all G.I. Joe and Rambo.

Woman Inside, The (1981)
DIRECTOR: Joseph Van Winkle WRITER: Joseph Van Winkle

EDITOR: John Duffy CAMERA: Ron Johnson (CFI color) MUSIC: Eddy Lawrence Manson PRODUCER: Sidney H. Levine DISTRIBUTOR: Twentieth Century Fox VIDEO: Yes

Hollis/Holly (Gloria Manon). A wounded Vietvet starts cross-dressing and has a sex-change operation.

Year of the Dragon (1985)
DIRECTOR: Michael Cimino WRITERS: Oliver Stone, Michael Cimino; Novel by Robert Daley EDITOR: Francoise Bonnot CAMERA: Alex Thomson (Technicolor) MUSIC: David Mansfield PRODUCER: Dino DeLaurentiis DISTRIBUTOR: MGM/UA VIDEO: Yes

Stanley White (Mickey Rourke). White, a policeman, battles with the Chinese Mafia.

Youngblood (1978)
DIRECTOR: Noel Nosseck WRITER: Paul Carter Harrison EDITOR: Frank Morriss CAMERA: Robbie Greenberg (CFI color) MUSIC: War PRODUCERS: Nick Grillo, Alan Riche DISTRIBUTOR: American International Pictures VIDEO: No

Rommel (Lawrence-Hilton Jacobs). Rommel uses his combat training on the streets of L.A. to wipe out a drug gang.

Willem Dafoe (smoking) in *Wild at Heart*.

A Vietnam War Filmography

This filmography contains the year of release and the major credits for films set in Vietnam during the Vietnam War.

Apocalypse Now (1979)
DIRECTOR: Francis Coppola WRITERS: John Milius, Francis Coppola EDITOR: Barry Malkin CAMERA: Vittorio Storaro (Technicolor) MUSIC: Carmine and Francis Coppola PRODUCER: Francis Coppola DISTRIBUTOR: United Artists VIDEO: Yes

Bat 21 (1988)
DIRECTOR: Peter Markle WRITERS: William C. Anderson, George Gordon; Book by William C. Anderson EDITOR: Stephen E. Rivkin CAMERA: Mark Irwin (Deluxe color) MUSIC: Christopher Young PRODUCERS: David Fisher, Gary A. Neill, Michael Balson DISTRIBUTOR: Tri-Star VIDEO: Yes

Boys in Company C, The (1978)
DIRECTOR: Sidney J. Furie WRITER: Rick Natkin EDITOR: Michael Berman CAMERA: Godfrey A. Godar (Technicolor) MUSIC: Jamie Mendoza-Nava PRODUCER: Andre Morgan DISTRIBUTOR: Columbia VIDEO: Yes

Clay Pigeon (1971)
DIRECTOR: Tom Stern, Lane Slate WRITERS: Ronald Buck, Buddy Ruskin, Jack Gross Jr.; Story by Buddy Ruskin, Jack Gross, Jr. EDITOR: Danford Greene CAMERA: Alan Stensvold (Metrocolor) MUSIC: Gavin Murrell PRODUCERS: Tom Stern, Lane Slate DISTRIBUTOR: Metro Goldwyn Mayer VIDEO: No

Don't Cry, It's Only Thunder (1982)
DIRECTOR: Peter Werner WRITER: Paul Hensler EDITORS: Jack Woods, Barbara Pokras CAMERA: Don McAlpine (Deluxe Color) MUSIC: Maurice Jarre PRODUCER: Walt deFarla DISTRIBUTOR: Sanrio Cinema VIDEO: Yes

84 Charlie Mopic (1989)
DIRECTOR: Patrick Duncan WRITER: Patrick Duncan EDITOR: Stephen Purvis CAMERA: Alan Caso (Du-Art color) MUSIC: Donovan PRODUCER: Michael Nolin DISTRIBUTOR: New Century-Vista VIDEO:Yes

Flight of the Intruder (1991)
DIRECTOR: John Milius WRITERS: Robert Dillon, David Shaber; Novel by Stephen Coonts EDITOR: C. Timothy O'Meara CAMERA: Fred J. Koenekamp (color) MUSIC: Basil Poledouris PRODUCER: Mace Neufeld DISTRIBUTOR: Paramount VIDEO: Yes

Full Metal Jacket (1987)
DIRECTOR: Stanley Kubrick WRITERS: Stanley Kubrick, Michael Herr, Gustav Hasford; Novel, *The Short-Timers* by Gustav Hasford EDITOR: Martin Hunter CAMERA: Douglas Milsome (Rank color) MUSIC: Abigail Mead PRODUCER: Stanley Kubrick DISTRIBUTOR: Warner Bros. VIDEO: Yes

Go Tell the Spartans (1978)
DIRECTOR: Ted Post WRITERS: Wendell Mayes; Novel, *Incident at Muc Wa* by Daniel Ford EDITOR: Millie Moore CAMERA: Harry Stradling, Jr. (CFI color) MUSIC: Dick Halligan PRODUCERS: Alan F. Bodoh, Mitchell Cannold DISTRIBUTOR: Avco Embassy VIDEO: Yes

Good Morning, Vietnam (1987)
DIRECTOR: Barry Levinson WRITER: Mitch Markowitz EDITOR: Stu Linder CAMERA: Peter Sova (Deluxe color) MUSIC: Alex North PRODUCERS: Mark Johnson, Larry Brezner DISTRIBUTOR: Buena Vista VIDEO: Yes

Green Berets, The (1968)
DIRECTORS: John Wayne, Ray Kellog WRITERS: James Lee Barrett; Novel by Robin Moore EDITOR: Otho Lovering CAMERA: Winton C. Hoch (Technicolor) MUSIC: Miklos Rozsa PRODUCER: Michael Wayne DISTRIBUTOR: Warner Bros. VIDEO: Yes

Greetings! (1968)
DIRECTOR: Brian DePalma WRITERS: Charles Hirsch, Brian DePalma EDITOR: Brian DePalma CAMERA: Robert Fiore (Eastmancolor) MUSIC: The Children of Paradise PRODUCER: Charles Hirsch DISTRIBUTOR: Sigma III VIDEO: Yes

Hamburger Hill (1987)
DIRECTOR: John Irvin WRITER: Jim Carabatsos EDITOR: Peter Tanner CAMERA: Peter MacDonald (Rank color) MUSIC: Philip Glass PRODUCERS: Marcia Nasatir, Jim Carabatsos DISTRIBUTOR: Paramount VIDEO: Yes

Hanoi Hilton, The (1986)
DIRECTOR: Lionel Chetwynd WRITER: Lionel Chetwynd EDITOR: Penelope Shaw CAMERA: Mark Irwin MUSIC: Jimmy Webb PRODUCERS: Menahem Golan, Yoram Globus DISTRIBUTOR: Cannon VIDEO: Yes

Iron Triangle, The (1989)
DIRECTOR: Eric Weston WRITERS: Eric Weston, John Bushelman, Larry Hilbrand, Marshall Drazen EDITOR: Roy Watts CAMERA: Irv Goodnoff (Metrocolor) MUSIC: Michael Lloyd, John D'Andrea, Nick Strimple PRODUCERS: Tony Scotti, Angela P. Shapiro DISTRIBUTOR: Scotti Brothers VIDEO: Yes

Jacob's Ladder (1990)
DIRECTOR: Adrian Lyne WRITER: Bruce Joel Rubin EDITOR: Tom Rolf CAMERA: Jeffrey L. Kimball (Technicolor) MUSIC: Maurice Jarre PRODUCER: Alan Marshall DISTRIBUTOR: Tri-Star VIDEO: Yes

Last Message from Saigon (1965) AKA *Operation C.I.A.*
DIRECTOR: Christian Nyby WRITERS: Bill Balinger, Peer J. Oppenheimer EDITORS: Joseph Gluck, George Watters CAMERA: Richard Moore (black and white) MUSIC: Paul Dunlap PRODUCER: Peer J. Oppenheimer DISTRIBUTOR: Allied Artists VIDEO: Yes

Losers, The (1970)
DIRECTOR: Jack Starrett WRITER: Alan Caillou EDITORS: James Moore, Richard Brockway CAMERA: Nonong Rasca (Eastmancolor) MUSIC: Stu Phillips PRODUCER: Joe Solomon DISTRIBUTOR: Metro Goldwyn Mayer VIDEO: No

Missing in Action 2--The Beginning (1985)
DIRECTOR: Lance Hool WRITERS: Arthur Silver, Larry Levinson, Steve Bing EDITORS: Mark Conte, Marcus Manton CAMERA: Jorge Stahl, Jr. (TVC color) MUSIC: Brian May PRODUCERS: Menahem Golan, Yoram Globus DISTRIBUTOR: Cannon VIDEO: Yes

More American Graffiti (1979)
DIRECTOR: B.W.L. Norton WRITERS: B.W.L. Norton; Characters
by George Lucas, Gloria Katz, Willard Hyuck EDITOR: Tina Hirsch
CAMERA: Caleb Deschanel (Technicolor) MUSIC: Various artists
PRODUCER: Howard Kazanjian DISTRIBUTOR: Universal VIDEO:
No

Night Wars (1988)
DIRECTOR: David A. Prior WRITERS: David A. Prior; Story by
David A. Prior, Ted Prior, William Zipp EDITOR: Reinhard Schreiner
CAMERA: Stephen Ashley Blake (United color) MUSIC: Tim James,
Steve McClintock, Mark Mancina PRODUCER: Fritz Matthews
DISTRIBUTOR: SVS Films VIDEO: Yes

Off Limits (1988)
DIRECTOR: Christopher Crowe WRITERS: Christopher Crowe, Jack
Thibeau EDITOR: Douglas Ibold CAMERA: David Gribble (Deluxe
color) MUSIC: James Newton Howard PRODUCER: Alan Barnette
DISTRIBUTOR: Twentieth Century Fox VIDEO: Yes

P.O.W.: The Escape (1986)
DIRECTOR: Gideon Amir WRITERS: Jeremy Lipp, James Bruner,
Malcolm Barbour, John Langley; Story by Avi Kleinberger, Gideon
Amir EDITOR: Marcus Manton CAMERA: Yechiel Ne'eman (TVC
color) MUSIC: Michael Linn PRODUCERS: Menahem Golan, Yoram
Globus DISTRIBUTOR: Cannon VIDEO: Yes

Platoon (1986)
DIRECTOR: Oliver Stone WRITER: Oliver Stone EDITOR: Claire
Simpson CAMERA: Robert Richardson (CFI color) MUSIC: Georges
Delerue PRODUCER: Arnold Kopelson DISTRIBUTOR: Orion
VIDEO: Yes

Platoon Leader (1988)
DIRECTOR: Aaron Norris WRITERS: Rick Marx, Andrew Deutsch,
David Walker; Book by James R. McDonough EDITOR: Michael J.
Duthie CAMERA: Arthur Wooster (Rank color) MUSIC: George S.
Clinton PRODUCER: Harry Alan Towers DISTRIBUTOR: Cannon
VIDEO: Yes

Purple Hearts (1984)
DIRECTOR: Sidney J. Furie WRITERS: Rick Natkin, Sidney J. Furie
EDITOR: George Grenville CAMERA: Jan Kiesser (Panavision,
Technicolor) MUSIC: Robert Folk PRODUCER: Sidney J. Furie

DISTRIBUTOR: Warner Bros. VIDEO: Yes

There Is No 13 (1974)
DIRECTOR: William Sachs WRITER: William Sachs EDITOR:
George T. Norris CAMERA: Ralph Bode (Eastmancolor) MUSIC: Riz
Ortolani PRODUCER: Robert Boggs DISTRIBUTOR: Unset VIDEO:
No

To the Shores of Hell (1966)
DIRECTOR: Will Zens WRITERS: Robert McFadden, Will Zens
CAMERA: Leif Rise (Technicolor) EDITOR: Michael David MUSIC:
William Schaefer PRODUCER: Will Zens DISTRIBUTOR: Crown
International VIDEO: No

A battle scene in *Full Metal Jacket*.

Bibliography

Secondary literature on the films
Adair, Gilbert. *Hollywood's Vietnam: From the Green Berets to Apocalypse Now.* London: Proteus, 1981.

Auster, Al and Quart, Leonard. "Hollywood and Vietnam: The Triumph of the Will." *Cineaste*, Spring 1979, pp. 4-9.

Axeen, D.; Dempsey, M.; Kinder, M.; and Callenbach, E. "Four Shots at *The Deer Hunter*." *Film Quarterly*, Summer 1979, pp. 10-22.

Berg, Rick. "Losing Vietnam: Covering the War in an Age of Technology." *Cultural Critique*, Fall 1985, pp. 92-125.

Canby, Richard. "Review of *The Crazies*." *The New York Times.* 24 March 1973, sec. 1, p. 20.

Corliss, Richard. "Guns and Buttered Popcorn: Vietnam Movies." *New Times*, 20 March 1978, pp. 65-68.

Dempsey, Michael. "Hellbent for Mystery." *Film Quarterly*, Summer 1979, pp. 10-13.

Dickstein, Morris. "Bringing It All Back Home." *Partisan Review*, Winter 1978, pp. 627-33.

Fore, Steve. "Kuntzel's Law and *Uncommon Valor*, Or Reshaping the National Consciousness in Six Minutes Flat." *WideAngle*, Winter 1985, pp. 23-32.

Felker, Mike. "Vietnam Again: *Platoon* and *Full Metal Jacket*." *Jump Cut*, February 1988, pp. 28-30.

Freedman, Samuel G. "The War and the Arts." *The New York Times Magazine*, 31 March 1985, pp. 50-55.

Galperin, William. "History into Allegory: *The Wild Bunch* as

Vietnam Movie." *Western Humanities Review,* Summer 1981, pp. 165-72.

Gelman, D. "Vietnam Marches Home." *Newsweek*, 13 February 1978, pp. 85-86.

Jeffords, Susan. "Friendly Civilians: Images of Women and the Feminization of the Audience in Vietnam Films." *WideAngle*, Winter 1985, pp. 13-22.

Just, W.S. "Vietnam: The Camera Lies." *The Atlantic*, October 1979, pp. 63-65.

Kauffmann, Stanley. "Hunting of the Hunters: Vietnam." *The New Republic*, 26 May 1979, pp. 22-23.

_____. "Tell the Real Lies: Films about Vietnam." *The New Republic*, 2 March 1968, p. 26.

Kilday, G. "Rambo's Children." *Esquire*, October 1985, pp. 122-23.

Maloff, Saul. "Vietnam Mon Amour." *Commonweal*, 3 February 1978, pp. 84-87.

Marin, Peter. "Coming to Terms with Vietnam." *Harper's*, December 1980, pp. 41-56.

McConnell, Frank. "A Name for Loss: Memorials of Vietnam." *Commonweal*, 9 August 1985, pp. 441-42.

McInerney, Peter. "Apocalypse Then: Hollywood Looks at Vietnam." *Film Quarterly*, Winter 1979-80, pp. 21-32.

Michaels, W.B. "Road to Vietnam." *MLN*, December 1979, pp. 1173-75.

Morrow, L. "Vietnam Comes Home: *Coming Home* and *The Deer Hunter*." *Time*, 23 April 1979, pp. 22-24.

Norman, Michael. "*Platoon* Grapples with Vietnam." *The New York Times*, 21 December 1986, sec. 3, pp. 17-18.

Palmer, William J. "The Vietnam War Films." *Film Library Quarterly*, Winter 1980, pp. 4-14.

Pym, John. "A Bullet in the Head: Vietnam Remembered." *Sight and Sound*, Spring 1979, pp. 82-84.

Rickey, Carrie. "It's a Birdbrain, It's a Plane, It's...Supervet!" *The Village Voice*, 25 November 1981, p. 52.

Saltzman, Arthur M. "The Betrayal of the Imagination: Paul Brodeur's *The Stunt Man* and Tim O'Brien's *Going After Cacciato*." *Critique*, Spring 1980, pp. 32-38.

Sayre, N. "At War in the Movies." *The Progressive*, February 1980, pp. 51-54.

Siskel, Gene. "Candidly Kubrick: A Private Man Talks Openly about Life, Movies and the Fate of the Free World." *The Chicago Tribune*, 21 June 1987, sec. 13, pp. 4-23.

_____. "A Test for Platoon: Battle Vets Say the Film Lacks Only the Taste and the Smell of Death." *The Chicago Tribune*, 4 January 1987, sec. 13, pp. 4-5.

Smith, Julian. "Between Vermont and Violence: Film Portraits of Vietnam Veterans." *Film Quarterly*, Summer 1973, pp. 10-17.

_____. *Looking Away: Hollywood and Vietnam.* New York: Scribner's, 1975.

_____. "Looking Away: Hollywood and Vietnam." *The Progressive*, October 1975, pp. 58-59.

Suid, Lawrence. "Hollywood and Vietnam." *Film Comment*, September 1979, pp. 20-25.

Tuchman, Mitch. "Celluloid Vietnam." *The New Republic*, 31 May 1975, pp. 28-30.

Turner, R. "Worst Years of Our Lives: Vietnam Movies." *New Times*, 20 March 1978, pp. 54-84.

Wilson, James C. *Vietnam in Prose and Film.* Jefferson, NC: McFarland & Company, 1982.

Wood, Michael. "Bangs and Whimpers." *The New York Review of Books*, 11 October 1979, pp. 17-18.

Yakir, Dan, and Romero, George A. "Morning Becomes Romero."
Film Comment, May/June, 1979, p. 64.

Zoglin, Richard. "An Outbreak of Rambomania." *Time*, 24 June
1985, pp. 72-73.

Personal narratives
Baker, Mark. *Nam*. New York: William Morrow, 1981.

Downs, Frederick. *The Killing Zone: My Life in the Vietnam War*.
New York: W.W. Norton, 1978.

Edelman, Bernard, ed. *Dear America: Letters Home from Vietnam*.
New York: Norton, 1985.

Emerson, Gloria. *Winners and Losers*. New York: Penguin, 1985.

Goldman, Peter and Fuller, Tony. *Charlie Company: What Vietnam
Did to Us*. New York: William Morrow, 1983

Herr, Michael. *Dispatches*. New York: Alfred A. Knopf, 1977.

Lewis, Lloyd B. *The Tainted War: Culture and Identity in Vietnam
War Narratives*. Westport, CT: Greenwood, 1985.

Santoli, Al. *Everything We Had: An Oral History of the Vietnam War*.
New York: Ballantine, 1981.

Social film histories
Braudy, Leo. *The World in a Frame: What We See In Films*. Garden
City, NY: Anchor Press/Doubleday, 1977.

Cavell, Stanley. *The World Viewed: Reflections on the Ontology of
Film*. New York: Viking, 1971.

Jarvie, I.C. *Movies as Social Criticism: Aspects of Their Social
Psychology*. Metuchen, NJ: Scarecrow Press, 1978.

Sklar, Robert. *Movie-Made America: A Cultural History of American
Movies*. New York: Random House, 1975.

Thomson, David. *America in the Dark: The Impact of Hollywood
Films on American Culture*. New York: William Morrow, 1977.

_____. *Overexposures: The Crisis in American Filmmaking*. New York: William Morrow, 1981.

Wood, Michael. *America in the Movies: Or, "Santa Maria, It Had Slipped My Mind!"* New York: Basic Books, 1975; reprint ed., New York: Dell, 1978.

Critical literature on genre, genre film, myth, and system
Basinger, Jeanine. *The World War II Combat Film: Anatomy of a Genre*. New York: Columbia University Press, 1986.

Biro, Yvette. *Profane Mythology: The Savage Mind of the Cinema*. Bloomington: Indiana University Press, 1982.

Borget, Jean-Loup. "Social Implications in Hollywood Genres." *Journal of Modern Literature*, April 1973, pp. 199-200.

Brownlow, Kevin. *The War, the West, and the Wilderness*. New York: Alfred A. Knopf, 1979.

Campbell, Joseph, with Moyers, Bill. *The Power of Myth*. New York: Doubleday, 1988.

Cawelti, John G. *Adventure, Mystery, and Romance*. Chicago: University of Chicago Press, 1976.

_____. *The Six-Gun Mystique*. Bowling Green, OH: Bowling Green University Popular Press, 1970.

Cripps, Thomas. *Black Film as Genre*. London and Bloomington: Indiana University Press, 1978.

Derry, Charles. *Dark Dreams: The Horror Film from "Psycho" to "Jaws."* South Brunswick, NJ, and New York: A.S. Barnes and Company, 1977.

_____. "More Dark Dreams." *American Horrors: Essays on the Modern American Horror Film*. Gregory A. Waller, ed. Urbana and Chicago: University of Illinois Press, 1987.

Grant, Barry Keith, ed. *Film Genre Reader*. Austin: University of Texas Press, 1986.

Hellman, John. *American Myth and the Legacy of Vietnam*. New

York: Columbia University Press, 1986.

Kagan, Norman. *The War Film.* New York: Jove, 1974.

Kaminsky, Stuart M. *American Film Genres.* 2nd ed. Chicago: Nelson-Hall, 1985.

Laszlo, Ervin. *The Systems View of the World.* New York: George Braziller, 1972.

McNeill, William Hardy. *Mythistory and Other Essays.* Chicago: University of Chicago Press, 1986.

Neale, Stephen. *Genre.* London: British Film Institute, 1980.

Perlmutter, Tom. *War Movies.* London: Hamlyn, 1974.

Rubin, Steven Jay. *Combat Films: American Realism, 1945-1970.* Jefferson, NC: McFarland, 1981.

Schatz, Thomas. *Hollywood Genres: Formulas, Filmmaking, and the Studio System.* Philadelphia: Temple University Press, 1981.

_____. "The Structural Influence: New Directions in Film Genre Study." *Quarterly Review of Film Studies,* August 1977, pp. 302-12.

Shindler, Colin. *Hollywood Goes to War: Films and American Society, 1939-1982.* London: Routledge & K. Paul, 1979.

Siska, William. "Modernism in the Narrative Cinema: The Art Film as a Genre." Ph.D. Diss., Northwestern University, 1976.

Slotkin, Richard. *Regeneration Through Violence: The Mythology of the American Frontier, 1600-1860.* Middletown, CT: Wesleyan University Press, 1973.

Suid, Lawrence H. *Guts and Glory: Great American War Movies.* Reading, MA: Addison-Wesley, 1978.

Todorov, Tzvetan. Trans. Richard Howard. *The Fantastic: A Structural Approach to a Literary Genre.* Ithaca, NY: Cornell University Press, 1975.

Wood, Robin. "Ideology, Genre, Auteur." *Film Comment*, January/February 1977, pp. 46-51.

Works on film history and the film industry

Allen, Robert C. , and Gomery, Douglas. *Film History: Theory and Practice*. New York: Alfred A. Knopf, 1985.

Dunne, John Gregory. *The Studio*. New York: Limelight Editions, 1985.

Gertner, Richard. *The International Motion Picture Almanac*. New York: Quigley Publishing, 1982-1990.

Gomery, Douglas. *The Hollywood Studio System*. London: British Film Institute, 1986.

Kratsus, Richard, ed. *The American Film Institute Catalogue of Motion Pictures, Feature Films 1961-1970*. New York and London: R.R. Bowker, 1976.

Litwak, Mark. *Reel Power: The Struggle for Influence and Success in the New Hollywood*. New York: William Morrow, 1986.

McGee, Mark Thomas. *Fast and Furious: The Story of American International Pictures*. Jefferson, NC, and London: McFarland, 1984.

Nash, Jay Robert, and Ross, Stanley Ralph. *The Motion Picture Guide*. Chicago: Cinebooks, Inc., 1986-1990.

Parris, Michael "The American Film Industry and Vietnam." *History Today*, April 1987, pp. 19-26.

Premiere magazine, 1987-1991.

Variety Film Reviews, vols. 10-19. New York and London: Garland Publishing, 1983-1988.

Willis, John. *Screen World*, vols. 35-38. New York: Crown Publishers.

Historical works on the Vietnam veteran

Bonior, David E.; Champlin, Steven M.; and Kelly, Timothy S. *The Vietnam Veteran: A History of Neglect*. New York: Praeger, 1986.

Boulanger, Ghislaine, and Kadushin, Charles, eds. *The VietnamVeteran Redefined: Fact and Fiction.* Hillsdale, NJ: Erlbaum,1986.

Brende, Joel Osler. *Vietnam Veterans: The Road to Recovery.* New York: Plenum, 1985.

Carroll, Edward M.; Rueger, Drue Barrett; Foy, David W.; and Donahoe, Clyde P., Jr. "Vietnam Combat Veterans with Post-traumatic Stress Disorder: Analysis of Martial and Cohabitating Adjustment." *Journal of Abnormal Psychology*, Fall 1985, pp. 329-337.

Helmer, John. *Bringing the War Back Home: The American Soldier in Vietnam and After.* New York: Free Press, 1986.

Hendin, Herbert, and Haas, Ann Pollinger. *Wounds of War: The Psychological Aftermath of Combat in Vietnam.* New York: Basic Books, 1984.

Keane, Terence M.; Scott, Owen W.; Chavoya, Gary A.; Lamparski, Danuta M.; and Fairbank, John A. "Social Support in Vietnam Veterans with Post-traumatic Stress Disorder: A Comparative Analysis." *Journal of Consulting and Clinical Psychology*, Winter 1985, pp. 95-102.

Klein, Joe. *Payback: Five Marines after Vietnam.* New York: Alfred A. Knopf, 1984.

Kolb, Lawrence C. "Post-Traumatic Stress Disorder in Vietnam Veterans." *The New England Journal of Medicine*, March 1986, pp. 641-42.

Lifton, Robert Jay. *Home from the War: Vietnam Veterans--Neither Victims nor Executioners.* New York: Basic Books, 1985.

Myths and Realities: A Study of Attitudes Toward Vietnam Era Veterans. Washington, DC: U.S. Government Printing Office, 1980.

Patterson, Oscar, III. "Analysis of Coverage of the Vietnam Veteran." *Journalism Quarterly*, Summer 1982, pp. 308-10.

Wheeler, John. *Touched with Fire: The Future of the Vietnam Generation.* New York: Franklin Watts, 1984; reprint ed., New

York: Avon, 1985.

Fiction

Blatty, William Peter. *The Ninth Configuration*. New York: Harper & Row, 1978.

_____. *Twinkle, Twinkle, "Killer" Kane*. Garden City, NY: Doubleday, 1966.

Brodeur, Paul. *The Stunt Man*. New York: Atheneum, 1970.

Caputo, Phillip. *DelCorso's Gallery*. New York: Holt, Rinehart, and Winston, 1983; reprint ed., New York: Dell, 1984.

Daley, Robert. *Year of the Dragon*. New York: Simon and Schuster, 1981; reprint ed., New York: Signet, 1982.

Diehl, William. *Hooligans*. New York: Villard, 1984.

Fitzgerald, F.Scott. *The Last Tycoon*. New York: Charles Scribner's Sons, 1941.

Ford, Daniel. *Incident at Muc Wa*. New York: Doubleday, 1967.

Freemantle, Brian. *The Vietnam Legacy*. New York: Tor, 1984.

Gosling, Paula. *Fair Game*. New York: Coward, McCann & Geoghegan, 1978.

Hasford, Gustav. *The Short-Timers*, rev. ed. New York: Bantam, 1983.

Hastings, Michael. *The Unknown Soldier*. New York: Ballantine, 1987.

Heinemann, Larry. *Paco's Story*. New York: Penguin, 1987.

Hinton, S.E. *That Was Then, This Is Now*. New York: Dell, 1971.

Jenks, Tom, ed. *Soldiers and Civilians: Americans at War and at Home*. New York: Bantam Books, 1986.

Kennedy, Adam. *The Domino Principle*. New York: Viking, 1975.

_____. *The Domino Vendetta.* New York: Beaufort Books, 1984.

Kirkwood, James. *Some Kind of Hero.* New York: Thomas Y. Crowell, 1975; reprint ed., New York: New American Library, 1976.

La Fountaine, George. *Flashpoint.* New York: Coward, McCann & Geoghegan, 1976.

_____. *The Long Walk.* New York: Putnam's, 1986.

Leonard, Elmore. *Bandits.* Boston: G.K. Hall, 1987.

_____. *The Big Bounce.* New York: Dell, 1969.

_____. *Fifty-two Pick-up.* New York: Delacort Press, 1974.

_____. *Mr. Majestyk.* New York: Dell, 1974.

Mason, Bobbie Ann. *In Country.* New York: Harper & Row, 1985.

Miller, Ken. *Tiger, the Lurp Dog.* New York: Ballantine, 1983.

Moore, Robin. *The Green Berets.* New York: Crown Publishers, 1965.

Morrell, David. *First Blood.* New York: Ballantine, 1972.

_____. *Rambo: First Blood Part II.* New York: Berkley Publishing Group, 1985.

_____. *Rambo III.* New York: Berkley Publishing Group, 1988.

Proffitt, Nicholas. *Gardens of Stone.* New York: Carroll & Graf, 1983.

Rossner, Judith. *Looking for Mr. Goodbar.* New York: Pocket, 1976.

Schulberg, Budd. *The Disenchanted.* New York: Donald I. Fine, 1978.

_____. *What Makes Sammy Run?* New York: Random House, 1941; reprint ed., New York: Bantam, 1964.

Stone, Robert. *Dog Soldiers.* Boston: Houghton Mifflin, 1974.

Woods, William Crawford. *The Killing Zone.* New York: Harper's Magazine Press, 1970.

Sylvester Stallone as John Rambo in *First Blood.*

Index